UNDER THIS BEAUTIFUL DOME

UNDER THIS
BEAUTIFUL DOME

*A Senator, a Journalist, and the
Politics of Gay Love in America*

TERRY MUTCHLER

SEAL PRESS

SEAL PRESS
A Member of the Perseus Books Group
1700 Fourth Street
Berkeley, California 94710

Library of Congress Cataloging-in-Publication Data

Mutchler, Terry.
  Under this beautiful dome : a senator, a journalist, and the politics of gay love in America
/ Terry Mutchler.
    pages cm
  ISBN 978-1-58005-508-6 (hardback)
1. Mutchler, Terry. 2. Severns, Penny, 1952-1998. 3. Lesbians—United States—Biography.
4. Gay journalists—United States—Biography. 5. Gay politicians—United States—
Biography. 6. Homosexuality—Political aspects—United States. I. Title.
  HQ75.4.M87A3 2014
  306.76'63092—dc23
  [B]
                                         2014021397
10 9 8 7 6 5 4 3 2 1

Cover and interior design by Domini Dragoone
Printed in the United States of America
Distributed by Publishers Group West

για την Μαρια

CONTENTS

PREFACE   AN OPEN SECRET..1

ONE   THE CALL...5

TWO   THE REPORTER AND THE SENATOR 12

THREE   FIRST TIME FOR EVERYTHING.....................................19

FOUR   THE FUTURE'S KNOCKING 37

FIVE   FOUNDATION OF SECRECY 46

SIX   NAKED BEHIND A FURNACE
AND OTHER DAILY INDIGNITIES.............................56

SEVEN   THE MARRIAGE PROPOSAL 64

EIGHT   FINDING THE LUMP 74

NINE   MAKING A DEAL WITH GOD.....................................86

TEN   DIAGNOSIS: MALIGNANT POLITICS 92

ELEVEN   THE LAST FRONTIER 101

TWELVE   BONE MARROW TRANSPLANTS, LAW SCHOOL,
AND OTHER FORMS OF HELL..................................115

THIRTEEN   BEHIND THE EIGHT BALL: RETELLING ALASKA.................132

FOURTEEN   PLANS INTERRUPTED 140

FIFTEEN   GIBSON GIRLS 152

SIXTEEN RACE TO THE FINISH 156

SEVENTEEN VALENTINE'S DAY WILL 164

EIGHTEEN LOOKING AT THE ART 181

NINETEEN "YOU BE STRONG" 190

TWENTY ANNOUNCING HER DEATH 208

TWENTY-ONE SILENT EULOGY 215

TWENTY-TWO FIFTEEN ROWS BACK 226

TWENTY-THREE AND JUSTICE FOR ALL? 235

TWENTY-FOUR MORE AFTERMATH 238

TWENTY-FIVE LOCKED OUT 247

TWENTY-SIX "NO HOMELESS HERE" 258

TWENTY-SEVEN "I COULD DIG A DITCH" 270

TWENTY-EIGHT BACK TO SPRINGFIELD 276

TWENTY-NINE THE $1,000 OFFER 282

THIRTY DATING AND THE ABYSS 290

THIRTY-ONE THE SEASONS OF GRIEF 299

AFTERWORD CHICAGO 302

AN OPEN SECRET

On a cold, sunny February morning in 1998, with the unusual sight of three rainbows arcing the Midwestern sky, the family and friends of Senator Penny Severns gathered in the opulent chamber of the Illinois Senate to memorialize Penny, their fallen colleague, and to pay tribute to the rich tapestry of her life's work.

Inside Lincoln's Statehouse, Senate President James "Pate" Philip banged the oversized wooden gavel three times, calling to order the upper chamber of the Ninetieth General Assembly. Senator Severns's family, followed by close friends, was escorted to the front of the chamber as senators stood in respect. The chamber, laden with a thousand ethical reckonings, was orderly and still.

The Secretary of the Senate, a personal friend of Penny's, stood at the dais, a level below the president's chair, and looked over her half-glasses at the audience. Then-Senator Barack Obama (a seatmate to Senator Severns who'd mentored him when he was a freshman lawmaker), then-Representative Jan Schakowsky (now congresswoman), and others from the House and Senate looked on, grieved and heavy. Senator Severns's seat was draped in a black cloth, stark against the white calla lilies centered on her antique rolltop desk.

The clerk cleared her throat and, fighting tears, read Resolution 168, outlining the accolades of the rising young star in the Democratic Party whose life was cut short by metastatic breast cancer one month to the day after her forty-sixth birthday.

Every detail of her life was preceded by the Senate tradition and political lingo of a resolution—the word *whereas*. Those listening were then reminded of the life Senator Severns lived:

> "Whereas, at the age of twenty, while still a student, Penny Severns was elected as a delegate to the Democratic National Convention, then the youngest delegate in the Convention's history. Whereas, she was appointed to a prominent post within the United States Department of State, and as a Special Assistant, traveled to Thailand, Nepal, and India evaluating and auditing countries and addressing poverty for the Agency for International Development (USAID). Whereas, while she worked for the State Department, she was an Agency representative at the Camp David Peace Accords and was in attendance when the historic document was signed. On a trip to Israel with other high-ranking lawmakers, she met Israeli leaders Shimon Perez and Yitzhak Rabin ... "

The resolution detailed Penny's political accomplishments, including winning a Decatur City Council seat with the largest number of votes in city history; her victory in the Senate, unseating a popular ten-year Senate Leadership Republican incumbent; her service as the first woman budget negotiator for the Senate Democrats; and her history-making bid as part of the first all-female major-party gubernatorial ticket in American history, when she won the nomination for lieutenant governor of Illinois and the late Dawn Clark Netsch won the gubernatorial nomination.

Her colleagues listened as her academic credentials were recited: a degree in political science and international relations at Southern Illinois University; a fellowship at Harvard University's Kennedy School of Government; a Toll Fellowship, for which she was chosen from among the nation's elite lawmakers to study public policy in an intellectual boot camp in Lexington, Kentucky; and an appointment to the German Marshall Fund to study job creation in Denmark and Germany.

Some colleagues cried as the resolution, beautifully written and tenderly read, regaled Senator Severns's love of family, music, history, art, nature, and friends. They each had their own memories of their beloved colleague and friend.

Whereas, then came the lie.

The lie that contradicted the rumors, rightly whispered and wrongly denied. The lie had been culled from Penny's obituary, which I had written just days before in my own hand. The obituary contained a three-word lie; perhaps the most painful words I have ever written. I wrote of Penny Severns, my partner and mate: "She was single."

> *Whereas*, Senator Penny Severns is survived by her father, Donald Severns
> Sr., and his wife, Audine Moery; her twin sister, Patty Severns Love, and
> her husband, Douglas, and their three children, Kristin, Weston, and
> Graham; her brother Rod Severns and his wife, Jane; her brother Don
> Severns Jr. and his three children, Jennifer, Emily, and Matt Severns; her
> nephew, Nick Wilber; and her great nephew, Kyle Wilber. Senator Severns
> was preceded in death by her mother, Helen Severns, and her sister
> Marsha Severns Hamilton.

There was no mention of the life that Penny and I had created and lived together. No mention of the marriage proposal she made to me three months into our relationship. No mention that we had forged our marriage with the symbols of ring and bracelet. No mention of our love. No mention of the conversations we had about whether to have children. No mention of the unbelievable extent to which we went to hide our relationship. No mention of our shared finances. No mention of how we dreamed of retiring together. No mention of our life as we struggled with the news of her returning cancer. And no mention of how tenderly we took care of each other or how I tended her as she was dying. There was no mention of me at all, in fact.

The best years of our lives were written in invisible ink.

In the aftermath of Penny's death, I struggled in every way to make that life visible, to preserve that life, to be recognized in a life that we strove to keep hidden and yet in retrospect was very much an open secret at the most basic levels. Our families addressed holiday cards and birthday invitations to both of us; they insisted we sleep in the same bedroom while staying in their homes, even when there was only a twin bed to share. Penny and I were inseparable at every holiday and family function and bought joint presents for our nieces and nephews. Our relationship seemed common yet was underground knowledge on the political circuit. Political friends had whispered about our relationship and political enemies threatened to use it for political gain. Years after Penny's death, I learned that our relationship became a bit of a parlor game among reporters: over brandy and cigars they'd ask, "Were Penny and Terry lovers?"

Two years after Penny died, I was still shut off from her family and from any say in the process of death's aftermath; I was completely consumed with grief and confusion. With no hope that Patty, her twin sister, would ever acknowledge me as even a friend of Penny's, let alone her spouse, I drove to Patty's house to talk to her about the love Penny and I shared. I decided to speak the truth with the hope of cutting away the confusion and curing my grief. I wanted to declare aloud what Patty already accepted and honored until Penny's death: that Penny and I were lovers and considered ourselves married. I hoped we would weep together over the incalculable loss of her twin and of my spouse. I hoped that I would retrieve my possessions and revive the friendship and love Patty and I had shared. I hoped to grieve together with Penny's identical twin and move with her through death's dark jungle, easing the pain with the very presence of each other.

Those hopes were met with the reality that I was treated more foe than family, all marks of friendship and love erased. As a last-hope effort of reaching Patty's consciousness, I said: "What if, God forbid, Doug died, and you were locked out of *your* house? Or if Doug died and your father-in-law started going through *your* mail, or made *your* husband's funeral arrangements? How would *you* feel?" I was certain the parallel would resonate.

"Don't say you were married, Terry," Patty interrupted, shaking her head emphatically. "You were not married. You were *friends*. Penny took you under her wing. That is all."

Under This Beautiful Dome makes visible the hidden life I lived with my spouse, Penny Severns, and lays bare the consequences of living a lie and of denying gays and lesbians marriage equality. For some people, this will be a story of betrayal. For others, it will be a story of great strength or great weakness. For others still, this story will reinforce the doctrine of punishment for moral failings.

For me, though, this story will always remain a love story.

Whereas, now be it resolved . . .

CHAPTER ONE

THE CALL

We cried about the cancer only once.

Penny had finished five months of a chemotherapy-radiation regiment the previous January, and her regular checkups indicated she was doing well. Now, ten months later, a few days before Thanksgiving 1995, blood tests showed something was amiss. We were waiting for her oncologist to call with results of a body scan and more extensive blood work.

The phone rang on that November day with billowing gray clouds hanging low. Standing in the kitchen, Penny and I looked at each other, and nothing short of terror flashed between us. Internally, I froze. This was it. Penny walked into the dining room and picked up the green handset that we kept as a private line in the house. We sat at the walnut table where we always shared dinner, usually New York strip from Peter's House of Meats in Decatur, or grilled vegetables when we were sticking to Penny's vegetarian plan. "It's K. H.," she mouthed, referring to Dr. Karen Hoelzer.

Penny's black Mont Blanc pen scribbled the rest of her life in numbers on a white lined index card. I read over her shoulder. *C28 (?) high. Cancer returned. Mass in lungs.* My stomach lurched as if I'd high-dived off a ledge into an abyss. Sometimes, to this day, I feel like I am still falling.

Penny kept talking and I began pacing, feeling the white Berber rug against the soles of my bare feet. I stood behind her and put my right hand on her left shoulder. I was listening, but I was looking out the sliding glass door at our deck. Leaves from the cottonwoods that we loved so much hid the unstained wooden planks. I thought about the many times we swore we would stain the deck in order to preserve it. I looked at the teak furniture from Smith and Hawken, at the Adirondack chairs that seemed out of place. Their loneliness, their framed emptiness, caught me; I chided myself for thinking of empty chairs and death when I didn't even know the full news yet. I looked down at Penny as she hung up the phone.

She took a deep breath, eyebrows up, and quickly turned her head as if to say, *Oh boy.* "Well," she said, "that wasn't the news we wanted."

I nodded. I felt as though I had swallowed a hard biscuit, whole, and it was stuck in my throat. I pursed my lips, holding back every thought and desperate prayer.

"It's gonna be all right," I said, sitting down beside her. My voice sounded smooth and tender despite the clawing within my soul as I searched for the fundamentalist faith of my childhood that had provided an answer to every hard question or trial.

"It's not the news we wanted," Penny said again. "But we'll just move forward. We'll deal with it."

There was a pause.

"Right?" she asked.

In that pause, an entire unstated conversation passed between us as it had so many times on the campaign trail or at the capitol. It was the same invisible conversation we'd had when I stood in the press box as the Associated Press Statehouse Bureau Chief and she on the Senate floor as the Senate Democrat's Chief Budget Negotiator. Our eyes had locked on each other, speaking a silent, emotional Morse code. In some ways, our entire life was framed in that pause—an unspoken reality we both understood.

"We're definitely going to deal with it, P," I said. "We are going to get through this."

We both exhaled.

"I better call Pat," she said, referring to her identical twin.

I sat at the table fingering the green and cream placemats that Penny loved. I'd ruined them after washing them with blue jeans. The cream cotton weave with five green-stitched herbs with their names underneath had blurred. The blue bled into the fringes. I traced my fingers over the basil and the purple-tipped sage, wishing I hadn't ruined something she liked. She kept talking to her sister, a registered nurse, relaying the news and the numbers.

"We'll just move forward with this new challenge," she said near the end of the conversation, displaying the same resolve she'd shown throughout her career as the Senator from Illinois's Fifty-first Legislative District, as if she were giving a news conference at the capitol.

She hung up the phone, and we looked at each other. Her eyebrows arched up. Another exhale.

"How's she doing?" I asked. Patty herself was in remission from the same disease that had claimed their youngest sister, Marsha, at thirty-six, and was now chasing Penny.

"She's all right," she said, deflated. "I think we all wish this would've been different."

And as all press secretaries and politicians know how to do, we started spinning the news of our private truth into the weave of our public lives. At our table, we talked about whether we needed to say anything to the public, and we concluded that yes, we did need to disclose this news—but not immediately. The political/press realm was familiar, and we eased into that river easily, ignoring the falls that lay ahead. We knew what we needed to do. We knew how to behave.

"I definitely think we need to tell the public eventually," Penny said. "After the biopsy, when chemo starts again, we'll hold a news conference and talk about how this is another bump in the road." *Just another bump in the road*. That was a phrase she used even up to a few days before her death.

Her voice picked up the steam that it always had when she was thinking about other people. "You know, this really isn't any different than what thousands of other women go through while balancing jobs and health," she said, and instinctively I knew that I would write that phrase into the press release. Her voice seemed to inflate again even though I knew she was trying to convince both of us.

She reached across the table, across the bowl of purple and green papier-mâché grapes that we'd purchased in a market in Zihuatanejo, Penny bargaining with the merchant as though an undiscovered Chagall were on the line. She grabbed the Thanksgiving issue of *Bon Appétit* with its dog-eared pages and started flipping through it. I reached for the *Colorado Cache Cookbook* and started looking for the apple dip recipe we liked. I stood up and kissed the crown of Penny's black head, stepped to the stereo under the dining room window, and put on some Van Morrison, *Avalon Sunset*. I knew she liked Van Morrison. But then I wondered if I should have chosen this album, since Penny often told me that Marsha had liked Van Morrison.

I had a chilling, unwelcome thought: *Had Van Morrison become the requiem of the sisters?*

I walked through the arch of the dining room past the distressed leather couch that we'd paid more for than I'd paid for my car. I walked into the bedroom. I sat down on the bed's edge and began to shake so badly that my legs were jumping. I didn't want Penny to see my fear, but I needed to be near her, so I quickly walked back to the dining room. Penny was again scribbling furiously, this time a Thanksgiving grocery list that I still have.

We knew if she tried to go food shopping these few days before Thanksgiving she'd be mobbed and wouldn't get through the vegetable section without holding a town meeting.

"I'll go," I offered, knowing I would get stopped by people less than she would.

"Nah, let's go together," she said. Something in her eyes said she really didn't want to go at all.

"P, you know that Kroger's is going to be wall-to-wall people."

"I know, but I don't want you to be stuck with it."

"It's all right. Besides, you can do the laundry," I said, holding up the ruined placemat.

We laughed and went to the kitchen.

"Do you think we should cancel Thanksgiving and go up to Patty's?" I asked. "We could have a quiet Thanksgiving with Patty and the kids, walk around the lake, and we'd skip all this stress of having twenty-six people over."

She leaned in for a kiss. I felt my heart breaking and wondered if I felt hers breaking too. She laid her head on my shoulder, and we stood there for a moment, her head in my neck, my chin on her head, and my arms wrapped around her.

"Let's just do it. It'll be fun."

I'm not sure where the time went that day. I went to the store, and when I came home, Penny seemed frantic. She walked around the house picking up laundry and putting it down, moving it instead of gathering it. Then she would switch to working in the kitchen, cutting apples and celery with fury. I can still hear the sound of the knife chopping and see the green celery lying against the scratched white cutting board. I brought the brown plastic grocery bags in and set them on the handmade cherry table that we designed together on a piece of scrap paper. Nothing I said or did seemed to slow her pace, so I moved into her rhythm, trying to keep up.

Everything I touched seemed empty. I felt odd, as though I were the one dying and touching things for the last time, but I pushed those leprous thoughts away. I picked up her brown leather bomber jacket from the corner of the couch and hung it in the closet. All I could think was that she was not in the jacket, nor was she in the shoes I picked up in the bedroom closet.

Empty shoes. Empty chairs. Empty jackets.

We just kept moving—she in the kitchen, cutting, me cleaning up. We talked about our mothers. We wondered aloud how Star, my mother, and Helen, Penny's mother, with seven and six kids respectively, managed to accomplish Thanksgiving preparation while doing laundry and keeping the house clean—all by themselves. We talked about my classes at law school. We talked about our next vacation to Puerto Vallarta. Of course, we talked politics.

The preparations continued after dinner and into the night. Around 2:30 AM, we decided to go to bed. She turned out the lights. I shut the doors to the fireplace. She walked through our master bedroom and into the bathroom. She stood in front of the double sinks while brushing her teeth. Sometimes, moonlight would spill in through the skylight and bathe our shoulders as we sat in the Jacuzzi. But when I walked into the bathroom that night, the only light was from the vanity lights, which Penny hated because she thought they were too bright and harsh. She was brushing her teeth in slow motion, heavy, sawing a log.

She slid out of her jeans and pulled off her shirt, leaving them in a soft pile bedside. The coolness must have given her some energy because she climbed into bed, laughing at how cold it was and telling me to hurry up.

"Sure, you just want me to warm up the bed," I teased.

"Quick. Hurry!" she said, laughing through the chill. Penny was in the center of the bed and threw the white down comforter back as I stepped from the bathroom. I slid in, laughing too. She pulled the covers up over our heads, and we breathed hot air under the down, trying to warm up. She was lying on her left side, her back to the window. I was lying on my right side, facing her.

"We *could* just turn up the heat a notch," she said wryly.

"Oh, is that like, *Honey, is that the bathroom light?*" I said, referring to a joke from the first house we shared together. I'd be in bed and she'd come to bed leaving the bathroom light on. Lying down and getting comfortable, she'd say, "Honey, is that the bathroom light?" For the first few months, I would say, "Oh, I'll get it." Then, finally, it dawned on me that it really wasn't a question. So I began to reply with a lighthearted sarcasm: "Dear, what light do you *think* it is? Of *course* it's the bathroom light. *You* just want *me* to get up and turn it off." She would close her eyes tightly, and promise that wasn't the case. I would get up anyway, laughing.

We laughed again, and I rolled over to slip out and turn up the heat. She clutched my arm, and we lay still for a moment as though we'd just heard a plate glass window smash.

At that moment of frozen terror, there were three of us in our bed: Penny, me, and truth, all of us naked.

She started weeping. I did too. Not the slowly building kind of tears, but that immediate wail, that burst, that deep convulsing that comes straight from the bottom of your belly and moves through you, soaking your skin.

"I thought . . ." she choked, haltingly. "I thought I'd have more time."

"Oh Penny," I wailed, unable to even hear her words. We were speaking over each other, our words wet with tears, drunk with pain, almost slurring.

"Penny, I—" and the weeping took over again. "I can't live without you," I finally choked out.

"I don't want to live without *you*," she said.

Our bodies clutched each other so hard that my ear throbbed from being pressed against hers. Our weeping slowed as though we had just come through the whitewater and were washing ashore, gulping and choking for air. She pulled her head back to look at me. She took my face in her hands and held it there, fiercely. "I *love* the way you make me feel."

I kissed her deeply, still crying, still aching, still cursing, still pray-ing. Her cheeks and neck were wet from tears. Our words were now silenced with kisses more ferocious than I had ever experienced. Half words. Half sentences. Mutterings. Pleadings. We made love with urgency and depth, weeping loudly through all of it, and then, finally, surrendered to exhaustion.

When I awoke, Penny was still curled into me, but her head was nearly covered by the comforter, her black hair stark against the white. I rubbed my eyes awake and lay there, trying to be still. I looked at the blond rocking chair in the left corner of our bedroom with an array of Hermes and Anne Taylor scarves thrown over the spindles. A red wool tam caught my eye, and my memory flashed to the first time I ever laid eyes on the woman now lying in bed next to me.

CHAPTER TWO

THE REPORTER AND THE SENATOR

I was on deadline, and I was hungry.

The first woman appointed AP Statehouse Bureau Chief in Illinois, I had been on the job about a month and was editing a story by one of my reporters. His reporting was superior, but his writing was terrible. Editing his work felt as easy as sucking gravel through a broken straw. I was irritated that he wrote 900 words of copy for a story that should have been 350 at most.

I had eaten breakfast but had skipped lunch because the Legislature was in session, which meant the House and the Senate had a full day of committee hearings and legislative debate on the floor. I was still learning the players and the politics of a state with a storied history of graft and corruption at all levels of government.

It was about four in the afternoon that Tuesday, April 27, 1993. I had a few stories of my own to write, plus, as bureau chief, I had to finish editing the staff stories before sending them to the "desk"—a collection of editors—in Chicago.

In addition to fielding calls from the desk, I also needed to reduce all of our print stories into broadcast copy for the radio and television stations that AP, the world's largest newsgathering operation, served. I knew I wouldn't leave the office until well after eight at the earliest. A Snickers and a Diet Coke seemed in order. I walked out of the newsroom, which was strewn with cups of stale coffee and stacks of day-old news.

I walked up the marbled steps of the crowded capitol rotunda to the snack machines. At the top of the stairs, amid what looked like a clothing rack from Brooks Brothers, my eye caught a splash of red. A woman with a shock of black hair wearing a red suit stood next to the round brass rail. She held an overstuffed, scratched leather briefcase in her left hand and was slapping a pinstriped shoulder with her right. A jolt of electricity passed through me. I froze on the steps, staring. I felt stupid actually, standing still amid the chaos of a session day—a day where reporters scramble for lawmakers, lobbyists scramble for staffers, and the public scrambles out of the way.

But still, I stood on those steps and stared. She passed in front of me on the landing, walked down the hallway, pulled open a mammoth, unmarked oak door, and walked into a room I did not know. Dazed and mesmerized, I walked up the landing, made a right past the wall of phones, pumped quarters into the vending machine, and watched a Diet Coke roll out.

"She's probably a lobbyist I'll never see again," I said to myself, walking back to the newsroom with a new energy in my step.

I returned to the acrid story on my computer screen, but I couldn't concentrate. It was one of those rare occasions that I had the tiny capitol newsroom to myself because my staff was out gathering news, so I picked up the phone and called Anne Matthews Conners, an old reporting buddy who was working for Rockefeller University in New York City.

"You're not going to believe this," I said to Anne. "*I* don't believe this. I just fell in love."

"With who?" she asked excitedly.

"I don't know," I said.

"What? Well, what's her name?"

"I don't know."

Anne chortled. "Terry," she said, not unkindly, "why don't you call me back when you have more details."

You have to love reporters. If you don't have the facts, it's not a story. I laughed and hung up the phone. This *was* silly. In three minutes, I'd fallen for somebody I knew nothing about. I didn't know who she was, whether she was married or single, gay or straight, where she lived, what she did for a living, or, at the most basic level, whether she was mean or nice. Nothing. It didn't make sense for me to be so captivated. Yet this unknown woman held my attention. I could not, and still can't, explain it, but when I saw her, I felt something inside of me shift.

Several days later, sucking more gravel through that same editing straw, I yanked the Illinois Blue Book of state officials off the dusty newsroom shelf to double-check the political party affiliation of a person we were writing about.

I flipped open the book and checked the index. On the opposite page, the woman who had been standing at the brass rail was staring back at me. I couldn't believe it. There she was, just as I remembered her. My eyes scanned to the left of the picture, through the committees, the chairmanships, her education.

"Who cares about committees," I muttered impatiently as my finger traced the words. "Just tell me who she is." Somehow I'd missed her name in big, bold letters.

Senator, Fifty-first District, Penny L. Severns, D—Decatur.

I laughed out loud, prompting one of my colleagues to ask me what was so funny.

"Nothing," I said, chuckling. "I just saw something."

"In the *Blue Book*?" he said dryly. "Must be somebody's mug."

"Yeah," I said. "Somebody's mug."

I was incredulous. A Senator. Damn. Not good.

I grabbed an X-Acto knife that was squatting in my cup of pens and sliced the page holding her picture. I popped her into a Federal Express envelope and jetted the Penny L. Severns page to my pal in New York with a note.

"Anne, get *this*," I scribbled. "She's a senator. Yes, I know. The very body of people I irk in ink for a living."

Anne called me the next day and skipped the salutations. "Lay low, Terry," she ordered flatly, in infamous advice we still laugh about. "She's a *senator*. You're a *reporter*," she declared, reminding me of the crass bit of caution a Philadelphia newspaper editor once gave my classmates and me when we were journalism students: "You're reporters. I don't care if you screw the elephants, so long as you don't cover the circus."

"And *you*," Anne lectured on, "are the first woman bureau chief there. You gotta lay low. There's too much riding on this."

I'm sure that friends, employers, and even some enemies could provide a long list of my personal or professional characteristics. "Laying low" generally isn't one of them.

And lay low I surely did not. Everywhere I went in the capitol, I scanned the crowd for this woman.

On Tuesday, May 11, I saw her at the capitol newsstand glancing at magazines, something I would learn was a serious hobby. She had considered being a journalist and read at least six newspapers a day. Later that day I ran into her again at the vending machines, and I couldn't stand it any more. "Senator Severns, I wanted to introduce myself," I said. "I'm Terry Mutchler, the new—"

"Yes, I read about your appointment," she said. "The new AP reporter. Congratulations. It's always nice to see women in positions of power."

I thought she was politicking and didn't have any idea at all who I was.

"I think it said you're from Pennsylvania," she went on, proving me wrong. "I got a ticket on your turnpike once."

We laughed.

"Well," she continued, "if there's anything I can do to help, you let me know."

"I'll do that, Senator. Thanks."

That Friday night, May 14, I had scheduled a dinner meeting with my all-male staff to get to know them. At the end of the night, new in town with nothing to do, I decided to go back to the newsroom to prepare for the following week. When I walked to the mezzanine level, I glanced up and saw that Senator Severns's light was on. It was 10:00 PM. *There's no way that could be her,* I thought. But after sitting in my deserted office, I figured I'd go and check anyway.

As a cover, I grabbed a reporter's notebook and walked upstairs to Room 311. I looked into the outer office and sure enough, sitting at her desk was Penny Severns herself. I walked into the outer office and she looked up, smiled, and said, "Well, hello."

"Hello, Senator," I said.

"Please. Call me Penny."

"Okay, well, Senator, I'm surprised you're here this late on a Friday night. I was working on a story about the state's sunshine laws and thought you might be able to offer some insight."

"Sit down," she said, gesturing over her desk to the couch that faced it. "Can I get you a Diet Coke?"

"No thanks," I said, trying to steady myself. I felt like I was doing a television live shot. No re-taping. Every word counts.

"I'm surprised that you're at work this late," she said.

I wasn't sure what to say and started muttering about a pending Senate bill that would negatively amend the state's Freedom of Information Act, and what did she think of that?

She gave me a quote or two about transparency in government, but before long, a staffer, Donna Ginther, interrupted us. Penny made the introductions, and the three of us talked amicably. Ginther was working on some Senate budget numbers, and after a bit she walked back to the staff offices.

I really had no reason to stay, but my heart was pounding and I wanted to keep talking to her. I blurted out: "I think I'm pretty much done for the night. Any chance you're interested in grabbing a drink and talking more about this story?"

My words hung in the air like a long ball hit from the plate, every eye in the stadium on the three-inch roll of stitched white leather, waiting to see if the center fielder can make the over-the-shoulder catch.

"Sure," she said. "A beer sounds good."

Yes! The lanky athlete gets ahold of the ball, pulling it down and holding it tight. It wouldn't get away today.

Just then, Ginther walked back in and said, "I'm starving. Anybody up for dinner?"

I didn't say a word.

"Well, we were just going to grab a drink if you want to join us," Penny said. "Let's go to Saputos."

Did I recognize a note of regret in her voice?

"Sounds good to me," I said, crestfallen and relieved. "I have some work to finish up. Why don't we meet in fifteen minutes and we'll go from here?"

Ginther said, "Great," and walked out.

"I hope you don't mind," Penny offered. "But I thought I should invite her."

"I don't mind," I lied, secretly pleased with her caveat.

I nearly bounced back to the newsroom.

We arrived at the Italian restaurant, and Penny asked for a table in the back. The waitress came, and I ordered a Scotch and soda, Penny an Amstel Light, and Ginther the Saputos' signature homemade green noodles with garlic and oil.

We sat and talked. At one point, I noticed Penny staring at me. I flushed, wondering what she was thinking. I felt exposed as she was studying my face.

Or, my mind panicked, *maybe that's my imagination.*

"Can I taste that?" Penny asked, motioning to my Scotch.

"Sure," I said, offering the smoky amber liquid. She smelled it and said, "Mmmm." Then she sipped and nearly choked.

"Well, it *smells* great," she said.

In the mellow darkness of that restaurant, I could hardly look at Penny—her eyes sparkled and her hair framed a face with high cheekbones and perfect lips.

We talked politics, what it was like to cover politics in Pennsylvania, and what it was like working in New Jersey, my previous AP assignment. We swapped funny stories about a mutual acquaintance. As we continued to talk shop, I learned that Penny was chief budget negotiator for the Senate Democrats and was the first female budget negotiator at the table. Coming back into my journalistic self, I asked how the budget was shaping up, hoping for a scoop, or at least a few new details for a Sunday story. Education funding, she disclosed, was going to be the holdup.

I could have sat there all night, but it was late and I needed to be at the local university in the morning. U.S. Senator Carol Mosley-Braun was going to be a guest on a publicly taped talk show that I would be covering. Saputos was closing. We paid the check and left, but once we stepped outside, it seemed none of us wanted to leave, and so we stood laughing and talking for another half an hour before calling it a night.

The next morning, I walked into the auditorium at Sangamon State University, now the University of Illinois at Springfield, and to my great delight, Penny was there too. She was a guest on the show.

I remember the newscaster asking her about the budget delay and how that was affecting people's personal lives. The reporter asked if it was easier on Penny, since she didn't have a family. Without missing a beat and with an edge in her voice, Penny said, "I do have a family," and she spoke of her mom, her sister Patty, her brothers, and her nieces and nephews. I liked the way Penny gracefully dispelled the notion that those without children don't have a family. I jotted a note that said, "I really enjoyed the drinks last night. By the way, you missed your calling in television. Terry."

I folded it, scratched her name on it, and left it with one of the producers. As I was leaving to go back to the newsroom, we ran into each other in the hallway. "I enjoyed the note," was all she said, but I floated on those words all day. I was hungry to get to know her.

That night, a friend and I went to the St. Louis Symphony.

At intermission, something struck me. On the playbill, I did a little journal writing, questioning what it was about Penny that stirred me. I envisioned in ink us sharing a New Year's Eve at this very symphony hall.

Penny later told me that weekend she'd kept my note in her jacket pocket, rereading it throughout the day because it made her giddy. Even these many years later, our story having taken many dark turns, I still laugh to think of the serious, dignified, Ivy League financial wizard, giddy like a schoolgirl.

CHAPTER THREE

FIRST TIME FOR EVERYTHING

"There's is a fine line between courage and stupidity," Penny used to say to me. I'm glad we had been living together for a long time before she shared that analysis with me, or I might have never pursued her as I did. Doggedly pursuing a senator when you are a reporter can be dangerous business for your career—let alone your ego.

On Monday, May 17, 1993, I walked into her outer office—this time to try and get some inside information about the budget negotiations. My motive clearly was to see her, but I was also new to the Capitol Press Corps and I needed a story to send the message that *The Chicago Tribune* was not the only game in town. I asked to see the Senator, and after a brief wait I was escorted to her inner office. While she took a quick call, I studied her office—a bust of Abraham Lincoln, several pictures of John F. Kennedy and Robert F. Kennedy, hand-blown glass paperweights, political biographies, political mementos, a dark-green desk lamp—a replica of the ones at the New York City Library.

When she finished her call and I was done with all the small talk I could think of, I felt I had stepped out of myself. I heard these words sail through the air: "If you're free this week, Senator, we should have dinner."

Not a question. Just a statement.

"You'll have to check with my scheduler," she said pleasantly.

I thought she was blowing me off. As a reporter, I had never had an inside view of a lawmaker's life and didn't realize that most of a lawmaker's evenings, particularly for one that wants to be governor, were packed with events, meetings, and planning sessions. Later, when I saw Penny's daily schedule on a regular basis, I realized that her statement didn't mean what I thought it meant.

"I'll do that," I said shortly. I felt stung. Now laying low didn't seem hard at all. The experience brought me to my news-reporting senses. *If she can't even control her own personal schedule enough to know if she is free to have dinner, then why should I even ask?* I thought to myself, irritated. This confirmed the stereotype I had of lawmakers: they had easy jobs, somebody else did the work for them. Having covered politics for almost a decade at that point, I had only seen a handful of hardworking people representing the people.

The next day, I had to cover the daily goings on of the upper chamber because one of my colleagues who regularly covered the Senate heard that the Senate President made some racist, provocative remarks, so he was working the phones. One of us needed to be in the Senate. I would have been excited to get a chance to see Penny, but I was still put off by the "check with my scheduler" comment and didn't really want to be available to her in the Senate. But all the other reporters were on assignment. I didn't have a choice. For all the steeling and internal griping I did, when Penny stepped on to the Senate floor, I melted, and my stomach turned to butterflies.

She smiled at me. In the press box, I gave my best poker-faced nod and went on taking notes of the Senate debate, ignoring her. A little while later, Penny wandered over. There were only two of us in the press box, the other a Copley reporter sitting a few seats away. I leaned in to hear Penny, who stood near the lip of the wooden dais. She said she had heard that the Senate President had made some off-the-cuff comments about blacks and lottery tickets—was that true? I was a little surprised that she wouldn't know that, since it had been buzzing through the Capitol all morning. Yes, it was true, I said, adding that a colleague already had something out on the news wire. I suggested that she should have her press secretary check it out. I imagined that my body sounded like a bee buzzing near honey, and I could feel myself becoming intoxicated in her presence.

"By the way," she said, smiling, "do you like Thai food? Because there is a great Thai place here, and we should go this week."

I had never had Thai food and had no idea what it was, much less whether I liked it.

"Absolutely," I said. "That sounds great. You can fill me in on the players of this cavernous chamber over dinner."

She smiled and said, "Great."

"Should I buzz your scheduler?" I gently taunted.

"Friday looks good," she replied with a slight smirk, opening the volley of our unspoken understanding that would carry us for our too-short time together. She returned to her burgundy chair with the gold seal of the State of Illinois emblazoned on the back.

I slapped my blue-and-white reporter's notebook against my left palm and said, "Bingo." I'm certain that my press colleague, who couldn't hear our conversation but could see us talking, thought I had just landed a budget scoop. All the better.

That night, I called Anne Conners to find out two things: What's Thai food? And what should I wear?

"You are not laying low, Missy," Anne said, pulling out an old family nickname. After the scolding, Anne reminded me that there were many other attractive and smart people in the world, and she was sure some were in Springfield as well.

"You cannot get romantically hooked on a source when you are the first woman bureau chief," she said, clearly thinking that if I failed in this high-profile appointment, I would set women reporters back.

I thought Friday would never come. I had buzzed Penny late in the afternoon to find out what time she thought she would be leaving. Our schedules unclear, I told her to just stop in the newsroom when she was done.

A little before six, I was finishing up a telephone call and she popped her head into my office. I motioned for her to wait a minute. When I finished, she said, "So this is where the Pulitzers are written."

"Not lately," I said.

"What's the news for tomorrow?" she asked, her eyes sparkling.

I never stuttered in her presence, but she could discombobulate me with one flash of her smile.

"Well, let's see," I said, showing her the copy that was spewing off "the wire" machine. I showed her the story budget that would go to all the newspapers, radio, and television stations, providing a snapshot of the stories that the AP would offer to its members for their use in the next day's news. The Legislative budget was of course the top news of the day in Illinois.

"Shall we go?" I said, more interested in knowing her than the news.

When we walked into the communal part of the newsroom, another reporter, Eric Robinson from WAND, and Linda Hawker, the Senate Secretary and Penny's previous campaign manager and great friend, were standing there.

"Hello there," Penny said, and I immediately regretted having asked her to meet me in the newsroom. I wanted to have this dinner alone.

That wasn't happening. It was an awkward moment. Not knowing each other or whether this was a date, I didn't know what to say. It was clear we had been walking out together and now seemed a bit caught.

"We're gonna get some Thai at Magic Kitchen," Penny said. "Want to join us?"

"Sure," they said. Linda added that she would call her husband Roger Ryan to join us.

Great, I thought sarcastically. *My first dinner with Penny—just the five of us.*

I became more hopeful when Penny said, "Okay, I'll ride with Terry, and we'll meet you guys out there."

I can recall only two things from that drive to the restaurant: swinging by a nearby beer joint to grab a six-pack because it was BYOB, and Penny's blurry apology.

"Sorry about that," she said, which I didn't understand exactly, but surmised that she was sorry her friends were joining us. I also remember not being able to breathe very well with this woman near me, talking.

Dinner was easy and uneasy at the same time. There was lots of laughter, but most of the questions were directed at me, since none of them knew me. Where I grew up. Why I moved to Illinois. What it was like to be the first woman to head up a statehouse newsroom in Illinois. What I liked to do. It was like a group date.

While enjoying pecan pie and coffee at the end of the early night, Penny suggested we all go to the movies. Somebody had a copy of the local paper, and we decided to go see *Dave,* a romantic political comedy starring Kevin Kline and Sigourney Weaver. I certainly wasn't going to miss an opportunity to spend more time with Penny, even if it was in a group. I immediately began angling to sit next to her.

I thought, *You're the AP statehouse bureau chief, you have taken on Donald Trump, had the courage to walk up to John Gotti's front door and knock, and now you're behaving like an eighth grader, wanting to be sure you get to sit next to her?*

I disgusted even myself.

In the parking lot, Roger and Linda were trying to give me directions to the theatre, and I figured that meant Penny was driving with them.

"I'll just drive with Terry," Penny said, tossing another "we'll meet you there."

We walked into the now-defunct Esquire theatre and, happily, Penny sat next to me. The movie was funny, but the only sensation I focused on was the feel of her arm brushing mine on the arm of the chair.

That night, I drove Penny back to her car. I was trying to figure out how to see her again that weekend.

"If you're around on Sunday," I said, "I'll probably hit the links. You'd be welcome to join me."

"I don't golf," she said apologetically. "I'll tell you that story sometime."

"Well if you're free, give me a buzz and maybe we'll have lunch," I stretched.

"I hate to say it, but I have a ton of events in my district on Sunday," she said.

Okay, I thought, *just sit tight, Terry.* We got to her car, and I pulled in next to it. "I'll see you later," I said.

"Take care," she said.

She got out of my car, and because it was dark, I waited until she unlocked her car and got in. I had the car in reverse and my foot on the brake and was about to back up when she rolled down her passenger window. I rolled down my window. She said, "You know, there's some movement on the education funding issues in the budget. We are talking about moving the numbers up, but not much, about 5 million to 10 million at the moment."

"I heard that, but I didn't have anything concrete on the amount."

"Now you do," she smiled. "We're looking at doing something by Memorial Day. We have a meeting Monday," she said. "No name," she said, reporting shorthand for no attribution.

There was a pause before either window moved, it felt like we were both holding our breath, waiting for each other.

Even though it was nearly midnight, I decided to jump through the open window.

"Do you want to grab some coffee?"

"Why not?" she said quickly, smiling. It seemed we both exhaled, having made room for another moment together.

We pulled into a Shoney's parking lot on MacArthur Boulevard and walked in. We sat at a table as far from the door as possible. Even before there was anything to hide, we were hiding. The waitress brought over the laminated menus. We both declined.

"Just coffee for me," I said.

"Make that two," Penny said.

I finally had my few minutes alone with this woman, and now I was unsure what to do with them. An unfamiliar energy coursed through me, and I felt like I couldn't sit still. Trying to find a release valve for this mounting tension, I blurted out a non sequitur: "I need to get up early."

"Working?" she asked, lifting her coffee mug to take a drink.

"No, I take flying lessons," I said. Her eyes got big and she smiled.

"Just how old are you, anyway?" she asked, pulling the mug away before taking a drink, but keeping it midair.

I laughed, but in that moment the showdown was there. I remember feeling caught, or found out, and then afraid. I knew how old she was, forty-one, and I figured, even if she was interested, which I still didn't know, there was no way she would date a twenty-seven year old.

"Twenty-seven," I said with an edge, like a kid who added on the "half" to prove a little more maturity.

She set her coffee cup on the table. Her eyebrows arched up, and she cocked her head a bit as though she hadn't heard me correctly.

"Twenty-*seven*?" She threw her head back and laughed out loud. "Wow, AP statehouse bureau chief at twenty-seven. That is amazing."

I wasn't interested in my career climb at that moment.

"Does that bother you?" I said, realizing it was a very premature question.

She looked me squarely in my eye.

"No. Does it bother you?"

"Not in the least," I said, feeling a sense of relief, space, and happiness about a communication I didn't yet understand.

We sat there until nearly 2:00 AM talking politics, her family, my family, steering very clear of the obvious question: whether either of us was dating anybody.

I went home afterward feeling as though I had a field of butterflies in my stomach, and I tripped over an unpacked box. The collision broke my hypnosis, and I realized that I still had so much to do in my new apartment. If it had not been for my very organized sixteen-year-old niece, Rachel Parker Thrasher, who unpacked my kitchen, I'd still be rooting around in a box for silverware. I knew that if things progressed with Penny, I would invite her here. I went to bed, and the next day, after my flying lesson, I went right to work on making my apartment a home: hanging pictures, unpacking boxes, and buying new towels and sheets.

I didn't talk with Penny all weekend. I worked hard to prepare my house for her first visit—even though I had no idea when or if that would happen. It sounds crazy, but deep inside, I knew that Penny would come to my house.

That week, I got up without an alarm clock. Even my most basic morning routines, making coffee and walking to work, were filled with excitement at the prospect of seeing Penny at the capitol. I felt like Walter Mitty, my imagination bursting with images of what our life would be like together and the adventures we would have. I saw her a few times during the week, but she was always surrounded by staff or colleagues. Our interactions were reduced, on both our parts, to big smiles and waves.

The following weekend the Senate was in special session. On Sunday, I decided to correct the previous week's dinner date by inviting Penny to dinner again via a note. I wasted about ten pages trying to find the right words to get her to dinner alone. My house was the only place I could guarantee that isolation.

I finally scrawled something like: *Why don't you join me for steaks on my porch tonight after this illustrious chamber adjourns?* I added a sarcastic P.S.: *I'll ask Eric to bring the beer.* The postscript was risky. I was trying to be funny about the fact that five of us had gone on what I had wanted to be our first dinner date together. I hoped I had interpreted her apology in the car correctly. I knew I couldn't deliver the note personally because reporters are prohibited from the Senate floor. But I remembered part of the job of a Senate page is to ferry notes and messages among Senators, and they were forbidden from reading them. I summoned the blue-blazered teen and asked him to deliver this note to Senator Severns. Penny read the note, slipped it into her jacket pocket, and did not acknowledge me at all. No smile, no look. Nothing.

I panicked.

What if she was offended?

What if she called my editors?

Maybe I should retract the note.

I should just call the desk and explain that I had a misstep in judgment.

I called Anne for quick advice, spilling my guts as though I were in a confessional. As I spoke aloud, I realized how silly I sounded. Anne repeated her cautions but also advised me that I didn't need to do anything about the note. I was overreacting. I could easily explain it if needed. After all, reporters would do more for a story than offer up steaks and beer. If asked, I was "working a source."

She was right. I was making too much of this invitation. I breathed a sigh of relief, and as I was on deadline, I wrote my story and shipped it off to the editing desk in Chicago, then packed up to go home for the day. I decided I was over this Severns woman and the emotional energy she was sapping from me. But before I left, the news editor called me with some questions related to the budget story I just filed. The only person with the answers was Penny. I asked him if we could "write around it," but I knew the fact needed to be clarified because it was so central to the story.

I hated myself. She hadn't responded to my note, I was acting foolish with the whole crush-business, and now I was going to have to call her. *Damn.*

I dialed her office phone, praying that she would not answer and that I could tell the desk that I tried but couldn't reach her.

"Penny Severns," she said in a serious and clipped working voice.

I decided to be as straightforward and professional as I could with absolutely no warmth in my voice and without a pause. I said, "This is Terry Mutchler from the AP. Senator, the Chicago desk had a question about the budget issues and the number you provided." She clarified the calculations and gave me some new information. As I was saying thank you as fast as I could, she said, "Uh, Terry?"

"Yes?"

"If I am coming over to your house, I'm going to need your address."

Hell turned back to heaven, and I gave her the address.

"I'll give you a call on my way over," she said.

I rushed home to prepare the grill, and then I started to worry about my house. It was a beautiful apartment with hardwood floors and a built-in glassed bookcase, but it was so sparsely decorated. She was, after all, a Senator. Growing up in a family that didn't entertain, I had no coordinates on how this worked, and I didn't know whether or not my house was ready for such a heady visitor.

Panic washed over me again. *Should I call it off?* I thought. *Maybe she won't come.* I was alternately worried and relieved by the thought it might all be moot.

I'm embarrassed to admit how many times I changed my outfit before settling on a blue oxford shirt, knee-length tailored golf shorts, and penny loafers, which I polished in preparation for her arrival.

Seven o'clock rolled around. No call. Seven thirty. Nothing. I picked up my phone to be sure it was working and put it back in its cradle. Eight o'clock. Silence.

I had many monologues during these moments. Joyous glee sunk to anger. Then the chiding started: *You are an AP reporter, Terry, you know better. Anne's right—you should be laying low.* Penny Severns was proving exhausting. By nine o'clock, the grill cooled and I closed the lid on both the coals and my schoolgirl crush.

But at 9:35, the phone rang.

"Hello?" I said casually, sure it was one of my friends.

"Is the bar still open?" Penny said.

Another U-turn on the hell–heaven highway. I re-ironed my shirt and fired up the grill again.

I buzzed her into the building. When she knocked on my door, it felt like she was knocking directly on my heart. I opened it and welcomed her with a handshake, asking her to make herself at home while I did some things in the kitchen.

I didn't ask what she wanted to drink, but rather handed her an Amstel Light, saying I had picked some up to try this week on her recommendation. She walked around the living room and dining room asking how my day ended up. I told her about the story and thanked her for the inside numbers she provided.

"The Speaker's not going to be happy about that," she said, referring to Representative Michael Madigan, often referred to as the "velvet hammer."

She studied the antique hot-type alphabet letters I had hanging on the wall in their original wooden tray. She bent down to look at some antiques I had in a glass cabinet below the archway of my living room. Somehow her attention to the detail of things that were important to me made me feel like everything would be all right. We sat on the porch, eating and talking until two in the morning. Politics, careers, more about our families. Her political aspirations, my reporting goals and dream of becoming a lawyer, and our love of travel. When she finally left, I lay awake for a while thinking. I didn't need any more signs. I felt like she was, in fact, interested in me. Every fear and panic-laded moment ceased, my mind quieted, and for the first time in my life, I felt like I was truly home. I had never known that feeling before, and I wanted it to stay. I realized I was in love.

That week, I was excited about every aspect of work, wondering where I would see Penny next. I knew the chamber would adjourn on Thursday, and standing off of the floor while interviewing lawmakers on Wednesday afternoon, I spotted Penny and asked her for a quote. Then I asked her to give me a call when her week wound down.

"What do you have in mind?" she said with a sly smile. Lying about what I really had in mind, I said, "Dinner."

"How about Mexican?" she suggested. "There's a great restaurant out of town where we can go."

"Great," I said.

Still building a reputation as a hard-nosed news reporter, I didn't want to be seen in a state Senator's car. I thought that my car would provide a bit more privacy, so I suggested that I drive.

"Come up the circle drive around six and we can go," she said.

Our time talking on the porch a few nights before seemed to move us quickly past a strictly professional arena and into the outer perimeters of a personal one. But I was still unsure whether we were moving in a romantic realm or simply building a friendship.

I picked her up, and we drove about fifteen miles into the country, to a town called Pleasant Plains. The restaurant, La Casita, was adjacent to Pueblo Southwestern Art Gallery.

We ordered dinner, and I could do little more than push my food around on the platter. For the life of me, I couldn't get over my own nerves or speak about personal things. Because I knew I was falling in love with her, I was struggling with whether to share my feelings, but I was not brave enough. So I spoke of what I knew best: politics. She followed suit, although I sensed that she wanted to shift the conversation away from the political.

"You know, I rarely have dinners with reporters," she said, pausing. I knew it was a cue but could only manage to stab at my Spanish rice with my fork and say, "Hmm." I was having a full, rich conversation in my head, trying to coach myself to take this invitation and make something of it: ask her why that was, or why me—anything. I felt like I had a glob of peanut butter in my mouth preventing the formation of words.

Undeterred and patient, she tried again.

"And," she said, pausing to pick up her wine glass and take a slow sip, "even when I do have dinner with reporters, I never have dinner with them alone." She looked right at me. Her flirtation was unmistakable. My heart was pounding, I was out of sync with her smooth overture, and I talked myself out of the opportunity. I couldn't step up and instead relied on humor to protect me as I wound my way through love's labyrinth.

"So, how do I know that you're not just inviting me to dinner because I'm the AP bureau chief," I played.

Without missing a beat, she said, "You don't."

The atmosphere was charged. Sensing my inability to slip deeper and step into the romantic arena, she seemed to tacitly agree to go at my pace, yet she kept the slow burn of invitation present, mostly with direct eye contact.

My eye contact, on the other hand, faltered. I couldn't look at her. Each time our eyes met, I was certain she could see right into my soul and read my inner text: that I thought she was so beautiful; that I felt a strange giddiness and peace colliding inside me at the same time. When I was a child, my father would drive very fast over little mounds on the road, creating a sensation in my stomach that we dubbed "belly rides." It is the same feeling I get the moment when a plane's wheels leave the runway and I am simply climbing on current—no longer grounded, even the strongest metal is held airborne by the invisible current.

Being with Penny felt that way all the time.

The signs were there. She was flirting, throwing softball invitations. And yet, I kept thinking, *Am I right? Am I imaging these signs?* I had no bearing or coordinates. I just felt exhilarated. I craved to be near her, and I wondered whether, if we ever really took off, the cruising altitude would feel the same as this ascent.

As dinner wound down, she said to me, "You've barely touched your food." She sounded disappointed. "You didn't like it?"

I tried to cover the reality that my stomach was doing summersaults. I needed to step away, take a deep breath, and get grounded. I stood up, put my napkin on the table, and leaned in, and now *she* looked startled as if I were coming in for a kiss. I stopped halfway, pleased to have shifted the power: "I guess now you have me worried that you're just having dinner with me for my ink." Then I smiled and said, "I'll be right back."

Not wanting an argument over the check, I gave the waiter my credit card instead of going to the ladies room. When he returned it, Penny simply said, "Ah, I can see I am dealing with a clever one."

On the drive back to town, I threw in the one cassette tape I had in the car at the time, which had Joan Baez on one side and a demo tape of Mary Chapin Carpenter on the other. Mary Chapin's sister, Mackenzie, a reporter and friend of mine, had given me the tape before Mary Chapin had become well known. We listened.

"Do you sing?" Penny asked. Not ready to reveal that I'd been a vocalist in a newsroom band years before, I merely said, "A little."

Inexplicably and unbelievably, Penny then said, "Sing to me," as Baez was singing the sad lyric ballad "Jesse." I felt timid and unsure of whether or not to sing. I kept silent and let that song end. I wanted to please Penny, to offer something personal. I wanted to show her that, in fact, I could respond to the flirtation and be intimate. She had asked me to sing to her, and I wanted to deliver. In my mind, I equated her asking me to sing to her as a defining moment: the verbal version of a first kiss, walking past a platonic line. It felt as though she had touched me, and I wanted to respond.

When Baez started to sing "Amazing Grace," I simply said, "Okay, Penny, I will."

And I did.

I didn't look at her, I couldn't. Rather, I gripped the wheel, studied the road, and sang as though I were auditioning for the part of my life. When the song was over, I turned to her, and she looked at me with this stunned amazement. Perhaps she couldn't believe I had sung to her. I couldn't believe it myself. She pushed the off button on the cassette, leaving silence.

"That was really beautiful," she said quietly. "I mean *really* beautiful, Terry."

It felt as though something in our unspoken relationship solidified, and we moved to a deeper, quieter level.

We rode the rest of the ride in contented silence, watching sunlight and dust mingle over cornstalks and wheat, listening to the thrum of the tires on the pavement of the two-lane highway.

We pulled into town, but I was not ready to let her go.

"How about a drink?" I asked.

"Let's go to your place," she said. We left her car at the Capitol.

Another night on my porch meant another chance to express my feelings if I could find the courage. I vowed that I would settle into myself and respond in kind to her flirtation. I lived on the third floor of a Chicago-style brownstone with a wide, bricked balcony. At the end of my living room, a screened door opened to the balcony, where I had a spring-iron antique chaise lounge that I'd painted red and black, an antique black milk can, and a folding lawn chair facing out. Against the long concrete balcony wall in front of the furniture, I had a paint-chipped wooden bench. Penny lounged in the rocking chaise. I sat in the chair with my feet on the bench. Both still in our suits, we sat on the porch for hours talking and listening again to my limited music selection. She said, "I have to go to the ladies' room. Can I bring you another beer?"

"Sure," I said. The moon was large and low. I moved from the chair I was sitting on to the bench near the balcony to get a better view. My back was to the balcony, with my hand laid across the wide concrete ledge. Internally, I felt like I was running sprints between the hurdles of *What are you doing, Terry?* and *She's beautiful and seems interested.*

She returned, and to my surprise, instead of sitting in the lounge, she sat next to me on the bench. When she sat down, she leaned back against the concrete balcony, where my arm had been outstretched. Her back pinned my jacket sleeve. I didn't want to move, as I didn't want to pull away from her. And yet, I wasn't sure what to do. In essence, my arm was around her. I kept looking up and behind me, repeating, "What a beautiful moon."

She didn't move. We sat there without speaking, me looking up at the moon and my stomach doing flip flops because this beautiful, smart woman was sitting so very close to me. If I were going to express my feelings, this was the moment to do it. I inhaled. Before I could speak, she laid her head on my shoulder, her black hair against my cheek. I moved my arm around her and pulled her close to me, kissing the crown of her head.

"Oh, Penny," was all I could manage, and I began kissing her hair.

The night was still, the moon bright. In that moment, I thought of a line in Marge Piercy's book of poetry *The Moon Is Always Female*. She wrote about two women who "couldn't have monogrammed towels, or have children, or file joint tax returns, but that they could love, love, love."

I don't know how long we sat like this. It seemed hours and moments at once. Penny finally arched her head up, looked up at me, and paused. Our lips were inches apart. We leaned into each other and kissed.

And we kept kissing. Slowly, we created a rhythm: us kissing, and then Penny resting her head into my neck, and then lifting her head, and then us kissing more. Kissing and resting. Kissing and resting.

"Let's go inside," she said.

We moved into the living room and sat on the couch, growing hungrier for each other.

I couldn't believe what was happening and yet had a quiet confidence in all of it. For some reason, as my hands were under her jacket, up and down her nyloned legs, all over her body, I stopped for a moment and dropped my hands. "Are you all right with this?" I asked. It was the first spoken acknowledgment of our feelings for each other, of our developing relationship.

She reached for my hand, put it back a little lower than her stomach, and said, "Terry I don't know what's happening. I just know I don't want you to stop."

Every conversation in my head ceased. Every fear. Every question. Every wonder. There was a quiet calm, as though I had been groping for and had finally found the missing piece of my soul.

We stayed on the couch for quite a while, and the only thought that came to me was: *I want to do this right.* I had no idea what I meant other than I didn't want to rush this moment; I wanted this experience to be one of declared intention, honor, and desire. It was the first time I had ever felt that way. I surely didn't want either of us to have regrets: she was, after all, a source. I was, after all, a reporter. That wasn't really the core of it, but it was a fact that everything was on the line.

"Penny, I don't want to rush this. I want to do this right," I said, but half of me was saying to myself, *You idiot. You have this beautiful woman right here on your couch and you want to "do this right"?*

"Me too, Terry," she said quietly, but she kept kissing me.

We didn't move from each other and stayed there, fully clothed, kissing and caressing. I wanted to explore her to get to know her, date her before moving our relationship into a more sexual one.

She spoke first.

"Will you have dinner with me tomorrow?" she asked.

"Yes," I said, knowing it was Memorial Day Weekend and that I would have to rearrange a family visit that I was supposed to have with my sister Donna Parker.

The sun started to rise, and we both knew Penny had to leave.

"I have an apartment here in Springfield. It's really just a room I rent from some friends to use on long session nights. Can you drop me there?"

"Yes," I said.

We stood at my door, knowing we would not be able to kiss outside or in the car.

"Until tomorrow then," she said, kissing me for a very long time. We exited my house out the side steps, which were a fire escape off my kitchen. I drove her to Governor Street and dropped her off around 5:30 AM and quickly sped away.

I chose to focus on the ethereal rush of new love instead of seeing the ropes of secrecy gathering at the feet of our relationship, woven cords that already were an unspoken agreement that we would not kiss in public, we would exit my home from the side entrance instead of the front door, and of course, we would leave before dawn.

A few hours later, I had to cover a Senate hearing. I walked into the committee room with absolutely no sleep, and there Penny was, on the committee, which I hadn't anticipated. I slid into the seats reserved for the press, trying very hard not to look at her and trying harder to stop my face from flushing. We smiled at each other, but I had the discipline to ignore her. As she was leaving the committee, I purposely walked near her with my notebook as though I were going to interview her. She whispered, "We still on for tonight?"

"Oh damn," I said facetiously, hitting my forehead. "I forgot about that." Then I smiled and said, "Of course."

"You think you're funny," she said, smiling and walking away. "Okay, I'll see you around seven."

I returned to work, happy and excited that in just a few hours I would see Penny again. To save time, I ran to the grocery store over lunch and pushed the staff very hard to send their stories to me early. At 6:00 PM, I was still working. When I finished, I hurried home and took a shower and struggled with what to wear again. After reaching another detente with my casual wardrobe, I was ready. Sitting on the balcony, I saw Penny pull up and park. She wore jeans and a red and white striped shirt. She looked up and waved before popping her trunk and retrieving a cardboard box. She walked in and put the box on the table. It was filled with a six-pack of Amstel Light, two six-packs of Grolsh, and a bottle of Scotch only three years younger than me.

"You're going to think I'm trying to seduce you with all this liquor," she said, smiling.

"I'm glad you brought it," I said. "I worked late tonight and just got home about half an hour ago. I haven't even had a chance to start dinner."

"I actually ordered a pizza from Bernie and Betty's," she said. "It's great pizza. I just put in the order, and I'll go pick it up."

I gave her the code to the house so she didn't have to stand on the stoop waiting for me to buzz her in. I put plates and silverware on the porch, put the Amstel Light into a silver wine chiller, and lit some candles. She came back and we ate pizza, sat on the porch, and oddly, we both only drank water, leaving the alcohol alone. I stood to go inside, and she stood up as well.

"When you walked into 212," she said of the committee room, "I almost fell off my chair. I was talking to Vince Demuzio, saw you in that brown silk suit, and couldn't remember what I was saying. He knew something was up and looked over to see you walking into the room."

"Did he say anything?" I asked.

"No," she said.

I was standing, holding the screened door, and said, "I was blushing so hard that the entire room probably knows how I feel about you. I wasn't prepared for seeing you there."

We started kissing. We moved into the living room again and fell to the couch. I felt as though our bodies were gone and we were simply spirits mingling within one another, and yet every sensation was alive.

This time, *she* stopped.

"Terry, listen. There's something I have to tell you."

Okay, here it comes, I thought. *She's involved with somebody. She can't get involved with a reporter. I'm too young. She doesn't like me.*

"I really want to be here with you," she said in a rare moment of sounding flustered. "But . . ."

"But what?" I said a little too defensively. I held my breath.

"I don't know how to say this," she said, taking my hand and kissing my palms and fingers.

My mind said, *Just say it.* My mouth kept silent. She looked at me and said, "I've never been with a woman before, and I don't know what I'm doing."

I exhaled.

"That's okay, Penny," I said softly, quite relieved that was the only rev-elation. "We'll figure it out together."

I took her hand, and we walked down the long hallway to my bed-room, where we figured it out for nearly the entire weekend.

CHAPTER FOUR

THE FUTURE'S KNOCKING

O ur first weekend together was filled with lovemaking and lies.
Penny told me later that the walk from my living room down the
hallway to my bedroom was one of the longest walks of her life. She was
nervous, uncertain, and excited. She said she was sure that I could see her
blushing face in the reflection of my waxed hardwood floors. "I had no idea
what I was doing," she told me. "I just knew I wanted to be with you in every
way I could."

It was not the first time I had been in love, but it was the first time I
felt whole in the loving. When her fingers had unbuttoned my shirt, it felt
as though she were unbuttoning my wedding gown.

Our experience was simple: We talked, we laughed, we loved, we slept.
We woke and made love some more and slept some more. We stayed in bed
all day Saturday—the first time I had ever done that. We sat up, resting
against the headboard, talking and finding out about each other. For breakfast that morning, we ate grapes and toast in bed. For lunch, also in bed, we
ate grapes, crackers, and cheese and drank wine.

In retrospect, it seemed like a scene from a movie—the hungry feeling of not wanting to leave each other in the youngest of love. Penny had
a previously planned dinner meeting at Linda Hawker's house Saturday
night to discuss her options for a statewide race. Several people were
coming, and she couldn't excuse her way out of it. It was, after all, about
her political future. She was already late for this dinner, but we just kept
kissing. Kissing each step of the way, getting out of bed, getting into the

shower, getting out of the shower, dressing. She told me it would be a three- or four-hour ordeal. Only an hour later, she tapped on my apartment door that I had left ajar and walked in. I was sitting on the couch, reading. She shut the door, pulled the book from my hands, and pulled me up off the couch.

"I thought you were going to be three or four hours," I said. She didn't explain what she had told them; she just said, "I missed you." This time, she walked me down the long hallway to my bedroom, where we stayed for many hours.

I felt centered. I felt happy. I felt that my life was just beginning.

We made love and stayed up talking until nearly dawn. We slept in a little on Sunday morning, and when I slid out of bed to go make us a decent breakfast, Penny pulled me back into bed, saying, "Who wants pancakes?" So we had another breakfast of cheese and bread. We slept until about noon, woke, and made love again. We had fallen asleep afterward, but a sharp knock on my front door woke us up.

That knock changed the way we chose to live our lives from the very beginning of our relationship onward. To this day, I loathe that knock, and loathe even more our reaction to that knock.

"I wonder who that is. Nobody in this town knows me," I said, sliding out of bed, thinking, *Did something happen to my parents or family? Is it a neighbor?*

"Don't answer that," Penny said.

I thought she was kidding.

"Really, Terry, please don't answer the door," she said very seriously, her entire demeanor changed.

The knocking continued for quite some time. I put on a robe and walked to the living room, thinking, *This is ridiculous. Of course I am going to answer my door.* Nobody would know that Penny, or anybody for that matter, would be in the bedroom. As I walked through my dining room, the knocking continuing, I saw that the clock said 1:55 PM. The thought of opening the door suddenly gave me pause—I was in my robe at two in the afternoon; I didn't want whomever it was to think I was lazy. I stood near my couch while the rapid knocking continued. I figured that if it were the police, they would have said so. I tightened my robe and decided to simply open the door. And then the knocking stopped, and I heard foot-steps descending the staircase.

"I don't have a good feeling about that knock," Penny said with a fore-boding when I returned to bed.

"I don't think it's a big deal," I said. "Probably somebody had the wrong apartment."

Penny seemed pensive and worried. But a few minutes later, her worry gave way to want. We stayed in bed until the next morning.

The next day, as Penny was getting ready to leave for the Memorial Day parade she was scheduled to walk in, we discovered a note (which for some reason, I kept) slid under my door. It was written on a bank deposit slip with most, but not all, of the name ripped off. The full name wasn't necessary though, because Penny knew from the handwriting that the note was from Linda Hawker.

It read: *Penny. Call your mother. She's worried.*

Penny's energy and lightheartedness drained, and a cloak of fear seemed to descend over both of us, thrown back so quickly into our profes-sional roles. It more than startled me that the Secretary of the Senate would presume that Penny was with me, spend the time to find out where I lived, and come looking for Penny. How did she figure it out? I'd met her once, at a dinner with five people.

I was scared; Penny, on the other hand, seemed simultaneously angry and drained.

We took a shower, trying to shake off the note. I made her a sandwich to take with her and added a little bag of pretzels, an apple, and a note. *Focus on this note*, I wrote, and I scribbled a heart. We stood kissing in the kitchen for a while and said we'd see each other soon.

Penny left, again from the side-door entrance, but she called me a few minutes later from her car, which had been parked in the Springfield Clinic lot adjacent to my building. She sounded shaken. She said there was a sec-ond note on her windshield.

I asked her if the note was dry or wet.

"Dry. Why?"

"Well," I deduced, "that means that she left it this morning. It rained all night last night. If she left it yesterday, the note would have been wet or smeared. She must have come back this morning after leaving the note under the door yesterday."

I felt trapped and hunted. I felt scared. My body seemed to regress to a time when I was about ten years old, after I had been sexually assaulted. Those old paralyzing feelings of fear filled me. Instinctively, my body went into an old overdrive: *hide, keep silent, and keep the secret at all costs.*

Our happiness, new as it was, was being siphoned by someone who tracked Penny. The giddiness was gone. The natural unfolding of new love was marred by something neither of us had created, caused, or controlled. Instead of simply being able to enjoy this newfound happiness—or have time to explore our feelings for each other and decide whether our relationship was a fling or something deeper—we were immediately thrust into planning mode, forced to create lies to camouflage our true lives.

I saw that Penny was affected deeply and somewhat confused about how to proceed. I wanted to ease her mind. First, I knew Penny could no longer park in the medical clinic parking lot where her car, with state plates, was so visible. Her car had been there nearly the whole weekend, with the exception of her leaving to attend the dinner meeting. We could never do that again.

"Look, Penny. It's simple. When Linda asks where you were, tell her I invited you to St. Louis on Sunday to meet some friends and go to a jazz festival. Tell her I drove (my car was in a windowless locked garage behind my apartment) and you parked in the clinic lot for convenience. That explains why your car was there Sunday and Monday, and also why I didn't answer the door." She seemed relieved with the quick, clever cover, but it was clear our new love had suffered its first welt of reality.

"Yeah, that's good," she said. "But what about my mother? She calls me every day."

I wasn't sure what to say to that. While I was close with my mother, we long ago established boundaries over my life. And, being 800 miles a way certainly prevented the unexpected drop-in. At that point, it was Penny who seemed to revert to a younger version of herself. Talking more to herself than to me, she declared, "I'm forty-one years old; I don't want to explain my love life to Helen."

"We'll figure it out," I said, not really believing my own words and wondering if this cascade of reality would overshadow her feelings for me or if she would conclude that I wasn't worth the risk.

She seemed to sense that I was thinking this, and she shifted her attention back to us.

"I really had a great time, Terry. I am really sorry about all this. Hawker's just possessive of me and my career, I guess."

I had a few other words for Hawker, such as *crazy* or *stalker*, but I held my tongue.

"I'm not sure how to do this," Penny said, "but I'd really like to see you again, and I hope you feel the same way."

I was so happy she spoke these feelings before I did. I felt like I just had a rocket ride to the moon and was standing on top of the universe.

"I do, Penny. It was the best weekend of my life." *Did I really just tell her that? Don't tell her everything, Terry—it's too honest and sappy.* But it was true.

I quickly recovered: "Have fun in the parade, and we'll talk later."

"You know," she said, sounding equally as vulnerable. "I think this is the first time I am regretting having such a public life. I'd rather be in your bedroom."

A few days later, at the Capitol, I saw Linda talking to a group of people. She stepped away, and I thought we would just chat amicably. Instead, I felt like I was being cross-examined, and her first greeting was, "Hey, what did you do for Memorial Day? Being new in town and all?"

My conversations with Penny had only centered on what *she* should say. I hadn't circled back to see if she had told Linda anything at all, as I didn't anticipate that Linda and I would be talking. I wondered if Linda was trying to trap me into a lie. I decided the only thing I could do is to stick to what Penny and I had spoken about.

"I went and heard some music in St. Louis with friends," I said.

"Did you have dinner anywhere?" she pushed. I was really on thin ice. What if Penny had named a restaurant? I could bluff and say I didn't remember the name, or I simply could go for broke and take this lie the whole way, sounding definitive.

"Yeah, I had some Italian at the Spaghetti Factory. They have good drinks," I threw that last bit in for good measure, trying to sound "new in town." Anybody that knew St. Louis at all knew that the best Italian food was in an area called The Hill, and I wanted to play the perfect greenhorn. I realized that keeping this relationship secret was going to take some sophisticated effort, lots of energy, and a painstaking amount of the campaign skill they call "sticking to the message."

A few years after Penny's death, Linda and I, who had warmed to each other, had dinner together, and she told me that the moment she saw the way Penny looked at me at that first dinner with all of us, she believed Penny's career—and all the work Linda had put into it—was over. "I felt like all my work to shape her politically went right out the window when you came into the picture," Hawker said, not unkindly. "The chemistry between you two was unbelievable." I always appreciated her telling me that. Somehow, her candor about our chemistry made me feel better; someone had recognized it.

After Memorial Day weekend, Penny and I saw each other every day and night for the next two weeks. We would talk at the Capitol, purposefully arranging to run into each other, and decide what time Penny would be coming over. After work, she would leave her car at the Capitol and begin the short mile walk to my house. We would arrange for me to pick her up somewhere along the route: an alley behind the Dana Thomas House, a market on second street. She would get into my car, we would drive around a bit to be sure we weren't being followed, and then I'd park in my windowless brick garage. I felt like a clandestine operative, albeit more Clouseau than Bond.

Despite the bizarre effort of hiding in plain sight, Penny and I were still excited to see each other and could barely keep our hands off each other even in the few minutes we shared in the car. Most times she would stay at my house all night. Sometimes, we would wake at three or four, and I would drive her to a spot near the Capitol or near her apartment on Governor Street, drop her there, and then speed off.

One of those nights in early June, Penny had an evening event in Decatur, and she suggested I come to her house. Because there was no parking on Main Street in front of her house, I pulled into the single-lane driveway with a one-car garage at the end. I walked to the door, rang the bell, and greeted Penny. It was the first time I had been to her home. She hugged me, and she offered me a Grolsch. She stood in the kitchen, popped the white porcelain top, and then opened an Amstel Light for herself.

"Do you mind if we move your car?" she asked apologetically. I didn't mind. In fact, I was relieved. I was going to suggest it because I didn't like the idea of an AP reporter's car in a senator's driveway, particularly overnight. Since I didn't know the area, Penny came with me. We drove a few streets away and walked back to the house, unknowingly beginning a ritual.

No matter how happy we were, we couldn't shake the memory of the Memorial Day note or the feeling that we were being tracked. A piece of innocent happiness had been stolen, and so quickly. Now, we watched every move we made and every look that fell upon us.

Late on a Friday night, about two weeks after our first weekend together, we were in Penny's office, talking about the reality of our relationship as a reporter and politician and what the consequences of a relationship like ours would be. The complication, as we saw it, was entirely professional, and we never overtly discussed the fact that we were both women. The spoken machinations always, at that point, centered on politics: her being a senator and me being a journalist.

The first few weeks of hiding and planning our routes had taken a lot of energy, and we had been lying quite a bit about where we were to our friends and coworkers. I was turning down a lot of new-in-town invitations, and inadvertently started creating the inaccurate perception that I was a loner. Despite her desire to run for governor, Penny was altering her political schedule so we could spend time together, and she was lying about the reasons she was turning down political events. We talked about her position as the first female budget negotiator and my work as the first woman to head an AP statehouse bureau in Illinois. I would rightly be fired on ethical grounds if our relationship were disclosed. Her political aspirations in Illinois would be over. Both of us had a lot riding on our professional lives.

We kept coming back to the note under my door with incredulity and fear. The note itself had really scared us. But a deeper fear came from the idea that someone drove around looking for Penny. Looking for me. And worse, finding us. How long had Linda looked? Who else had she called? Once she spotted the car, did she drive by, checking periodically? Was she, or anyone else, spying on us? Penny was angry, an emotion that came later for me, as I was stuck in my fear of discovery rather than anger about being stalked.

That Friday night, we couldn't figure out a way to make this relationship work. Sadly, being honest about our relationship with our friends and coworkers did not seem like a viable option; we never even discussed the possibility of telling the truth about our relationship. Penny would say, "My mother would shit if she knew this," or, "Hawker would die if she knew the whole story."

"I'm falling very hard here, Terry," Penny said. "This will only get harder."

We couldn't be together outright. And every time one of us would say, "Maybe we should just walk away," the other would say, "I don't want to do that." And we would try again to strategize a solution or a plan.

"If one of us were a guy, this wouldn't be an issue," Penny said, disgusted and angry, sitting behind her desk. I agreed and told her about a time that I dated a man named Jack, a key staffer to House Speaker Robert O'Donnell in Pennsylvania. When I realized that relationship was going to be a serious one, I went to my AP bureau chief and told him I was dating Jack. My boss thanked me for telling him, and said, "You can't cover the House." It was clean, simple, and ethical. Here though, I didn't have the courage to tell my boss I was dating a senator, let alone a woman. And, in her conservative, Republican-dominated district, Penny could not face the truth either.

With nothing resolved after hours of discussion, I stood to walk back to the newsroom. Penny walked me to the door. Then she took my hand and pulled me into the adjacent office in the suite, which belonged to then-Senator Miguel del Valle. His office was dark, and we stood there in the shadows in case a colleague or staffer came to see Penny, who often worked late. We kissed and talked some more. She told me that she didn't want to let me go. I told her I didn't want to stop seeing her.

"All we want to do is love each other, Terry," Penny said, crying. But, unable to negotiate a way into the truth of our own lives, we agreed that the best course of action was to walk away from each other before we fell more deeply in love. We agreed not to see each other anymore.

I went back to the newsroom and looked at my Sunday story that was running. (It was a great piece, based on a tip from Penny that the House speaker was going to be buying a new fleet of planes for lawmakers to use). "At least I have a great source," I half-joked with myself. I felt sick. *Maybe I should just move back East*, I thought. How could I be near her and not be with her? I decided to go home.

As I stepped out of the newsroom onto the landing, I heard a door shut. I looked up and saw Penny. She walked to the top of the steps.

She looked up to the top of the dome and pointed up. "You know," she said loudly, "I never can walk in the Capitol without feeling privileged that this is my office. Look up," she said. "I am always awed at how the moon shines in through that blue glass under this beautiful dome."

She walked down the steps, the very steps I first saw her on, and from there we walked down the next flight of steps together, briefcases in hand.

We had not planned to leave together. And now that we were walking together, we did not speak of our recent breakup.

We walked across the rotunda to the exit. William Wozniak, a guard who several years later was killed when a troubled teenager walked into the Capitol and shot him in the chest with a shotgun, was on duty.

"Hello, Senator," he said.

"Please, Bill, Penny," she said to him.

"Where are you ladies parked?"

I pointed to the left and she to the right.

"Need me to walk you out?"

"No thanks," we both said simultaneously.

We pulled open the heavy doors and stepped into the Midwestern heat, alone. We stood for a split second looking at each other.

"So, are we going to my place or yours?" Penny said with a smile.

I laughed and my heart started pumping again.

"You pick. I'll follow you."

She pulled from the circle drive and I from an adjacent parking lot. We met at the first red light at the corner of Capitol and Second Street.

She rolled down her window and said, "I love you, you know."

"I love you too.

In the darkness, now having declared our love for the first time aloud, we hopped on I-72 and drove into the rest of our short life together.

CHAPTER FIVE

FOUNDATION OF SECRECY

Secrecy and fear were invisible siblings of my youth. But I realize that these twin cords of my DNA were formed early on, long before my parents had me, their seventh child of four boys and three girls.

My father, Donald, was born in Mt. Pocono, Pennsylvania, the second of six children born to Harry and Agnes (Lynn) Mutchler. Born in 1923, my father was raised Irish Catholic and lived through the Great Depression. His father battled alcoholism and, according to my father, had a terrible temper, and yet had the dual capability of being kind and loving. My grandmother, a first-generation immigrant, was a teetotaler.

My mother, Star, was born in East Stroudsburg, Pennsylvania, the seventh child of eight children. Her parents, Mabel (Smith) and Robert Brundle, were Canadians who moved to the States for my grandfather's work as a masonry builder. Star and her siblings were raised as Methodists. Her father also battled alcoholism, though his coincided with the death of Mabel when she was only forty-nine years old. In fact, my mother and father first met at my grandmother Mabel's funeral, when Star was just ten years old and Donald was sixteen and working for the Lanterman Funeral Home as a driver. Shortly after my grandmother's death, my mother, for reasons that were always treated as a secret and never disclosed, quit going to school when she was eleven and spent a great deal of time with her father while he was working. For his part, my father enlisted in the U.S. Army in 1941 to fight in World War II. He headed into to a four-year European combat tour as part of the Third Infantry Division, the group that landed with General George Patton's task force in North Africa before moving through Italy, France, and finally Germany. When my father returned from World War II in 1945, he discovered the Brundles moved from their home in the country to a house my maternal grandfather had built just a few hundred yards from my paternal grandparents' home. One day, helping Harry cut wood in the backyard, my father spotted my mother, who was helping her father build a stone wall. Apparently, my dad couldn't keep his eyes off her, drawing my grandfather's ire. "Are you going to look at her all day or help me cut wood?" Harry asked. Dad told us that when he saw our mother, who was then sixteen, he fell in love. I think those were the early plantings that "love at first sight" was a real phenomenon; I believed it, and it certainly was romantic.

My dad was still in the military and was set to return to his post in Georgia. I don't know the story of their first date, but they married in 1946, and two years later, they had their first son. The early years of their fifty-six-year marriage, while tough, were also peaceful, according to my older siblings. But that changed when my father was deployed to fight in the Korean War. When he returned home, he was drinking heavily and eventually joined Alcoholics Anonymous. He stayed dry through being stationed in Germany in the late 1950s, but he relapsed when he returned to the States in the 1960s. When the Army wanted to deploy my father to Vietnam in the early 1960s, my mother had had enough of the military life and raising children alone and apparently gave him an ultimatum. In 1964, a year before I was born, my father retired as a as a highly decorated military veteran. The Mutchler clan moved back the Pocono Mountains and into the house where I would live until my college years. My father again began drinking heavily and would continue for the next decade. With my two oldest brothers dispatched to Vietnam in the Marine Corps, my father entered the construction business, worked hard, and spent a great deal of money on alcohol—the fuel for the machinery of poverty and crises.

Our home had all the makings of an idyllic retreat. We rented a large Georgian-style house that overlooked a five-acre lake and had grounds that rivaled Monet's garden: wild roses, rows of peonies, lilac trees, fruit trees, maples—all surrounded by 160 acres of woods. A high school coach once told me it was her dream house. But I knew she would rethink that if she knew the kind of violence that lived there. There were generally two types of scenes that played out in our home when I was growing up: one was tender and loving, the other was violent and bloody. I never understood the staunch paradox but always felt that undercurrent of fear—even the tender scenes were one comment away from violence. For example, my family enjoyed summer afternoon picnics on these large shaded grounds. Nearly every summer weekend we grilled outside and played horseshoes, badminton, and croquet. While alcohol was officially forbidden, my older brothers, nearly twenty years older than me, usually kept a cooler in the garage or in the back of their trucks and they would take breaks and drink. I never understood why my parents didn't forbid this in reality as much as they forbade it in speech. It seemed that as long as my brothers attempted to hide their alcohol use, to keep it a secret, my parents looked the other way.

Eventually, as the games and alcohol intake wore on, a tension would build that I could always feel. Before the picnic was over, a fight would ensue, and the peaceful summer afternoon would end in violence, fistfights, and days of recovery, followed eventually by handshakes and forgiveness. And even if the police were called, which they sometimes were, we were strictly forbidden from speaking about whatever had transpired. Telling a neighbor, teacher, or any one outside the family would draw a severe lecture from my parents.

One night, I woke to terrible screams and the sound of glass smashing. Deep male voices were shouting, but amid them, I heard my mother screaming, "Donald, help me!" She was trying to break up a fight between two of my brothers—one was standing on top of the other's new car and was smashing the windshield with a two-by-four. My father had suffered several heart attacks, and I was afraid that he would die if he got involved. I was paralyzed at the thought of my mother getting injured. Usually, when these routine domestic terrors would happen, I would get in a closet, cover my ears, sing, and pray. I lived with a tightness in my stomach and felt on the verge of throwing up at any given time. Sometimes, if things were bad enough, I would simply run out of the house barefoot, even in winter, into the vast woods behind our home and wait until I could hear nothing but my pounding heart and my prayers that my mother and father would be okay. I would stay until I could no longer bear the cold sting and numbness in my feet and body. Sometimes, hours later, I would go back home and slip into the house: it would be silent, but broken glass and pushed-over furniture often remained.

When I woke to my mother's screams for help that night, I panicked and ran a quarter mile to my neighbor's house—she was a high school English teacher (we often didn't have a phone in our home, so calling 911 was not an option). She and her husband were just arriving home, and when he opened the door to his car, I started pulling on his arm, begging for help.

Suddenly, I came to—sort of snapped awake and realized I was standing in my bathrobe and bare feet in my high school English teacher's driveway. I was certain she could see the hole in my chest, shame's embers glowing naked. Her husband insisted on walking me home. I begged him not to. He walked me to the edge of our yard, and I thanked him and sprinted away. The next morning, when the dust had cleared, my mother and brothers mocked me for "being a sissy" because I ran for help. "We don't tell people our business," my mother scolded. My father intervened and said that I had done the right thing by calling for help, but at the time, I didn't believe him.

It took many years for me to unravel the role alcohol played in these havoc-laden scenes of my youth, and I eventually realized the way it depleted our family finances. Often my father did not come home on Friday night payday and instead went drinking. Those nights were tense; my fear would build with each hour of his absence. Sometimes my older brother Joe was dispatched to find him. When Dad finally came home, usually early on Saturday morning, we were given two directives: get the keys from his truck and do not speak to him other than to say, "Hello." My mother forbade us to be disrespectful to him or to engage in argument. He was always kind to us, but the two of them would often fight. One night, my mother told my father, "I can't take it any longer," and I heard the parsed words from my father that he was sorry and "good for nothing." They were both crying. I fell asleep in my parents' bed and woke to muffled struggles. They each had both of their hands on a rifle that was hidden in their closet. It was somehow clear to me that my father wanted to end his drinking one way or the other, and my mother wrestled the gun away from him, screaming, "You can't do this to the kids!" I think she was only able to get the gun because he was so drunk.

My father would eventually go to bed, and early Saturday mornings brought on their own unique routine. My mother would wake me early, fear still present, and we would go on a bill-paying odyssey. She would take the remaining money from my father's pockets, and we would go pay the gas bill, the phone bill when we had one, the car payment, and our tab at a gas station where the owner, our neighbor, permitted my parents to run a line of credit. I didn't learn for years about paying a bill by mail. Then we would return home, often to another family picnic or gathering, and the weekly cycle would begin again.

For me, fear was always present in this environment, an invisible governess that lived in every room of the house. In the kitchen, I feared whether or not there would be enough food. In the living room, I feared dating, or even just socializing, because having people over to the house, for the most part, was strictly forbidden, and clear reasons were never offered. In the bedroom, I feared those ethereal feelings of adolescence because I was told so many times that every boy simply wanted to have sex, which of course was a vulgar thing. Spending time with boys was generally forbidden; spending time with girls was abided. Fear even steeped into our driveway: Would the cars start and get everyone to work? Would the transmission fall out? This literally was a question posed aloud on a regular basis.

There was the fear of spending money. Fear of the landlord. Fear of the doctor, who cost money. Fear of the utility bills. Fear of the bank. Fear of driving. Fear of sex. Fear that my brothers would marry young. Fear of Christmas with its stress of money and company. Fear of telling my Catholic aunts we were baptized by immersion in water. This last one, as it turned out, was not an unfounded fear. Sitting on my grandmother's porch behind a row of blue hydrangeas in full bloom, my father told his sister that he let me be baptized in a nondenominational church, leaving Catholicism behind.

"You son of a bitch!" my godmother yelled.

When I was eight years old, my young life was thrown into more havoc. One day, I rode my bicycle down to a nearby creek where I often fished. There, I was sexually assaulted by a teenage neighbor. I immediately pedaled home and told my mother, who was paralyzed with fear and angst, holding her head in her hands and simply repeating, "Oh my God." She forbade me from telling my father, fearing he would harm the boy or perhaps blame her, and instead she dispatched my twelve-year-old brother to speak to the assailant. When my brother returned and declared that the neighbor reported, "I only kissed her and I was only kidding," the matter was dropped. We never called the police, a doctor, or the boy's parents. The ensuing confusion and shock haunted me, and I felt as though I had split into two people, neither worthy of help, and both unable to speak. I was no longer allowed to ride my bike on that road or play anywhere beyond our yard and woods. Shortly thereafter, when a relative began sexually abusing me on a regular basis, I was on my own. I rationalized that if my mother couldn't help me when the abuser was a neighbor, she would certainly never be able to help me when the abuser was a member of the family. In trauma, I could not speak up for myself. I thought about going to my father, but my mother had forbidden it. Instead, I harbored the secret and the enduring pain for years to come.

This cycle was broken for a while because of religion. In the 1960s, my family was still staunchly Catholic, and we went to Mass every week. At that time, two of my mother's sisters had discovered the teachings of an evangelist named William Branham, who was widely considered the father of the charismatic evangelical movement. He was a minister that never took any monetary offering, believing that if God wanted him to preach around the corner or around the world, He would provide a sponsor. My aunts felt compelled by this revival preaching, which was Bible-based. Moreover, the healings and miracles that came with this man's ministry were profound, undisputed, and widely written about. In fact, during a service in 1951, Congressman William Upshaw of Georgia, who had been bedridden for sixty-six years due to an accident, was completely healed after being prayed for by Brother Branham, and he walked normally for the rest of his life. His healing was widely publicized, and he told the story of this healing on the floor of the U.S. House of Representatives in 1951. I have always believed Brother Branham to be the prophet promised in Malachi 4:5 of the Old Testament. A very humble man, Brother Branham dismissed the fame that came to him and never took credit for these miracles. He constantly told people that no man can heal another man, only God can heal. He told them that healing occurred because of a person's faith. During another healing service, Reverend Branham picked my aunt Mary Smith out of the crowd—though they had never met—and he correctly identified her and told everyone what she was praying for: a granddaughter that had asthma. For years, my aunt encouraged my parents to consider following this striking evangelical teacher. My parents, attracted to the humility of this preacher, eventually attended meetings in the early 1970s and were baptized, leaving Catholicism behind.

Switching religions didn't immediately change the tumult of our lives. What changed was praying about our problems, and we now believed that God was a personal advocate interested in each of us, individually. And with our new faith, we had something to strive for: living a Christian life. Given the dysfunction of our family, the idea of structure and rules was appealing, and we embraced them with enthusiasm, not resistance. Women were to behave and dress as stereotypical women, and men were to behave as stereotypical men; and there was to be no drinking and no gambling, and everyone would keep themselves well groomed and act polite. Each night, before my father went to bed, he would gather us around our dining room table, and we would hold hands and pray. There was a comfort in it, a closure to whatever tumult the day produced. No matter what craziness was happening, each day ended in prayer. The daily struggles remained the same for a long time—stretching paychecks, alcoholism, my brothers' run-ins with the law—but we built a faith and believed that in time, things would improve with God's help.

During my youth, I mistakenly blamed my faith for another rule that was present in our house: we weren't permitted to have friends stay with us for sleepovers and we were not permitted to stay with friends, and I assumed this was a rule of our religion. Instead, I now see it was because of my mother's fear: what would happen if I had a playmate at the house and my father came home drunk or my brothers came home drugged? What if there was a fight while I was at a birthday party and my mother was unable to retrieve me?

Despite the negative effects this deprivation, poverty, and shame had on my youth, I now see that it helped me hone my ability to conduct political spins. One year, we were so broke that my father apologized to me that he and my mother could only afford a drugstore doll as a Christmas present. I was deeply moved by his admission, and his tenderness and vulnerability only served to make me love my parents more. I thought it was odd that they had thought it one of the worst Christmases, because for me it was among our best. It was a peaceful Christmas that year, subdued somehow. We picked a Christmas tree as late as possible on Christmas Eve, as we always did. (This "tradition" coincided with payday). There were no screaming matches or fistfights, and I later correlated that to another fact: there was no alcohol present that year. When I returned to school in January, my classmates recited their long lists of presents, and they asked me what I had received. I felt vulnerable and embarrassed, so I shifted into what I would now call a high-gear political spin—I told them I received a doll.

"What else?" they asked.

"Oh, no—you don't understand," I said. I explained this was a *special* doll—a very valuable antique, a collector's item, the one-and-only present I wanted more than anything else, and the one my parents searched the entire year for. I weaved political clothes for my shame.

Eventually, with the help of faith, my father quit drinking and remained sober until his death in 2002. The years of his sobriety improved our lives dramatically. We still struggled financially, but much less. My father's tender side emerged, and he played the harmonica and the accordion and wrote poetry and songs. My parents laughed more. Alcohol was no longer draining our resources, and by then, the only children still living at home were my sister Linda, my brother Scott, and me, which also improved their financial situation.

Throughout much of my young life, even with faith, I felt as though I were standing barefoot on the edge of a high cliff getting ready to jump into a swimming hole. Overcoming fear always produced an adrenaline rush that was often disproportionate to the reality of any given situation. Fear didn't hold us back; in fact, it propelled us forward. And paradoxically, our fear-driven life was mixed with faith and religion.

One positive side of growing up in that atmosphere was that it made me courageous, and it gave me a very high tolerance for discomfort and secrecy. Professionally, it made me fearless.

In 1989, rumor had it that the famed mob boss John Gotti bought a house in the Pocono Mountains, and it was the talk of every coffee shop

in Stroudsburg, Pennsylvania. A cub reporter, I spent weeks doggedly trying to obtain Gotti's new address. I obtained the address from his deed, a
public record. I parked in the driveway, walked up to John Gotti's door, and
knocked. I had no idea what my first question would be if he answered. But
he didn't answer. So I walked around the back through a gate. A bikini-clad
woman was in the pool, and a beefy-looking fellow sat on a barstool under
an umbrella reading a newspaper (the one I worked for, as it turned out). The
woman saw me and must have thought I was a neighbor. We chatted. Then
she asked who I was, and when I said I was a reporter for *The Morning Call*,
the fat fellow hopped off the barstool and escorted me, with a bit of a push,
through the gate and into the driveway. I returned to my office, wrote the
story, and the editors played it on Page 1 and sent it to the wires—and then
The New York Times picked up portions of the story for their own piece.

A day or two later, a federal agent called my unlisted home number.
The fact that Gotti bought a house in the Poconos was just a "fluff" story,
he complained. Did I want to do a serious piece on the history of the mafia
in the Poconos and explain why this resort town was now transforming
into a bedroom community for the New York underworld? Of course I said
yes. For months I spent my spare reporting time meeting the federal agent
for coffee and listening. He introduced me to an informant in the Witness
Protection Program, and the agent brokered a phone call. After that interview, I co-wrote a series about mafia infiltration in the Poconos with my
fellow reporter Tom Lowry, and we won second place in the Keystone
Awards—the first going to the reporting of hidden mass graves in Africa.

The adrenaline rush of researching and writing this type of story was
powerful, and the edge of danger was also appealing to me in some way.
The feeling I'd get in my stomach while working on these types of stories
was not unlike the way I felt during times that I had endured hardship
as a child. That standing-on-the-edge-of-a-cliff feeling—the fear and pressure—that this work produced was familiar, an old friend, and so it didn't
paralyze me. I believed in what I was doing. I believed I was right, and the
fear training I received as a child certainly enabled me to stand my reporto-
rial ground.

The Associated Press hired me to cover politics in Harrisburg,
Pennsylvania, and I quickly made a mark as an investigative reporter. After

two years there, I was promoted from reporter to correspondent in Atlantic City, New Jersey, where I took on many high-powered stories—some that involved Donald Trump—before moving with the Associated Press to Illinois, where I met Penny.

I see now that my strength to stand alone professionally came from my family roots being grounded in faith and sheer stubbornness. I learned a certain toughness growing up in a fundamentalist family—standing for a belief, or on conviction, even if you were alone, trumped any other concern. This was reinforced through every David and Goliath story I heard and in each of my father's favorite union-versus-management stories. Being the only person in school that wore a skirt every day built character. I learned early to spin the reality into whatever message I wanted to send. The political strategy of my youth was to do the exact opposite of whatever I was feeling or wanted to hide. If I was withering with shame on the inside, the key was to become an extrovert—so visible that surely my clothing and I would be invisible to my antics.

In retrospect, it seemed that my entire young life was grounded in practicing secrecy and learning the art of spinning facts to my own advantage. Fear and secrecy helped shape me, and they also propelled me out of my troubled childhood, into and through my career. Secrecy and fear paved the way for building, protecting, and living secrets to the extreme and vast ways that Penny and I did. I even came to understand that my relationship with Penny, the secrecy of it, produced a familiar old feeling that hinged on the same rules of my youth: protect family privacy at all costs. Despite my efforts to break away from the shackles of fear and secrecy, here they were again manifesting in my love life.

CHAPTER SIX

NAKED BEHIND A FURNACE AND OTHER DAILY INDIGNITIES

As my relationship with Penny deepened, we spent more and more time together, which meant we had to become more secretive and more creative about hiding our relationship. With such secrecy training in my youth, this did not feel odd at first. From the beginning, it was understood that we could never be out—it would've been the end of both our jobs and political suicide for Penny. But the deepest unspoken reason we didn't want to be out, at least at the beginning, was homophobia. On both of our parts. Given my conservative religious and family background, I struggled with my sexuality. But for some reason, I didn't think to consider whether Penny had any spiritual qualms about being a lesbian. She was raised Lutheran and believed in God, and she had converted to Catholicism for a man she was engaged to but rejected that faith when the local parish refused her communion because she was pro-choice.

In the first month of our relationship, we never talked directly about homosexuality and faith. But one Saturday afternoon, when we had been seeing each other for about six weeks, Penny's roof started leaking, and the topic came up.

We were in Penny's guest room waiting for the handyman to come and repair the red Spanish-tiled roof above the back bedroom. Penny was laying fully clothed on the bed, resting against the headboard, thinking. I was sitting on the opposite edge of the bed, assessing the many books lining the walls, noting that she had no fiction. We discussed whether to drive to Champaign, about forty-five minutes away, for dinner and a movie, or to stay in that night.

"What do you think God thinks of our relationship?" Penny asked, out of the blue.

I didn't know what to say. As a child, I had learned that homosexuality was a perversion. It was never talked about in my home directly as an issue, but negative references to it were abundant.

My great uncle Frances was a closeted gay man, and my parents treated him with deep love and respect. Although they reminded me the Bible forbids and condemns such a lifestyle, at the same time, they would say things like, "Only God knows a person's heart." Their message was confusing, but I always seemed to adhere to the darker, negative interpretations rather than any possible positive ones. Though both my parents would treat any out homosexuals in our community quite normally, there was a clear understanding that gays were somehow flawed human beings, abnormal, and worse, that they were going to hell.

When Penny so easily asked about God's opinion, I froze. On one hand, I desired to have a real conversation with her about the struggle I experienced off and on in my life but that I generally chose to ignore on a daily basis. I couldn't drop into a real conversation, although I wanted to. Fear overrode that desire because I convinced myself that if I shared this with her, I might lose her. The line had been drawn in my spiritual sand, and at the time, I wasn't yet up for the windstorm. I had been involved with a woman before, but secretly, and only one friend knew of that relationship: Anne Conners. At this point, I had not yet told any family members that I was gay—although my brother Scott had said to me just a few months prior to Penny's question: "Hey, I want to ask you something. You're not one of those funny women, are you?"

"Yeah, Scott," I replied. "I'm hilarious." We both laughed nervously, but I knew Scott saw the truth through my humor.

I looked over at Penny. "What do *you* think?" I asked quickly, diverting the question from me with my reporting skills.

She smiled. "I don't see how He could see anything but our love."

"Yeah, me too," I said, believing something quite different, as I had been taught by my parents that God would more than likely reject anyone who was gay. I was relieved that she didn't push me to answer further. That seemed to end any spiritual questions Penny had about being gay, as she never brought it up again. Her struggle, it seemed, was more political than spiritual. She worried that the voters of her district would never elect an out lesbian lawmaker.

Whatever our private thoughts, though, we kept moving deeper into our relationship. In the two short months we were together, we already had lying and subterfuge down to a science, but the sheer logistics to keep our relationship hidden proved exhausting and often humiliating.

When Penny and I first met, Penny lived on Main Street in Decatur. When I visited her, I parked two miles from the house as a rule and walked the rest of the way, no matter the weather, so that my car would not be seen. When we stayed at my apartment in Springfield, Penny would leave her car at the Capitol and walk to my house. We used code words when we had to speak of our private lives in public or when talking on cell phones, which we were convinced were not secure. "C's" was our name for Penny's house, named after Columbia, Penny's cat. "The Porch" was the code for my Springfield apartment. Later, we dubbed our Chicago apartment "C's North."

We lied to everyone about where we were on weekends, where we were at night, where we were vacationing. Even in these earliest months of our relationship, when we'd meet Penny's family for dinner, we'd say that I happened to be in Decatur and stopped by and she invited me to come along. We never, ever took walks together while it was still daylight unless we were out of town. I would leave parties and other social gatherings early, if I went at all, so I could meet Penny and spend time with her. I would tell friends in Springfield that I was going to meet my brother Chuck, a long-distance truck driver who sometimes delivered to Archer Daniels Midland ("supermarket to the world") in Decatur. I varied the location though: I'd "meet him" in Taylorville, Champaign, Peoria. I did this so often that one night as I started to exit early from drinks and dinner with some reporting pals, a radio reporter, Becky Enrietto, said off-handedly, "You're in the FBI, aren't you? You're doing an undercover sting on corruption at the Capitol." I laughed. She pushed. "Come on, you always have *somewhere* to go, and you are always so cloak-and-dagger. Where are you going?" I nervously laughed it off again, but the remarks scared me deeply, and I wondered if my colleagues would turn their reporting skills on me. A few months later, another reporter and very dear friend, Jennifer Halperin, rightly didn't believe my cover of going to see my brother when I showed up at her house for a Saturday night party and only stayed for a short time. That Monday, she lightheartedly told me she checked my mileage and knew I had not gone to meet my brother. Penny and I spent days dissecting whether or not she actually looked at my mileage. Again, instead of addressing our folly, we spent countless hours creating elaborate machinations to be sure we weren't discovered. For this one, we came up with the bright idea that we should cover our odometers with index cards. I'm not sure why, but we never did. We just vowed to be more careful.

On vacation though, once we'd finagled secretive travel plans with the help of a discreet travel agent, we were free, and we took our freedom to the maximum limits. We usually traveled three times a year, and all but one of our vacations (our last) were out of the country, far from prying eyes. We exercised the freedom to hold hands, kiss in public, and tell people we met that we were together, and it made us so happy. But inevitably, the vacation would come to an end, and we always ended our travels with the same questions: *Why can't it be this easy in the States? Why can't we be our true selves in our own home?*

Back in central Illinois, our days began at 4:00 AM if we were in Decatur and 5:00 AM if we were in Springfield. We eventually moved in together and lived in the Decatur house on Main Street from 1993 to 1994, but our routine stayed the same.

The weekday morning routine was early and bizarre. I would wake to the alarm clock, kiss Penny, and slide from the warm covers, which were usually twisted around us instead of covering us. Sometimes, I was calm and gentle, hoping she would sleep a little longer. Sometimes, I would complain bitterly in my head that this was it, we had to figure something else out because I could not keep getting up at 4:00 AM.

Many times, Penny would get up with me. She would make me a sandwich of smoky cheddar, pickles, lettuce, mayo, and mustard while I brushed my teeth and threw on my clothes. Most times, I let her sleep and would just grab a blueberry Nutri-Grain bar and a Diet Coke for the forty-five-minute trip to the Springfield apartment, which at this point was kept merely for appearances' sake. I sometimes would stop there for lunch, or to get my mail, but rarely stayed there overnight unless Penny was with me.

I would slip out of the house in darkness. I'd always leave from the back door, walk around the east side of the house, and stop at the black wrought-iron gate with the pile of firewood covered in brown canvas to the left and the bushes to the right. A portion of our dining room, shaped like a turret, offered a little protection so that I could see if anyone was nearby. I would look both ways to be sure no early morning joggers were about, and then I'd hurry onto the sidewalk as though it were some magic safe place—as though crossing the property line would somehow protect our secret.

Then I would walk to my car wherever I had parked it the night before. The location varied. Sometimes, I would park at the Holiday Inn in Decatur and walk the two-plus miles to our house. Other times, I would park five or six streets away and try to slip in to our home unnoticed.

Friday mornings added a particularly crazy layer to our routine and gave birth to a toxic ritual that to this day makes me sick. The alarm buzzed earlier than usual so we could get up to clean before Nancy, the cleaning lady, arrived. We'd pull the duvet back, and my long hair would be laying on the sheets, and we'd chuckle, wondering what Nancy, unaware of our cohabitation, would say if she found them, given that the senator had short black hair. We searched the sheets for long hair, a travel-size lint roller an accomplice in removing the evidence of my existence. We'd examine the pillowcases and the sheets, and then I'd move to the bathroom to sweep up the long strands of hair there. We made sure any papers or books or errant socks or clothes of mine were removed to my car or were buried in the bottom of a closet. We would do a final scan of family photos to remove any that linked our lives. Eventually, we simply decided to stop displaying them altogether, as the effort to hide them on Friday morning only to return them to their locations Friday night became a wasted exercise.

Weekends were a little different: We would sleep in. If we decided to head out for the day, Penny would back the car out from the garage. Then she would loop back and pull into the drive, and I would dash into her car and lay the front seat back until we were five minutes from the house, and then I would sit back up. We would either spend the day together or she'd drop me off by my car, and we would head our separate ways.

Never once while we lived at 1942 West Main in Decatur did I park in the driveway or the garage overnight. The idea of somebody seeing my car there was too overwhelming for either of us. And yet, how could we have really believed that no one saw this comedic and sad morning routine that began the first time I went to Decatur, a few weeks or so after we started seeing each other? If anyone noticed, they never said so.

Usually, running into the neighbors was not an issue because I slipped out so early in the morning and arrived so late at night. But walking to or from the house at all hours and the thought of being caught made me feel exposed. My heart would race until I would get inside the door or until I would be on the sidewalk walking toward my car. Going home at night is supposed to produce relief after a long day; home should be a refuge and a place to relax. Just getting inside our home caused so much anxiety, I am surprised we endured it for as long as we did.

Despite this complicated schedule, I didn't really mind the arrangement; I was deeply in love, young, and happy. But one morning, I ended up naked behind the furnace.

Not feeling well, I had slept in later than usual. Penny had already left for a breakfast meeting, and I didn't wake up until seven or so. I decided to have a somewhat normal routine, now that the sun had already risen. I had gone downstairs to make coffee. I didn't throw on my robe. I took a shirt that needed to be ironed to the basement, turned on the iron, and walked back up to the kitchen. While listening to the percolating coffee and reading the paper, I heard a key in the front door. I panicked. The steps to the upstairs were right in front of the front door. I couldn't go out the back door because I had no clothes on, and I certainly couldn't stand in the kitchen. I slipped open the black bolt that locked the basement door, went downstairs, and listened. Don and Helen, Penny's parents, who at that point I had not yet met, had come to the house to do some chores for their senator-daughter.

I was completely panicked and completely naked. If they found me, I would look like a crazy woman, and I wouldn't be able to explain who I was and why I was there. *Maybe they're just picking something up,* I hoped.

Maybe they'll leave in a few minutes. I heard Helen go upstairs, and my mind raced ahead of her, trying to figure out what, if anything, I had left in the bedroom or bathroom. My clothes and shoes from yesterday were there. I didn't hear anything for a minute, and then I heard Helen say to Don, "Hon, put these towels in the washer." My stomach plunged. You would have thought she said, "Hon, toss the three children of Israel in the fiery furnace."

Don walked through the kitchen, and I heard the basement door open. I had no choice but to hide. But where? The basement was an open room, and it was too late to grab my shirt. Naked, I shimmied behind the furnace and the water heater, literally holding my breath. I hate spiders and yet tucked myself among cobwebs hanging behind these appliances. Don threw the laundry in the washer, and looked around for a minute. I remember seeing him and thinking of the signs on the backs of semitrucks: "If you can't see me in my mirror, then I can't see you." I prayed he wouldn't take to checking out the furnace or doing some other dad-like chore. Crazy thoughts raced through my mind, and then suppressed church-giggles bubbled up.

He saw that the iron was on, and turned it off. He went upstairs. I breathed a little easier. But it didn't take long for the next wave of panic to arrive. It dawned on me that I was in a real jam because I didn't know how long they were going to stay, and it certainly appeared that they would wait around long enough to throw the towels in the dryer. I was a mix of suppressed comedic energy and angry rage.

The only sense of time I had that morning was the sound of the various cycles of the washer—wash, rinse, spin. Don came down the steps thirty minutes later and dutifully moved the towels to the dryer. He went back upstairs, and as he shut the door, I thought I heard the bolt.

I was really pissed. I was not feeling well to begin with, which is why I was even in the house this late. I was naked. I was behind a furnace amidst spiders and cobwebs. I was cold and angry. My feet hurt from standing on the concrete and from not being able to move. I was late for work and had no way of letting anyone know where I was or that I was safe. I tried to avoid the thoughts of whether my staff would send someone to my apartment to do a welfare check. And I became increasingly alarmed that I was going to be leaving the house in daylight, something I had never done before. Now, if I was locked in the basement on top of all of that, Penny was just going to have to drive back to Decatur to let me out—I didn't care if the Senate *was* in session or *what* committees she was chairing. I was fuming, rageful in fact. Then, the cold hard facts of my life at that moment started to hit me. I was invisible in my own life. I was in love with someone and could not tell anyone. I felt a lump forming in my throat. I was fighting tears when I heard the front door open. I felt like I could breath again, but I didn't move until I was sure I heard *two* car doors slam. Don and Helen finally left. Not willing to face the possibility that I was locked in the basement at that moment, I calmly ironed my shirt and walked up the steps, defiant, certain that I was locked in.

I pushed the door latch with my thumb, and to my great relief, the door opened. I called Penny's private line at the office to regale the tale. A pall hung over that conversation for both of us. "My stomach hurts," she said quietly. "Mine does too," I said.

"I'm so sorry, Terry," she said sadly. Then her voice became angry. "We really need to figure this out. We are going to figure this out this weekend. Living like this fries my ass."

That phrase, which she used often but which I never really understood, reminded me of being naked behind a furnace. We both started laughing at the thought of her father finding me naked in the basement and what I would have said. That milky laughter drowned the anger and humiliation, giving way to one thought: all I wanted to do was see her, and we decided that I would stop in the office for a few minutes when I arrived at the Capitol, under the pretense of needing a quote. I called my office and told them I would be late. And, like every other morning, I hopped on I-72 and traveled to Springfield. But that morning I had an unusual driving companion: the sun.

In retrospect, I wish Don and Helen had found me, or that the basement door had been locked; perhaps it would have pushed us through our folly. Instead, we continued to create crazy mazes of living that soon became a regiment of ruse whether we were traveling, spending holidays with family, or simply doing yard work.

CHAPTER SEVEN

THE MARRIAGE PROPOSAL

Penny and I had been dating about six weeks when we decided to live together in mid-July. We had not slept apart since the night of our breakup, when we declared our love. She was well established, and since she was in the public eye, the only logical thing was for me to move in with her. "I don't want us to be apart anymore than we have to be," she'd say.

In early July, my sister Donna and her family were traveling from Indiana to spend July Fourth weekend with me after our rain check for Memorial Day. Although I had not told Donna about my relationship with Penny, I was very close to her. She worked for missionaries, and while I wasn't ready to tell her I was involved with a woman, I wanted her to meet Penny. I introduced Penny as Senator Severns and said that we had become friends. I said that because I was a reporter and Penny was a senator, we had to keep the friendship under wraps. A few weeks later, Penny wanted me to meet her twin sister. She invited me to a casual family dinner at a Cracker Barrel in Bloomington, where her parents liked to eat. When we arrived, Don, Helen, Patty, her husband, Doug, and their three children were already seated. Penny introduced me and told them that I was the new AP reporter at the Capitol and had stopped by Penny's house after a golf outing in Decatur and that Penny invited me to join them. Because I was an AP reporter and she was a source, we'd appreciate if they didn't mention our friendship too much to anyone. The dinner went smoothly despite the awkward introductions and weird characterization of our relationship as a friendship not to be talked about.

On the way home, Penny said, "Terry, I don't like having to explain you as a last-minute guest, or that we can't tell them we are dating."

I, on the other hand, didn't care. Secrecy was familiar to me. I was still struggling with my sexuality and overtly denied the factual obvious: I was in love with and was sleeping with a woman. I had been involved with women in the past as well, but because I had also dated men, I refused to acknowledge to myself that I was a lesbian. Explaining my relationship with Penny to most of my family was not something I seriously considered, because internally I was still worried that I was damned to hell, and I was too ashamed to admit the truth. I unfairly presumed their reaction would be negative. Although Penny and I were in love, I didn't know if this would be a long-term relationship, and so I was relieved not to have to address our situation with my family at this point.

That quickly changed. Soon after I met Penny's family, an unexpected surgery forced me to introduce Penny to my parents, Don and Star, when they came to stay with me while I recovered. This introduction let me see a side of Penny I had not yet discovered: a fun-loving risk-taker. Penny's reputation at the Capitol was that she was no-nonsense, dignified, and solely focused on her work. Some of the young staff later told me they were afraid of her and her perfectionism. I had arranged a short dinner for Penny to meet my parents on a Thursday, the night before I had surgery. My parents and sister were to stay with me through the weekend at my Springfield apartment. Penny had a packed schedule of events, and I wasn't supposed to see her until Monday. On Sunday night, however, after canceling some of her events, she made an unexpected visit. She walked in wearing jeans and a pale yellow silk shirt and had a gallon of ice cream in her hand. She greeted Don and Star again, walked to the kitchen, and called, "Terry, can you give me a hand for a minute?"

I was a little thrown off because I hadn't planned for all of us to be together again, and I was nervous.

"What's up?" I said as I walked into the kitchen.

She pulled me by the hand out of sight of my family and began kissing me and hugging me as though I were on fire and her kisses would douse the flames.

"I love you so much. I missed you so much this weekend," she said.

I was stunned. Happy. But stunned. Penny—conservative, by-the-book, and discreet-as-they-come Senator Severns—had grabbed me in the kitchen while my family was twenty feet away and kissed me passionately and playfully. And she wasn't quick about it either.

"P," I whispered, laughing and pulling away. "My parents are going to wonder what we are doing."

"Serving ice cream," she said, kissing me over and over. "Star and Don," she yelled to make verbal contact with my folks.

"What are you *doing?* " I whispered incredulously, panicked and exasperated, worried they would walk in.

"We're bringing that ice cream right out," she informed. Then she whispered, "Send them home. Right now." She laughed. "We could be in bed in minutes."

I started to scoop the ice cream, and she came up behind me, kissing my back and wrapping her arms around my waist.

"Will you stop? They're gonna see us," I warned.

She walked out with two bowls in her hands for my folks. I followed.

"I'm telling you. This is the best I've ever had," she said, turning and giving me a wink.

Later that month, our relationship still deepening, Penny took a full day off from work and political events, unheard of for her. She called me Friday morning at work to say she was making a special dinner, and she asked if I could come home a little early. I was taken aback that she was scratching her entire workday and wondered what the special occasion was. When I arrived home, after walking more than two miles from where I parked, the house was spotless and candles were lit in the living room, dining room, and on a glass table in an alcove of windows that faced the wooded backyard. Penny seemed happy. We sat in the living room for a while, having drinks, and Penny would pop into the kitchen to tend to dinner. She had made a strawberry walnut salad with homemade strawberry vinaigrette, fish, and a homemade cake for dessert. She said she wanted us to eat in the backyard, but we couldn't because the neighbors might see us. Instead, we sat on chrome and leather chairs at the small glass table overlooking the wooded backyard. Barber's "Adagio" played in the background.

We ate dinner slowly and more peacefully than we usually did—often we joked that if we both arrived home by the ten o'clock news, it was an early night. "This is really nice," I said.

"Normal for once," she added.

"We're just busy," I said, feeling for the first time that maybe the hectic life of reporting and lawmaking caused us to miss something.

We spoke of how quickly our relationship had blossomed and how that had surprised both of us, particularly since we were so career driven. She said, "I've never known a love like this, Terry. I never knew I could be so happy." She must have written that phrase a hundred times in love letters and cards to me, which I still treasure.

At dinner, she wanted to talk about where we would retire. Being only twenty-seven years old, I hadn't really given serious thought to retirement yet, let alone what region of the country I'd want to spend that period of my life in. I had often thought I would live in Maine for a while, or travel oversees as a foreign correspondent, and I knew I would go to law school someday, but I never mapped it out more seriously than that. In fact, until I met Penny, I was convinced that Springfield was only a very short stop on the way to somewhere else. We dreamed aloud that night about what our house would look like and whether we would have a fireplace in the bedroom and what our kitchen would look like. It was an easy, fun conversation void of any politics or work, but Penny also seemed to be driving at something. She seemed more purpose-driven about our personal life, but I couldn't put my finger on where she was headed. She was excited, happy, and very unusually in slow-gear. It felt as though she wanted to cement our life together for a long time to come, if only by daydreaming our future. As we lingered at dinner, she said to me again, "I love you, Terry, and I am happy unlike I have ever been happy. I never knew I *could* be this happy."

Though I was usually one to be talkative and expressive, I didn't reply. I was passionately in love with Penny, knew that I wanted to spend my life with her, had declared my love in letters and cards. But in that moment, I sensed that Penny needed to express these feelings alone, giving them the full measure of their weight without the follow-up tag of "me too."

Then, the doorbell rang. The sensation of the "outside" world coursed through me. I jumped perhaps as firefighters do when the bell pulls them from a sound sleep. Because I was a nonentity in the house, I quietly slipped up from the table, although you couldn't see me from the front door. I tip-toed into the back of the kitchen near the basement door in case I needed to hide there. It turned out that our visitor was a neighbor kid who was selling something, and Penny took a few minutes to talk with him and buy what-ever he was peddling. She came back and sat down, almost with a dejected thud at the interruption. "I'm tired of us living here on Main Street. We have absolutely no privacy."

The tender moment had been broken, and she became quiet and her mood somewhat dark.

"You sit," I said. "I'll clean up." We both ended up clearing the table and doing the dishes, but her lightness and energy was gone. "Let's read for a while," I said. She was a voracious reader and read two to three biog-raphies a week. We took our cake upstairs to the library/den. She picked up one of her countless biographies, and I grabbed the novel I was reading. After midnight, we brushed our teeth and went to bed (after I got up to turn off the bathroom light). I fell asleep with the sensation that Penny wanted to say something to me that she did not say, but that feeling was in my periphery, so I didn't force it.

Despite my routine of waking at 4:00 AM to sneak out of Decatur, I'm more of an owl than a robin. And so I was irritated when, only a few hours after we had gone to bed, Penny tried to wake me as I lay sleeping next to her that Saturday morning before dawn.

"Terry," she whispered, her warm breath above my left ear.

"What?" I asked, my throat cracking its morning layer. I squeezed my eyes shut tightly and then sprung them open wide, trying to wring out the night, so I could hear what was on Penny's mind.

"Are you awake?" she asked. I didn't need to tax my reporting skills to see that she was wide-awake and had been for a while. I pushed myself up on my elbows. I wondered if Penny were not feeling well, or perhaps had finally decided whether she would pursue the Illinois treasurer's race or the comptroller's race in the 1994 elections, in which case I was fully prepared to be irritated. Over the last several weeks, that decision-making process for my senator-lover mirrored a Wimbledon match. Treasurer. Comptroller.

Treasurer. Comptroller. Did I really need to know the final answer before dawn on a Saturday, when we planned to sleep in?

"You okay?" I asked.

She was staring at me, a watery glaze in her eyes.

"Terry, if I could, I would marry you tomorrow. I love you."

Her face was intense. Her voice seemed to be coming right from her sparkling brown eyes.

"Penny, if I could, I would marry you today. I love you too," I said.

We made love, and afterward, we lay talking.

"I'm sorry we can't marry," she said.

"I'm sorry that we can't even walk into a room together as partners," I said. "I can't even be a date for you at a wedding, let alone your spouse."

How we just accepted that premise in 1993, the year of "Don't ask, don't tell."

"What made you think of that this morning?" I asked.

"I've been thinking about it for a while," she said, lying on her back, talking with her eyes closed. I figured I was right that she had been thinking about this the night before. "I was thinking about Ken and Sheryl," she said.

Sheryl Cummins was one of her best friends who had met Ken Frye about the same time that Penny and I met. Just recently, they announced that they were engaged. Sheryl lived just a few doors down from us, and when she had told Penny she had fallen in love, Penny came home a little sad. She told me that she was so happy for Sheryl, but that she wanted to be able to tell Sheryl that she too had met someone and fallen in love.

"I felt like I couldn't tell her a part of my life," she said, grimacing as though the omission scratched her. "I know Sheryl would have been fine. She wouldn't have cared that I was involved with a woman. She would just be happy that I am happy."

While there was such happiness in her words and intent, a veil of sadness seemed to descend on us. It was as though we both wanted this but accepted without challenge that we could not have it. At the time, we did not discuss privately committing to each other or exchanging tokens of our love. It seemed Penny just wanted me to know that if she could marry me, she would. The intent and the expression of just how much we loved each other seemed enough in that moment, and we were very happy.

We were leaving in a few days for separate international trips, and we spent most of the day Saturday cleaning the house and making to-do lists. We moved into that hot Midwestern day of tasks, but the day was now different than any other we had ever experienced alone or together. We behaved as though we were betrothed. We felt and acted differently. Our home brimmed with a new hope and lightness, and a new beginning together. We seemed particularly gentle and soft with each other, as any other newly engaged couple would be.

In her capacity as senator, Penny was going to Israel with the Jewish Federation. In my capacity as AP reporter, I wrote about her junket in a story that appeared on page one of her local paper. While the Legislature wouldn't provide a list of those members attending the event, Penny gave me the list, adding to her staff's irritation with me.

Penny was permitted to bring a guest, and we talked endlessly about whether that could be me. We decided it could not, and though I had tried to convince the Federation to let me go along as a reporter at AP's expense, they declined, saying lawmakers wouldn't be as free to experience the trip if a reporter joined them. I decided to take a vacation instead and go visit my brother Scott, a military paratrooper stationed in Germany. We would return from Europe in time for Penny to attend a political rally at the Illinois State Fair and for me to cover the political event. After that, we planned a vacation to Mexico for a few days, our first vacation together.

Penny had told me that she had a bad habit of putting off everything she needed to do to get ready for a trip until the last minute and was usually up very late the day before she was supposed to depart. I laughed when she told me this because I suffered from the same procrastination problem, often cutting airport arrival way too close. We decided that we would try and solve this for each other by making a list: do laundry, find passports, pick up medicine, make last-minute political calls, make sure Penny explained the cat-sitting routine in writing for her mother. We planned to leave for Chicago early that afternoon, giving us enough time to stop and see Patty before going out to dinner. We would spend the next morning shopping and having a leisurely day before our evening flights.

Our good intentions failed, and we didn't finish doing errands and packing until 11:00 PM. We drove to Chicago that night, and despite how late it was, Penny wanted to stop and see Patty before she left for this trip. Around midnight, we met Patty at a drug store parking lot in Bloomington for just a few minutes. Patty said hello to me as I sat in the driver's seat, and she handed me some Diet Cokes and snacks for the road. Penny got out of the car and went to talk to Patty. When Penny got back in the car and Patty leaned in for another kiss to say so long, Penny said, "Oh, I almost forgot." And she handed Patty an envelope. When we drove away, Penny told me that she had given Patty a few thousand dollars, something that became a routine before we parted for every vacation. Penny told me later that sometimes she felt guilty that she had found so much happiness and felt bad that Patty didn't have the same opportunities to travel. We checked into the airport Hilton and slept in until noon. We decided not to go downtown and instead hung out at the hotel.

Before we left, we traded presents. Penny had given me a package to be opened on the plane. I opened it after takeoff and found a portable CD player with some of our favorite music and a card that read, *Terry, our love is deeper than any ocean we will ever cross. Love, P.* I had given her a stack of letters, cards, and notes for each morning and night she was away from me. I had wrapped the love letters in a red silk ribbon.

We had not planned to talk to each other during these two weeks, but when I landed and checked into my first hotel, I had a message waiting from Penny. Silly as it was, in the throes of young love, we ended up calling each other twice a day, billing it back to our home phones. On one call, Penny told me about a lawmaker who was traveling with his wife and that all they did was gripe. "I feel like marriage is squandered on them. If we were here together, this would be an even more wonderful trip." On another call, she said lightheartedly, "I have a confession to make."

"What's that?" I said.

"I opened all your letters on the plane, and I don't have any more to open. So I am just rereading them."

Eighteen hundred dollars in phone calls later, Penny returned from abroad first and stayed in Chicago until I arrived the next day. She was waiting for me with a dozen roses when I exited customs at O'Hare. We hugged—tightly, quickly, and, we thought, casually. We fumbled over each other, wanting to hold each other's hands but knowing we could not. We got to the car and our feelings were too much to contain, and we began kissing, laughing, and crying with happiness.

Exhausted, we drove the three hours to Decatur, stopped at the store a few towns over because we were together, and then went home.

That night, Penny said, "Do you remember what I said to you before we left, about marrying me?"

"No, I don't recall that," I said teasingly.

"Well, then, I guess you don't want these," she said nonchalantly, tossing two wrapped boxes onto the glass coffee table. One was a ring box. The other a long, rectangular box.

I was surprised, excited, and nervous.

She started to unwrap the boxes. "We can't wear wedding rings, but we can wear a matching ring and a bracelet." She fastened the bracelet on my wrist, I put the ring on her finger, and we kissed and went upstairs. When we awoke wearing only our jewelry, Penny said to me, "We can't marry, but we've joined in our hearts."

Later that day, Penny went to see her parents and I stayed home. I wrote her a letter, an overly flowery product of a twenty-something's new love. I found this letter after her death amid the hundreds of love letters she saved:

Sweetheart,

If the sky were my parchment and the ocean my inkwell, I could never have the room nor the ink to adequately write of what you make me feel. Our shared new experience together, a life bound by our hearts, will guide and sustain us in what is ahead. I would marry you if the laws would permit and humanity would accept. As you said this morning, we have, in our hearts, joined. I have never been so wanting and excited in sharing that than I am with you. I'm swirling in space, swirling about in intense delight. You take me to the highest mountain and dive me through the deepest ocean. You make me feel like I am part of you and have been all of my life. You seem to know just what I need at the right moment, whether it's a touch, a look, a smile, or a laugh. My body responds to you as do my mind and heart.

Know, my friend and lover and heart's mate, that I cherish, respect, love, honor, want, thank, need, and love you. May the path we have chosen

be easy on our feet, light on our souls, soft to our touch, and gentle to our
spirits, who make us who we are.

My love and trust always,

Terry lee

Of course, there would be no newspaper announcement, no press release, no public ceremony and celebratory reception attended by friends and family. Instead, we trothed ourselves to another purpose: keeping our love and marriage secret from everyone we knew, starting with the press.

CHAPTER EIGHT

FINDING THE LUMP

Shortly after I arrived home from Europe and Penny from the Middle East, we departed on a two-week trip to Mexico for our first vacation together. Although we didn't discuss it as such, our trip felt very much like a honeymoon. On the plane, I couldn't stop touching my bracelet to be sure it was there. She kept fingering her ring and smiling. Once there, we easily slipped into a routine free of the restraints we felt in the States. We walked hand in hand and were affectionate in public. We slept on the beach all day and explored the town each night, eating, drinking, and shopping to happy excess. Shedding the secrecy and lies we were used to let us simply live out loud. Of course, Mexico wasn't exactly Amsterdam, and so we were cautious, and yet in comparison to the strictures we created in central Illinois, we felt free.

I had told some friends and family I was going to Mexico but had led them to believe I was going alone. Because I had had dinner with Penny's family several times that summer, Penny had told Helen that we had decided to take a trip together, casually saying, "We both needed a vacation and decided it would be cheaper to go together." She cautioned her that we weren't telling our friends this and added a particular request: "Don't mention anything to Linda, Okay? She wouldn't like that I'm going away with a reporter."

When we returned, our whole outlook on life was different. People in each of our lives sensed the change and would confront us and say that they knew "something" happened. Friends repeatedly asked me if I was in love.

People who knew that Penny went to Mexico but believed she'd gone alone asked if she had fallen in love with a Mexican man. When we saw Helen the first time after our trip, she declared, "You two are positively glowing." Penny laughed and said it must be the "tan and the rest." Helen knew better. She put my hand in hers and patted it. "You remind me so much of my daughter Marsha," she said, her voice halting with emotion as she remembered her youngest child who had died of breast cancer. "I am so happy you are part of our family."

Helen was a very persistent and powerful presence, and I just could never bring myself to call her by her first name. Unsure how to respond, I simply said, "Thank you, Mrs. Severns."

Work, although incredibly busy, took a backseat for both of us, as we focused on spending time together, building a life.

"I've never bought really good china or silverware since I had my first apartment," Penny said to me one Saturday while we were cleaning. "Let's freshen up the house for a new start." Although I was young, it was thrilling to be building a home with the woman of my dreams. For the next few months, life calmed in a way I had never known. With the betrothal, the ring, and the bracelet, we behaved as though we were married. Our relationship had deepened in the quiet way one anticipates the unfolding of a long married life; we felt solid and safe in having committed to each other, and we were solely focused on each other. Even the crazy machinations and lies of hiding our lives somehow now felt muted because of how much we loved each other.

In October, Penny had finally chosen to run for comptroller of Illinois instead of treasurer. Preparations for this political race were intense. We had talked many times about the discomfort and ethical breach of a reporter being involved with a source. And although we had not yet arrived at a solution to this, we tried to minimize this conundrum where we could. As a reporter, I told Penny I would not be involved in any aspect of her race. I wouldn't give her advice, edit her materials, or assist in any way. I told her she should not talk to me about the inside of the campaign because if I found something out, I would write about it, as I had with her junket to Israel. She agreed. I was trying to rein in the ethical lines that we had long ago improperly crossed. The Democratic ticket was shaping up, and the major action was in the governor's race. In Illinois, gubernatorial and lieutenant governor candidates used to run separately in the primary election, but the victors then became a joint ticket in the general election. Dick Phelan was running for governor. He was a former special counsel to the U.S. House of Representatives Ethics Committee who had investigated Speaker Jim Wright for ethical and financial violations. Phelan's work resulted in Wright becoming the first Speaker of the House in history to resign. Phelan came up with the creative idea to tap a running mate early on, hoping voters would view and vote for them as a "ticket" in the primary. He was facing a formidable liberal senator and Northwestern University law professor, Dawn Clark Netsch, and knew that he needed to do something to capture the vote of women.

About five weeks after Penny announced for comptroller, Phelan called her and asked for a meeting in Chicago. He wanted her to be his running mate and serve as lieutenant governor. Although lieutenant governor is viewed generally as a do-nothing post designed solely to replace a governor if something happens to him or her, Phelan pledged that Penny would be a full partner in his administration, spearheading the budget. They would present themselves as a team and hope voters followed suit. Penny was more excited than I had ever seen her in her work with this opportunity to make something out of the normally boring position. But she was simultaneously more deflated than I had ever seen her because she had already announced for comptroller and therefore felt committed to that campaign and also because, as a woman, she felt a loyalty to Netsch, who was the first female candidate for governor of Illinois.

"There is no way I can back out of comptroller," she said a few days after Phelan made the proposal. For days, she met with her staff and campaign folks to find a plausible way to switch races and maintain her political integrity. And for days, she would come home depressed. I broke my own rule and asked her to tell me what she was thinking and what advice she was receiving. She said that she had already vacillated so much about running for comptroller versus state treasurer that she and her staff felt that she would be run out of politics if she dropped out of that race to ladder-climb to the top of the ticket.

I decided to intervene.

"I think you should run for lieutenant governor," I declared. "You're happy and energized, and Phelan is offering you a chance to be a real partner. I think you should do it."

"But how? I'm going to take a real hit for this. You of all people know that. And what am I going to say to Dawn? She's a friend."

"Look, Penny, the election is a year away. Do you *really* think that the voters are even focused on the election yet? Hell no. I cover politics and don't know the difference between comptroller and treasurer. People don't even know the comptroller office exists, or they think the same office has two names." Penny looked away, and I thought I hurt her feelings. But I knew this decision was important and I didn't want Penny to miss the incredible opportunity. So I continued.

"I've only been in the state a few months, but I've seen how people like that you are authentic and speak your mind to them," I said. "Use that. Start using the phrase 'public servant' instead of 'politician.' For this to work, you have to offer them something in this deal. Convince them that it's about them: They are getting something, and you are sacrificing something. And for God's sake, stop listening to the handlers. The politicos are uncomfortable because it's just never been done this way before. If Illinois needs you as lieutenant governor, then tell them you are willing to give up your personal preference of being comptroller and do it for them."

She loved it. She called Phelan and told him she had an idea and would like to meet with him. The next day she drove to Chicago and talked it through. Phelan loved it, and so did both their staffs. But Linda Hawker initially disliked the idea, and that worried Penny. Linda has great political acumen and had served as Penny's campaign manager previously, orchestrating an incredibly tough campaign to unseat a ten-year Senate incumbent against all odds. She had been throwing out different considerations. She strongly believed that no matter how Penny spun it, her credibility would suffer, and since Netsch was a friend, Penny should support her. In retrospect, Linda had a point about Penny and Netsch being friends, but she and I didn't dwell on that aspect then. Penny listened to Linda's concerns, but she pushed back a bit, pointing out that several women had approached Netsch about tapping Penny and that Netsch had wanted to wait. Despite Linda's advice, Penny opted to move forward with Phelan. The night before the announcement, Hawker finally revealed the root of her concern, and it had Penny in tears. For the first time, Linda raised concerns about Penny's friendship with me. She had told Penny that she overheard some Republicans talking about Penny's "Pennsylvania connection," but she refused to share who had supposedly said it. Penny didn't believe that Linda had overheard this. She believed that Linda was concerned and was putting this out there as a way of scaring us into ending our relationship.

I didn't have a problem with Hawker sharing her concerns about the race or her spot-on sense that Penny and I were more than friends. I did, however, have a problem with the fact that she was doing this the night before the announcement, and I also felt that if she were that deeply loyal to Penny, she would tell her the source of the allegation. I too believed she was using the claim to give voice to her own fears.

Penny and I talked well into the night, and my sole goal was to try and rebuild her confidence. The next morning, as she showered, I wrote her a note that said, *Part of me is filled with rage this morning at how much I believe "our friend" is deeply rude and negative. Keep focused, remain yourself (as you have advised me on other occasions), and remember you're going to do wonderfully. Keep the vision of why you are doing this. Wherever you are on the campaign trail, I am there with you.*

Phelan and Penny did a joint news conference. He started by talking about Illinois's financial problems and that the budget needed to be a top priority. He talked about a new partnership in the governor's mansion and Penny's budget expertise. They were off to an energized start. Some opponents pounded on Penny's flip-flop, but overall, the message that Illinois "needed her" worked. She got past the false starts of treasurer and comptroller, and eventually she won the Democratic primary. From the moment we created the successful flip-flop message, Penny consulted me on every political decision she made until the end of her life, even if she didn't always take my advice. And, honestly, whereas I had held the inside game of politics in great disdain previously, now I was hooked. In years to come, Linda, in talking with Penny, would sometimes still refer to me as "the Pennsylvania connection." Penny would come home and rant and rave about how she didn't like this but wasn't sure how to take it on without tipping the truth. I advised her to ignore it and not let it bother her. "It's not fair, Terry," Penny would say. "You're not a detriment to me. You're the love of my life."

While she devoted herself to the campaign, I devoted myself to more pleasurable hobbies like seeing more of my friends without leaving parties early, antiquing, and planning Christmas. Though I'd always been a last-minute shopper, I felt different this year. I wanted our first Christmas together to be memorable, and I started planning early. Earlier that spring, before we were even dating, Penny had told me she hadn't had a Christmas tree since her sister Marsha died. Marsha had loved Christmas, and Penny could not bear the painful memories a Christmas tree evoked. On a sheet of reporter's notebook paper, dated 1:00 PM, May 17, 1993, and inserted into my journal, I had written: *I'm not allowed to write this yet, but if I were: Dear P: Why am I bothered that you have not had a Christmas tree for two years? Why is it that I see snowflakes falling and disappearing as each kisses your face? Why do I see decorating a tree and loving you in front of a fireplace?* I had pledged in ink that if I was reading the relationship cards correctly and we got together, I would make it a priority to have a tree for her.

In mid-December, Penny was traveling for work. I went to a tree farm, picked and cut a tree, and waited until after dark to pull into our driveway and unload it. I set it up and strung lights, but I didn't decorate it, as I wanted us to do that together. Penny came home Sunday night, saw the tree, and started crying. We sat on the couch and I held her as she cried and told me about Marsha's illness and death and how very scared she was for Patty, who was in remission with the same disease that had claimed Marsha. Penny told me that returning Christmas trees to Christmas was the best present I could have given her. We built a fire, made snacks, played music, drank Baileys, and decorated the Douglas fir. That year, in love, with lots of time on my hands as Penny was campaigning, I went to the fabric store, bought bolts of velvet and silk, and wrapped all my presents to her in hand-sewn cloth and tied them with lace ribbons. For New Year's Eve, I bought us tickets to the St. Louis Symphony, and I gave Penny a copy of the playbill from the summer where I had written that if Penny and I dated, I would bring her to the symphony on New

Year's Eve. In less than eight months, my fantasy had become my reality, and I was happier than I ever knew I could be.

After the holidays, less than a year since our life together began, our lives changed forever. February flurries were flying outside our bedroom windows. I always liked the way our bedroom hung over the main part of that first house of ours in Decatur. The tiny rectangular windows with small white windowpanes gave it a tree-fort feeling. I loved it because it seemed fun, secluded, and very Swiss Family Robinson-esque.

We had slept in later than usual that morning. We opted to stay in bed instead of attempting to make it to the newsstand before it closed at noon. Our regular stack of Sunday papers included *The New York Times,* the *St. Louis Post-Dispatch, The Chicago Tribune, The Sun-Times,* the *State Journal Register,* and the *Decatur Herald & Review.* We never missed a Sunday run to the newsstand for anything—well, almost anything. Penny had walked downstairs to turn up the heat, and I asked her to turn on some music. She chose *Phantasy,* piano music by Danny Wright. I heard the front door open and knew she must be picking up the *Chicago Tribune* and the Decatur paper, the two delivered to our doorstep.

I lay on my stomach with my head on the pillow, looking with tired eyes at the open closet doors and the scores of shoes on the floor. Outside of a store, I had never seen so many colors and styles of shoes. I heard the refrigerator door open and close, and I figured two Diet Cokes were on their way with the ink. Penny got back in bed and pulled her hometown tear sheet from its plastic cover. I remember making some joke about squandering a Sunday morning to news instead of nuzzling.

"Patience is a virtue," she said.

"For the celibate," I replied dryly, eyes closed and still facing the closet.

She kissed the back of my exposed neck playfully.

"Oh, sure, now that you know you're not on page one," I said, feigning aloofness but turning around to look at her.

"And, look," she said, feigning shock and holding the newspaper at arm's length. "No page-one byline for the AP bureau chief." She tossed the paper off the side of the bed. "Slipping?"

"You wish."

We fell into making love that morning, teasing each other and talking as we explored instead of the more quiet way we usually offered ourselves. Penny was straddling my waist. I had begun to run my hands up her sides. Caressing her, my thumb grazed what felt like a lump under her left breast near her sternum, in about the same location as the tip of a rib might be.

"What is that?" I said, startled.

"What?" Penny said.

"This, right here," I said, taking her finger and placing it over mine and then moving my finger away.

She felt for a minute.

"A rib, I think," she said.

We both sat up as though we had discovered a ticking time bomb and tried to figure out what we were feeling. We walked into the bathroom to get a look in the mirror.

"It's a rib. I really think it's a rib," Penny said, and the location did look like it could have been a rib, as it was not on the flesh of the breast itself.

"I think we should have that looked at," I said. "You have an exam coming up in Champaign, don't you?" I asked.

"Yeah," she said.

I was scared and wanted to believe it really was a rib. The lump was small and hard, and it felt like the tip of a rib might feel, or at least how I envisioned the tip of a rib might feel. Neither of us could shake the feeling of worry. It was an eerie replay of a moment we had the summer before, shortly after we had met, when I had found a lump in my own breast.

Given Penny's family history with the disease, I opted not to tell Penny until I had at least a doctor's appointment in place, drawing heavy ire for making an executive decision without her. She insisted I get a quicker appointment.

"Time is everything. Don't you think I learned that with Marsha?" she said kindly but firmly.

More remarkable than her insistence that I speed up the appointment was that Penny insisted on going to the doctor with me. I had the mammogram, and Penny insisted on coming with me when the doctor reviewed the results. We walked in, and I introduced her to Dr. Burns as a friend. He recognized her, said he was glad to meet her, and Penny simply said, "I just thought an extra set of ears would be good."

It was simple. It was clean. Why didn't we apply that approach to the rest of our lives?

Penny knew way more than I did about breast health and was able to talk to the doctor about options as an expert. "What would you recommend if it were your wife?" she asked.

"I'd go with the lumpectomy," he said,.

Penny stood with my parents and sister as I was wheeled into the surgery room, had lunch with my family while I was in the operating room, and then left after I arrived in the recovery room. A few days later she showed up at my apartment with ice cream in hand. The surgery went well, the lump was benign, and our lives returned to normal.

Now, months later, we were trying to shake the jitters of finding a lump in her breast, in the middle of making love, no less. My knees felt weak, as if I had just averted a car crash. We got dressed and went downstairs. She made coffee. Ignoring daylight, I walked outside to get some firewood. I carried it in the house on the brown canvas carrier with leather handles, slipped off my shoes, and built a fire. We agreed that she needed to get to a doctor ASAP.

What I didn't understand and was not sensitive to was how terrified Penny must have been given her sisters' experiences. About two weeks later, the day that she had her scheduled exam in Champaign, I got up at the usual 4:00 AM, but I said I was going to take the day off and go with her. She would have no part of it. Pointing out how she came with me to Dr. Burns's office last summer didn't move her at all.

I decided I was going to forego the morning routine. If people saw me when I left the house, so be it. I was staying. We slept a little longer and then got up. We took a shower, and then Penny pulled out a suit, laid it on the unmade bed, and walked to the bathroom.

"Why don't you just wear jeans? We'll blow around Champaign when we're done," I said, trying to entice her into letting me go.

"I'm not going to the doctor today."

"What do you mean?" I said.

"I'm not going today. I'm rescheduling it."

"Penny, I want them to look at that lump."

"Rib," she declared.

"Okay, rib."

"An event came up, and I have to be there."

"Fuck the event."

"Terry, I'm not going today."

I walked into the upstairs den across from the bathroom and sat in the brown crushed-velour wingback. I tried to regroup and figure out what I could say that might convince her. Sometimes, I think back and wish that I would have had some kind of experience that may have helped me recognize her fear. I would have known as I do now, having lived through her death, that fear, like lightening, flashes in our souls and paralyzes us, often without explanation. At twenty-seven, I didn't understand the terror that Penny must have been feeling. Narrowly, I saw it as stubbornness. I saw it as a very poor choice between politics and life. If I could have just gotten myself, my pride, and my own fear out of the way and focused on *her* and seen things from *her* angle, maybe I would have understood that she was terrified and would have been able to help her better. *If only. If only. If only.*

I walked back into the bedroom and sat down on the edge of our bed.

"Penny," I said gingerly. "Honey, I don't want to push this, and I don't mean to nag you. But you know, if this were me, or if this were Patty, or your mom, you would insist that we go to the doctor now. How many times did you tell me that a month wasn't good enough when I had the appointment with Burns? You, of all people, know this. Why are you doing this? It's already been two weeks."

"Terry, I will reschedule the appointment."

Something inside me erupted. I started spewing about her stubbornness, her sick, fucked-up belief that politics was more important than her own life, her cavalier attitude, and the fact that when she made up her mind she didn't care who it affected. She was doing what she wanted to do. "Period. End of sentence," I said for emphasis. My stream of anger turned into a stream of tears. Despite the fact that I thought myself a wordsmith, a lawyer without the license, I made no headway. Nothing I said, nothing I did, nothing I conveyed moved her from her decision.

She would not go to the doctor that day.

"You want to roll the dice with your life?" I stormed. "Great, do it! I'm not going to be part of it! Go to your precious fucking meeting, Senator."

There are words that leave our mouths and travel on invisible currents of air, words that haunt us through the tired years when we are alone and aching. I hear those awful words in the rustling leaves. I see them on late winter afternoons when I drive past a row of naked trees in a field, their unclothed branches of truth staring at me. Sometimes, when the sun slips behind the horizon, blending the pain of its reds with the forgiveness of its turquoise and the healing of its mauve, I remember that inept closing argument I gave to a one-woman jury, and lost.

How I wish I could retract those words and put my arm around Penny instead. Name the paralysis and say to her, "I know you must be frozen in fear, but let's do this together." I should have told her that I understood her fear because of her experience with Marsha and Patty. Perhaps I should have called Patty. I wish I had said, "We are both afraid, so let's just slow down here and have a cup of coffee and figure this out." I am sure that my wanting to rewrite this history, to say the "right things," is really just masked regret—a hollow hope that if I would have been able to convince her to go to the doctor immediately, that maybe she would have lived.

I dismissed Penny, who was standing nearby, and strode down the steps. I sat on the last step, put my shoes on, grabbed my coat and hat, didn't say goodbye, and perhaps to express the depth of my anger, I strode out the front door, something I had never done on my way to work. I stuffed my hands in my pockets and kept my head down and my black brimmed hat tilted to the right, hiding my eyes—not because I was afraid someone would recognize me, but because I was ashamed that I couldn't stop the convulsing in my throat and the flow of tears streaming down my face.

About an hour later, my cell phone rang as I was pulling into Springfield.

"I'm sorry, Terry," Penny said in a voice so small it was nearly unrecognizable.

"I'm the one who is sorry. I said some awful things and I didn't mean to. I'm just worried and scared."

"Let's talk about this tonight, okay?" she said quietly.

"Okay," I said. And, for a moment, the world had righted itself. I felt my heart beating again, and the swirl of tenderness I felt for her started anew.

It was a quiet day at work, but I felt ill, like I had the flu—I didn't take in too much food or liquid and didn't want to talk too much. I felt better that she called, albeit bruised, but I wanted to be still and not stir up the acidic feeling within me that finally had quieted down.

That night, we both got home around seven, and instead of eating dinner, we went right to bed and made love. "I'm sorry I hurt you," I said very sadly. She instead became playful. She pointed to her elbow. "You hurt me here," she said. I kissed her. "And, you hurt me here," she said, laughing and touching her neck. I kissed her.

"Well, you hurt me here," I said, putting my finger over my lips. She rolled her eyes, apparently bored with my obvious choice.

"Let me see if I can guess where I hurt you," she said. And we just laid and laughed and loved.

I don't know how this is possible, even now, years later, as I sit in Penny's Senate chair in my home office and watch these black characters appear on my computer screen, but Penny made and canceled two more appointments over the next four months. She didn't go the doctor until June, and it took another month to schedule the lumpectomy. Even then, we spun the news: "Caught early, less than two centimeters."

Recently, I looked at a ruler. The same truth is that the lump was three-quarters of an inch. Many times, long before Penny died, we talked about whether those months had made a difference. That summer, Penny and I made a pact that we would not tell anybody how we really found the lump, or that we found it in late February 1994.

CHAPTER NINE

MAKING A DEAL WITH GOD

Two days had passed since the surgeon sliced open Penny's left breast. The doctor had pushed through the operating room doors on July 19, 1994, wearing a blue gossamer hairnet and booties that made his feet look like lumps of dough covered in cheesecloth. He said the lump appeared to be malignant.

"But we got good clean margins," he added, trying to include good news. I'll never forget that phrase, "clean margins." What does it even mean? It sounds like bleeding to death in the bathtub—at least you don't get blood on the white carpet. He said the confirming lab results would take about forty-eight hours.

Penny was still campaigning hard. She didn't want to tell anyone that she had a lump and was having it biopsied. She decided to keep this a secret until we knew whether the lump was cancerous. Before the surgery, she spoke to the doctor, grilling him, it seemed, more about his ability to keep a secret than to perform the surgery itself. She took a few personal days off from the campaign and told her staff it was a family-related issue. The doctor's office agreed to let her enter the hospital under a pseudonym. The doctor's nurse practitioner had come up with the fake name, Susan Hartman. It seemed surreal, and we agreed that she would never enter a hospital under a pseudonym again.

As we waited the forty-eight hours for the results, I was tormented in a private hell that I didn't share with Penny, or anyone. I felt as though my mind were a towel being wrung, with one hand saying, *You are in love with her,* and the other hand saying, *Being a lesbian is a curse and you caused her illness.* My rugged fundamentalist religious upbringing, which I have always cherished, didn't mesh with the life I was leading—living with a woman whom I loved deeply and considered myself married to. I began to believe that her illness was a punishment for choosing that life. Every positive and happy thought was being wrung out of me. From the moment I found the lump on Penny's breast, black thoughts saturated my mind like dripping water.

It's your fault.

Drip.

If you would have obeyed God, you wouldn't be in this mess.

Drip.

She *wouldn't be in this mess.*

Drip.

We all fall short of the glory of God.

Your sin will cause her death.

Drip, drip, drip, drip.

I felt I couldn't be honest with God, and yet I was praying every waking moment for Penny. I asked Him not to punish her for my transgressions. I was sure that I was the cancer's cause and equally confident He was its cure. I felt afraid to pray to God for *real.* I felt afraid to speak to Him as a friend and instead spoke to Him as a distant deity. If I had prayed honestly, I would have said, "Father, I don't understand any of this." I was afraid to say, "Lord, I love Penny with all that is in me." I feared God. I feared His anger. More deeply though, I know I feared His love. I feared His tenderness. I fear anyone's tenderness really, as I often feel unworthy. How could I be so silly as to think that He didn't understand the very heart I believed He created?

These thoughts knocked hard at the inside of my temples, denting me with self-doubt and self-loathing. And I knew these thoughts wouldn't let up as we waited to know whether the lump was cancerous. Worse, Penny and I couldn't spend much time together, as she needed to return to the campaign trail. The doctor encouraged her to take a few days off, but she refused. Phelan had lost his bid for governor, and Penny moved on to be partnered with Netsch. The Netsch-Severns ticket was also taking on national attention, and the media coverage was becoming even more intense. *The Washington Post* wrote about Netsch and Severns as the first two-woman gubernatorial ticket of a major party in American history. Three months before the election, eighteen- and twenty-hour days were now the norm.

Two days after the surgery, Penny called me late Thursday afternoon at the AP office.

"AP. Mutchler," I said.

"Sweetheart, can you talk?" she whispered.

Had it been good news, she would have just blurted out that things were okay. My colleagues were gone from the office, gathering news, and I said I could talk.

"Well, it's not the news we wanted. The lump was malignant. But he says he got everything. He wants to go back in and take some lymph nodes next week."

I started crying. I panicked. *I caused this, and there is no way around that truth. Can I atone? Can I offer to trade places?*

Penny's voice started cracking.

"It's going to be all right," she said. "We got it early."

Then I *really* started crying, remembering our February discovery of the lump.

"P," I said tentatively, about to remind her.

"I know."

"Where are you going to be tonight?" I asked. "Are you home?"

"No, I'm flying to southern Illinois."

"Why can't you stay in Chicago and fly in the morning? At least I could drive up." If I were in Chicago for the night, I could work the next day at our AP office there. Southern Illinois was four hours south, and it was already late in the day. Penny wouldn't get to the hotel until at least eleven, and if I went, I would have to leave at 3:00 AM to get back to work on time. Somehow, because my marriage was secret, it never occurred to me that I could simply take a day off, call in sick, or say I had a personal emergency.

"We have events all day, but we wind up in Springfield, and I am going to stay at home most of the day Saturday before flying to Chicago on Sunday."

"Have you told Netsch?" I asked.

"I wanted to talk to you first. I'm going to call Pat in a few minutes, though, and then I'm not going to say anything until we can talk this weekend."

We decided to wait until the next day to see each other. She said she had to go.

"I love you," she said, just as a colleague walked into my office.

"Thank you, Senator," I said, feeling caught instead of realizing he had no idea who I was talking to or what the person had just said.

We hung up. I wanted to pray right then and there. I wanted to fall to my knees and scream. If I am safe, my soul doesn't cry out. In crisis, I am quick to pray. I heard people speaking, but it was a din in the distance. I walked upstairs—the stairs where I saw Penny for the first time—and stepped into the ladies' room off the House floor. I remember splashing cold water on my face and how good it felt. My gut was jumping like a fish on concrete.

More thoughts flooded in.

This is your fault.

She would have been better off if she hadn't met you.

Everything happens for a reason.

Don't run.

Have faith. Be certain of God.

God is love.

I felt like I just experienced a bomb explosion. My hearing, my sight, and my breathing were stunned. I did not know what to do, who to turn to, where to go. I desperately wanted to talk honestly with Penny about this private struggle, but I talked myself out of that. She needed me to be strong, not get sidetracked with my own doubts. Nobody knew that Penny and I were partners. I couldn't tell friends—most were in the press. And even if I could tell them about Penny and me, I *surely* couldn't tell them now—it would mean disclosing that the lieutenant governor candidate on the Democratic ticket had breast cancer. I couldn't tell Anne Conners. After all of her help, I had lied to her early on, nonchalantly telling that her that nothing worked out with Penny. I wanted to call my sister Donna and tell her the whole truth, but I was not ready to be out, and I just wanted to talk about Penny's illness, not my sexuality. A thought flashed. I remembered a woman had told me about a Pentecostal church behind the Capitol and that she thought a great deal of the minister. I am not a Pentecostal—in fact, the interdenominational faith I grew up in would be considered to the right of that group.

I knew I could pray anywhere, but I wanted to be with other people. I wanted to be with long-haired women wearing skirts and men who were clean-cut and polite. I went to the church behind the Capitol. Hearing the traditional hymns "Old Rugged Cross" and "Amazing Grace" brought me deep comfort.

I prayed hard, but I did not pray honestly. I never told God what I was thinking. I never said, *I feel that I caused this. I feel that Penny's cancer is a punishment for me being a lesbian.* I just prayed for her and her strength and health. But the tormentors came back: *I'm to blame. If I hadn't fallen in love with Penny, if we were not lesbians, then maybe this sickness would have passed her.* Because we were closeted and isolated, no one could alleviate my crazy fears or even address them. Penny's and my whole life's mission, other than loving each other, was to ensure that no one knew we were partners. I felt that my soul was a piece of metal, crumpling like a crash-test car in slow motion.

Crying with my head down, I believed I had to atone. For a moment, I stopped praying and tuned back into the sermon. The minister spoke about how if you have the Holy Ghost within you, you have to speak in tongues to prove it. I thought of the scriptures that disprove this doctrine and was no longer interested in his sermon. I started to feel suffocated, and now I regretted coming here. My right hand gripped the nicked, rounded wooden pew in front of me, and I felt as though I were on the verge of throwing up. I bent over and watched my tears splash on the floor. Since the moment I found the lump, something in the back of my mind said, *If I left Penny alone, she would be better off.* Now that once-backburner thought was roiling. No matter how hard I gripped that pew, I couldn't withstand the swelling feeling in my heart, and I blurted a nonsensical prayer that has haunted me ever since:

"Father, if You will just spare her life—if You will just spare her getting sick and losing her hair from this chemo—Lord, I promise You, I will leave her. Please God, save her."

My shaking stopped. I was not calm, but I felt still, clammy.

Nothing mattered now.

I had turned off a part of me. I had made the unilateral deal. I didn't know how I would leave a woman I loved so deeply, but in my heart I wanted her to live more than I wanted to live with her. I couldn't go back on my promise to God. That was it. If He would make her well, I would leave her. It was as simple and complicated as that.

The service ended, and before I could leave, several congregants gathered and asked if I wanted to join their church. I told them no, that I went to an interdenominational tabernacle based in Indiana. Then assistant minister, Joseph Harrod, heard me say this and asked me if I knew William Branham. I confirmed that Reverend Branham was my minister, and Reverend Harrod lit up with great respect.

Standing in the back of that church, Reverend Harrod said to me and to the people gathered, "You won't believe this. My mother couldn't walk without braces. She was paralyzed. Back in 1946, in a little church in backwater Arkansas, Reverend Branham prayed for her, and she walked out of the church, without the braces. She walked normally for the rest of her life." The congregants gasped. He told us his mother followed Reverend Branham's ministry around the country. "He could preach for three hours and it felt like fifteen minutes, even when I was a boy."

I kicked into proselytizing. "And," I said, "he never took an offering. He believed that if God wanted him to preach around the corner or around the world, He would make a way. To this day, his ministry still does not ask for money." The people looked to Reverend Harrod to see if that fact was true. He nodded and then asked me if Brother Branham's sermons were ever distributed to other countries. I told him that yes, they translated 1,177 of his sermons and provided them to nearly every country in the world.

What were the chances of walking into the church and meeting a man who had a personal experience with a minister I followed, respected, and loved since my youth? This was no coincidence. I had offered the treasure of my heart to God. And whether right or wrong, logical or not, I interpreted Reverend Harrod's story as a divine sign: God's nod back to me that He accepted the deal. I interpreted this minister's story of his mother's healing as a sign that in fact I was the cause of Penny's illness, and in order to make it right, I must leave her. I had made a deal, and in my mind, God had accepted.

CHAPTER TEN

DIAGNOSIS: MALIGNANT POLITICS

At a time when Penny and I needed each other more than ever, we had to double down on the secrecy. Only Penny, Patty, and I knew the diagnosis. We had two days to figure out how to tell her mother, her brothers, the campaign, and the public. We badly needed time. Penny, at forty-two years old, needed time to come to terms with the fact that she had cancer. Her siblings needed time to deal with the fact that another sister was sick. Her friends needed time to absorb the shock. Penny needed time to find the right words to tell her mother, whose third daughter was now affected by this disease, before the news was splashed across page one of every newspaper in the state. We needed time to prepare for the political announcement and aftermath. And we had to do this with our lives underground.

Penny campaigned in Chicago on Friday, the day after receiving the diagnosis. I had worked all day, unable to leave the office till nearly 7:00 PM. I couldn't focus on my work, which made the day even longer. I became increasingly terrified, and in my isolation, I went further underground. I couldn't hold sway over the old patterns of thinking that had shaped my youth, nor could I focus on the positive ones. When I thought how much Penny loved me, or how happy I seemed to make her, I couldn't hold on to that. I had, after all, made a deal with God, and I intended to keep it. How, I didn't know, but I was going to.

When Penny arrived at home that night, I think I had expected that we would cry or spend hours processing this terrible news. Neither happened. When she opened the door, she had her hands full of papers, her briefcase, and luggage. She was trying to maneuver past the screen door. Oddly, I became angry. Here my love was coming home with terrible health news, and I couldn't even walk to the car to greet her and help her get her luggage? I was filled with anger for that and for not having made dinner or started the laundry, or doing any sort of irrelevant task at hand. She must have sensed my anger as I grabbed her luggage and held the door open with my foot. "It's okay," she said. We hugged each other and kissed and seemed to ignore the reality of the news.

"When did you get home?" she said casually.

"About twenty minutes ago," I said. "I slowed down, hoping you would see me and pick me up along the way so I wouldn't have to walk."

We laughed, but we both cringed at the joke that highlighted the folly of our lives.

"Man," she said, "I'm hungry."

"Yeah, me too." We paused, and I knew we were both internally processing: We couldn't just go out together for dinner in Decatur, driving to another town seemed exhausting, and we had nothing in the house to eat.

"Let's just get a pizza, Terry, and have a few beers." I picked up the phone to order, and then remembered I couldn't even do that; she made the call. The pizza arrived, and we ate and talked about everything *but* her health. I wanted to wait until she brought up the subject, giving her time to simply ease off the campaign trail and relax.

We finally started discussing her health, but only through the prism of campaigns and politics, not the prism of our lives. Penny wanted to talk mostly about what came next politically, and I knew that getting out of the race would not be an option in this political animal's mind. I got as far as, "Penny, are you sure about this? Are you really up for this?"

"This is what I want to do, Terry. It's who I am."

We made a short list of people who would need to know she had cancer before a campaign announcement. Her mother, of course, topped the list. She struggled deeply as we tried to decide how to tell her mother, not wanting to scare her or trigger the feelings of having buried her youngest daughter just a few years before. Penny thought that going to her parents' house to make this announcement would be best.

"We'll just have dinner first," Penny said, designing the disclosure to put as little stress on Helen as possible. I noticed that she did not mention or consider how this news would affect her father, but it didn't surprise me given their strained and near nonexistent relationship. "Then we can tell her."

"We?" I asked.

"I want me, you, and Pat to tell her."

My presence in a family that I was part of and yet not part of always pushed me into a muddy personal confusion. If you looked at it from her family's perspective, I was just a "new friend." Had I been her mother, I thought, I would have resented my presence in that discussion. In fact, in retrospect, I was starting to have a low-grade resentment to the half-life we were living. I was battling internally: I wanted to be there for my spouse, and yet I was uncomfortable. I considered this for a while, and then I offered a different option: We'd have dinner, and afterward, I would take Patty's kids—Kristin, ten; Weston, eight; and Graham, five—outside to play, giving Patty unfettered time with Penny to deliver the news to their mother.

I was honest with Penny about my discomfort of being in the room when she made the announcement. "Penny, if we were dating and they knew it, I could be in there, but now I can't. It's too weird. I'm just a reporter or a friend. I've only been in the picture for a year or so; it's not like you are taking Annette or Sheryl with you," I said, referring to her college roommate and her close friend. "Let me help by helping with the kids."

Penny talked with Patty, and the three of us agreed that we would go to their parents' house, have dinner, and afterward, I would take the children outside to play while the twins broke the news to their mother. Just as planned, we arranged a very early "family dinner" at her parents' house. Then I took the kids outside. Standing in the backyard of Penny's parents' home on Water Street that languid summer night, I felt surreal playing Red Light Green Light, Mother May I?, and Freeze Tag with the kids.

Though playful, carefree I was not.

Indeed, I could not have hated myself more for banishing myself from the opportunity to present ourselves as a couple. Penny had wanted me to be with her, and because I was uncomfortable, I exiled myself to playing children's games in the yard. I felt like I was abandoning Penny left and right. This served yet another example of how Penny would be better off without me. I don't remember how long they were in the house talking with Helen and Don, but it was dark when Penny came outside. The kids ran to her, Graham wrapping his arms around her legs. "Play Red Light Green Light with us," he implored, but then he ran off to tackle his brother. Penny's face said it all, and I asked the question everybody asks even though the answer is clear.

"You okay?" I said, putting my hand on her shoulder.

"I'm sick of this already, Terry."

We walked inside. Helen's face was ashen. She was crying. Don was at the dining room table, his hands folded, twiddling his thumbs. I sat down to talk to him. He spoke about a cancer he had had. As Penny started to walk past us into the living room to be with Patty and Helen, she looked at him with a flash of anger. Was it because he was speaking about his cancer? Because he wasn't in the living room tending to his upset wife? Perhaps he just couldn't deal with the fact that another daughter was gravely ill. Later in the car, Penny said to me, "He can never think of anything or anyone but himself." Knowing that family politics are the most treacherous of all to maneuver, I didn't say anything when she spoke of her disdain for her father; I just listened and often tried to soften the harshness. She could sense I had questions. "The only thing you need to know is that four of his six children don't speak to him unless they have to," she said curtly.

Having gotten through telling the family, we focused on the arena we knew and loved best. We devoted ourselves to discussing how this news would affect Penny's political aspirations. As the political and medical campaigns unfolded, Patty became part of the ruse in either hiding me or explaining my presence as a friend. At the time, the cover-up was founded on my being a reporter and Penny a politician, never outwardly discussing that it was really about our being a lesbian couple. Penny met with Netsch but told her only that she found a lump and that doctors were going to biopsy it on July 28. She was unsure how Netsch would react but wanted to keep the information as limited and positive as possible. She omitted the fact that she already had one surgery and that the lump was malignant. She decided to wait to see if it had spread before revealing everything. Netsch, Penny reported, was very supportive and said she would not ask Penny to step down from the ticket unless Penny felt she needed to focus solely on her health.

The campaign staff, however, went a little crazy. Penny had told me that the political handlers wanted to control all of the announcements related to her health and release them from the campaign. Penny could say nothing on her own without vetting it with them. I vehemently—although privately—objected to this. I had become a de facto handler to Penny, as I felt like no one was looking out for her personal interests in the campaign. I reminded Penny it was *her* health, and *she* needed to control how and when the information was released. When the campaign was over, win or lose, she was going to be stuck with her own facts and how she handled this very personal situation. She, not the Netsch campaign, needed to be in charge of this. To make the announcement, they wanted to go solely with a press release and then have Netsch and Penny comment on the campaign trail. It wasn't a bad idea for the first round of disclosure, but I told Penny that if the campaign thought the press was going to simply accept a news release without a formal press conference, they were nuts. If Penny were serious about convincing the public that she was in this race to win and was healthy enough for such a rigorous effort, then she needed to do more than a press release. As a student of politics, I drew on the Lyndon Baines Johnson moment of publically showing his gall bladder scar. I encouraged Penny to do a public news conference, her doctors in tow, announcing the treatment and fielding any questions the press posed.

"Okay, but I'm not showing my left breast," she deadpanned.

"That's perfect, you should say that," I said, knowing the stagecraft that is politics.

We both knew that anything less than full disclosure would look like she was trying to hide something. Penny left the campaign trail on Wednesday, July 27, after holding a political rally with Netsch on the front steps of Penny's parents home in Decatur. On July 28, she had the lymph node surgery. The cancer had spread to three of the nine lymph nodes that were sectioned. Once she was home and resting on Friday, the campaign released the first disclosure that Penny had a small tumor removed from her breast and that it was malignant. The Friday night press release sent shock waves into Illinois politics.

The press coverage of this gubernatorial race was already relentless on its own. It got more heated when the Republican incumbent Governor Edgar had a heart procedure and *his* health became a campaign issue. So when the story about Penny's "health crisis" broke late Friday night, the media went into overdrive, following her every move. The additional scrutiny added to our personal pressure of hiding more carefully. Everyone wanted an interview and more details, which the campaign held at bay. Scores of supporters and friends wanted to stop by and visit Penny while she recuperated, complicating my presence at our home. And because I was a reporter, there was no way I could be there without reporting on the Democratic lieutenant governor candidate's recuperation. Penny and I talked about these new difficulties and whether I should stay away for the weekend, which I did not want to do. She said she wanted me close to her. That was all I needed to hear in order to endure whatever awkwardness and risks would arise. This time, I overcame my own fears and decided to stay, despite the hectic pace of telephone calls, people visiting, and the always-present threat that an enterprising reporter would knock on the door for an exclusive interview. I was shocked, but grateful, that no reporters came to the house.

Penny was resting on the couch, watching television and reading the countless cards that already started pouring in. Patty and I would alternate between sitting with Penny or puttering around the house, tidying or cooking. When general well-wishers or flower deliveries came, I would hide upstairs, and Patty would get the door.

The one person Penny felt like she wanted to call but decided not to was Linda. Linda loved Penny and they were close friends, but Penny could never shake the "chased feeling" we both had felt since Linda left the note under my door during our first weekend together, and we couldn't forget the many times we felt she was trying to trap us into disclosing our relationship to her. To Penny's great regret, we didn't give Linda and Roger advance warning of the medical news. They learned about it on the radio while driving home from St. Louis on Saturday. Shocked and saddened, Linda had called Penny. She wanted to come by and see her friend.

I felt I couldn't be anywhere in the vicinity when Linda came by, but Penny wanted to talk about it because she didn't want me to leave. She threw out a few options of how I could be there when Linda arrived: I just happened to stop by; I wanted an interview; I was just checking if I could do anything for my friend. We agreed that none of them passed the smell test and that Linda would see right through them. We opted for another ruse, with Patty playing a key role, that would let me stay close by Penny until Linda came and then return later when she left.

When the doorbell rang, we sprang into action. Patty went to the door slowly. I kissed Penny and whispered, "I'll see you later."

She grabbed my forearm, pulling me close for another second.

"Don't go too far, okay?" she asked quietly and tentatively.

I paused. I almost decided to stay. She seemed so vulnerable in that moment. There was a split second when I thought, *I'll just stay and not explain anything. Let people think what they want.* I also had the urge to reveal to her my deal with God. Instead, I said, "I won't. I'm just going to go to Milliken and play the piano for a while." Milliken University was less than a mile or so from the house, and they had practice music rooms that generally were unlocked.

Patty greeted Linda at the front door and distracted her while I slipped out the back door of the kitchen. I crept along the side of the house as I had so many mornings in the dark, this time trying to stay below the dining room windows. Patty and Penny were going to occupy Linda and Roger in the living room until they were sure I was out of sight.

When I called Penny a few hours later, she answered and said, "The coast is clear," and hung up. When I came home, she was very tired, and we decided no more visitors and no more calls, and I unplugged the phone. Patty, Penny, and I talked for a while, and then Patty left to go home.

Penny told me that seeing Linda and Roger was nice and that she felt very bad about the way we let them find out that Penny had cancer. Linda, she said, was sad and shaken. She, Penny, and Roger were very close friends; before Penny and I met, they routinely spent many weeknights, weekends, and sometimes even vacations together. After Penny and I got together, it seemed Linda was looking for answers to make sense of Penny's changed behavior and their waning time together. Penny said that with this medical news, Linda seemed to shift away from chasing the truth and trying to confirm her belief that Penny and I were lovers and simply began caring for her friend again.

With everyone gone from the house, I sat down on the floor in front of the couch while Penny fell asleep with her arm draped over my shoulder. She slept and I watched television. When she awoke, Penny and her breast cancer led the evening news. The newscaster said that the senator had surgery to remove the lump, which was malignant. She was resting at home with family and friends. "I'm so sick of hearing about this. It sounds like a funeral," she said. "It sounds so negative. Like I'm already dead."

"I think I can change that. Did you make any work calls today?" I asked.

"Yes, I talked to Gail Handleman for quite a while about the press."

"Okay," I said. "And how are you feeling now?"

"I feel good," she said, frustrated. "Why are you asking all this?"

"Just give me a minute," I said.

I picked up the phone, called the Chicago desk of the AP, and told them I just talked with Severns by phone. I reported that she was feeling good, sounded impatient, and told me she was restless to get back to work and so was working the phones nonstop from her couch. The AP's "exclusive" interview made the next news show.

The campaign was not happy, as they forbade her from doing media interviews. Netsch's press secretary, Gail Handleman, immediately called Penny, demanding to know what happened. I knew they were wondering whether the number-two candidate had "gone rogue."

"Well, after you and I talked today, I hung up the phone and it immediately rang again. I thought it was you," Penny lied. "I got off the phone as quickly as I could."

The campaign seemed to accept that, particularly since the news had turned more positive.

Penny and I moved on to the next task, the press conference. The only real and in-depth discussions were not about Penny's health itself, but rather how she would fit her treatments into her campaign schedule and how much of her health status to reveal. We also talked about how best to prepare Penny's doctor for a press conference. We decided we needed to give the doctors a crash course on how to interact with the press and how to answer questions from a positive standpoint.

Four days after her surgery, Penny held the conference with her doctor and charmed the press with the LBJ story and her quip about refusing to show her left breast. In a serious tone, she told the press that she had given great thought to whether she could continue in the race and that she genuinely believed that she could. The press backed her play.

"By all means," the editorial board of *The Chicago Tribune* wrote on August 4, 1994, "Severns should stay in the race if she and her doctors believe she can handle the rigors of a campaign. Her vigor and determination are likely to give tremendous encouragement to other breast cancer survivors." The editorial went on:

> This has to be a traumatic time for Severns and her family, which has had all too much experience with breast cancer. Her sister Marsha died of the disease. Her sister Patty has also been treated for breast cancer. Severns is confronting the cruel knowledge that her family history greatly increases the odds that she will suffer another occurrence . . .
>
> Such is the political life. While voters generally don't reject candidates for treatable health problems, they do expect—and deserve—candor from them.

Oddly, Penny and I glazed over the import of the editorial regarding her health, and whether Penny would be alive in five years. Instead, we focused on the candor discussion the editorial board raised. We talked ad nauseam about the press and political part of candor, about the unforgiveable lack of ethics of my being a reporter romantically involved with a source. We talked about it regularly, and I knew we would talk about it again at length.

All the while I was supporting Penny during this crazy time, I decided to keep my pledge to God. Within days after her lymph node surgery, I spoke with the AP in Alaska. They had a position open, and I sent my résumé. A few days later, the bureau chief called me and said he would fly down for an interview in about two weeks. If all went well, I could transfer within two months. I knew I had to tell Penny, but I didn't know how or when I would do it yet.

CHAPTER ELEVEN

THE LAST FRONTIER

Penny refused to take time off and recover after the surgeries. Instead, she returned quickly to the campaign trail, and the press began hounding her for an interview. Giving me the interview was the perfect way to allow me to be at her radiation and chemotherapy treatments without raising too many eyebrows on the campaign or in the medical world. It was a surreal and hard experience to wake up with Penny at 4:00 AM, leave our house alone, travel to Springfield, and then greet Penny at the hospital at 7:00 AM and behave as a stranger as I watched her undergo radiation treatment.

"This is so strange," she said to me when she came out of the hospital dressing room in a gown.

"Which part?" I said, laughing.

"The part where we pretend that we don't know each other while I am getting zapped."

After her treatment, which usually lasted less than thirty minutes, I would travel with her all day, and after her driver dropped her off at our home around 11:30 PM, I asked to be dropped at the local Holiday Inn. Then I would walk the several miles back to the house. I did this for a week or so. Then I wrote the article detailing the medical and political life of this candidate. The story was true, except for one fact: how Penny found the lump. In the article, I wrote: "During a breast self-exam, Severns felt a little knot that doctors said was smaller than a dime."

The next weekend, I knew it was time to tell Penny I was leaving. I just didn't know how. I told her nonchalantly that I was "just thinking" about accepting a job in Alaska, when in fact I had already accepted the job offer.

Penny's face lost color when I said it. As I spoke to her about moving to Alaska, I felt numb and disconnected from myself, as though I were watching myself speak. Ever since I had made the deal with God, I couldn't feel anything and was divorced from the way I usually operated in the world. I stopped bringing Penny flowers and writing cards. My affect, according to my family, was flat.

In this conversation, instead of telling Penny that I felt that I was the cause of her sickness and that I had made a deal with God to atone, I instead drew on our old discussions about the ethical conflicts of a journalist and a source being involved. I told Penny that we both knew I could no longer remain a journalist if she was going to remain a politician.

"This will be good, really," I said of my move to Alaska, but hating myself with every word that came out of my mouth.

"Let's just wait a while," she said. " Maybe you can stop covering politics or get a job at a magazine, or just come to work for me full time."

"This is a chance of a lifetime," I said.

"I don't want us to be apart this much," she said.

"It won't be that long, Penny. You can come to visit, and I'll be home before you know it," I said again, my voice oddly devoid of emotion.

We never resolved anything in these conversations, and while I kept moving toward departing for Alaska, internally, I did not want to make the move.

The AP had arranged movers to ship my car and belongings. I would be living in Juneau, which can only be reached by boat or plane, and the shipping schedules were lengthy and very detailed. Each time the AP scheduled my move, I cancelled. Finally, with the third cancellation, the AP bureau chief demanded to know if I was serious about this move, and if I was, he wanted to know why I was delaying. I committed to a final moving date in early October. The morning that the movers were to arrive in Springfield, I was in Decatur. Penny and I had stayed up until about 3:00 AM talking, trying to find a different solution to what I posed as the ethical issue. She never knew I was trying to solve a different problem. That morning, I left to walk to my car a few miles away, but I vacillated once again about the move and returned to the house to talk to Penny. I called the movers and told them I would be about an hour late, and I asked if could they please wait for me without calling AP.

We were sitting on the couch, and Penny said to me, "There's a fine line between courage and stupidity, you know? It's a brave move to go to Alaska, but maybe the timing's off."

She started crying. I still felt nothing. But when she leaned into me, her warmth touched me, and I too started to cry and started to tell her the truth. "Penny, I . . ." I paused, quickly bracing myself and clamping my emotions down tightly. Instead, I said, somewhat coldly, "I have to go. I'll see you tonight."

Penny leaned over, kissed me, and hugged me.

"Don't fall in love with a polar bear, okay?" she said, smiling only a little.

I walked out the front door and started the two-mile walk to my car.

When I reached the end of the driveway, Penny came running out of the house in bare feet, and she put her hand up and said, "Wait a minute." I turned around and walked back to her, and we stood in the small front yard. She was crying. I thought she looked sexy in bare feet and jeans with the top few buttons undone.

"Don't go, T," she said. "We can figure something else out, can't we?"

I still couldn't reach my feelings. I had made a deal with God for her life. The choice seemed so obvious to me. Had I decided to be truthful with her, she would have seen that leaving her was my only option. If she only knew that this was for her own good, I reasoned within myself, she wouldn't ask me to stay.

"I gotta go, Penny," I said, completely disconnected from myself.

"Okay," she said, sadly. I turned away and started walking but looked back to see her holding the screen door and watching me. I smiled weakly and waved.

The next few days were scratchy between us. She became cranky at all the domestic chores that I didn't perform well. And there was an unusual sarcasm in her tone. "I won't have to redo this right when you leave," she'd say while reorganizing the dishwasher. Or, "I'll get a lot of reading done after you move." This undercurrent lasted for about three days. She softened to a point of sadness, and then those emotions transformed. She started to mention my inevitable departure to Alaska in a more positive way. She engaged in what she called "this adventure" and said we should go shopping for boots and clothes to prepare for the cold weather. We went on a shopping trip to Chicago to weatherize me, and Penny even bought winter clothes for herself, planning her first trip with a genuine upbeat excitement about traveling to the fiftieth state. She booked her plane tickets for a February visit, leaving just a few days between her last chemotherapy treatment and the trip to Alaska. We had a going-away dinner with Patty, Doug, and the kids, who gave me lots of warm socks, hot chocolate, books, and foot warmers. As with all things in our lives, we simply moved into whatever facts were present at the moment, not challenging the craziness of our decisions or lifestyle.

I knew I was making a mistake; I knew deep inside me this move didn't make sense. Even if I chose to leave Penny and keep my deal with God, there were many locations I could have gone that were closer than Juneau, an isolated town three thousand miles away. And even that wasn't far enough for me. I chose not to live in town but rather on a tidal island with a population of about 3,000 people. I decided that once I got there, away from Penny, and after her last treatment in January, I would tell her over the phone the true reason I left. I knew that she would be furious, both because she would see this decision as absolutely insane and also because I had shut her out of the decision-making process, something I never did. No matter how small a decision, we never made a move without one another. I cut her out of this decision because I knew she would highlight the irrationality of it. I had made a short four-day trip to Alaska in mid-September to find housing and look at the AP bureau, a beautiful office with wall-to-wall windows looking out to a waterfall. My final, one-way flight to Alaska was set for October 30, 1994. That weekend, a week before the general election, Penny was campaigning nearly twenty hours a day and was based in Chicago. We examined her campaign schedule and found all the Starbucks that were in the vicinity of her events on Saturday. We planned to "run into" each other three or four times that day just to spend some last-minute time together since I couldn't travel with her. Penny told me later that one of her campaign staff thought the coincidences were creepy and had asked her: "Do you think she is following us?" She said she decided to disclose to the staffer that we were in fact personal friends and had planned to meet up a few times before I left for Alaska.

On Saturday night, around midnight, Penny returned to the campaign apartment in Chicago and called her press secretary. She had a battery of churches to visit on Sunday in hopes of firing up the base of their support. She insisted, however, that she was going to take some time off that morning so that she could see me off at the airport. We had been saying goodbye ever since I told her I was leaving, and this last goodbye didn't seem real. The doorman buzzed the apartment. The cab was waiting. I hadn't built in any extra time in case of traffic or other problems, and I had wanted to stop at the Jewel grocery store and get cash and some lunch for the plane. When we got in, the cabbie said, "You're not going to go far. There's a marathon today, and the streets are blocked."

"See, God doesn't want you to go," Penny deadpanned. I flinched, wondering if she knew about my plan after all. Then she comforted me, saying we would be together soon and she was coming to see me. We pulled into the grocery store parking lot about a block away, and we were both nervous about me making it to the airport on time and Penny making it back in time for her late-morning campaign schedule. We decided to say good-bye there, so Penny could go back to the apartment instead of traveling to the airport. She gave me a letter to read later. I wondered if she was going to break up with me, tell me that I had betrayed her. Or perhaps she was asking all the questions I was asking myself: *How could I leave her during cancer treatments? Why not just come to work for her? Was I breaking up with her? Didn't I love her?* The letter was written on her personal stationery, in black ink, and was dated nearly a month before: September 29, 1994.

Dearest Sweetheart,

Know that my thoughts and prayers are with you on this most exciting journey! I've always said there is a fine line between courage and stupidity. Part of the many reasons I love you so very much is because you are so very courageous, as this decision most certainly is! I love your sense of

adventure over the love of ease. I love you and your decision with all my
heart. This is not only an exciting, once-in-a-lifetime decision for you, it is
also for me. Not only will I join you at length as often as possible, I will live
the excitement through you and with you. We will always be together—
I love you with all of my heart, my sweet, sweet love. You are now—and
always will be—the love of my life.

Don't let any bear fall in love with you!

All my love,

Penny

I read and reread the letter, running my hands over her familiar handwriting. I was still numb, and I wondered if this was how I would feel for the rest of my life. I felt like my skin had been burned and scarred over, and no feeling existed in me at all. Once I got away from Penny, far enough where I couldn't return in a day, then I would break up with her. Then my plan was to live in Alaska for a while until we both got over the shock of the breakup, and then once I knew she was doing well, I would go overseas and live there for the rest of my life, picking up work as a freelance journalist. I had been trying to build a relationship with international desk since my earliest days at the AP. My goal was to impress its editor with my reporting skills from Alaska.

When I landed and stepped into the cold, frozen air, my feelings finally started to crack. Alaska was vivid and beautiful, the snow-capped mountains jutted into the sky, and my sense of being seemed to awaken. My belongings hadn't arrived yet, and I would be staying at the Baranoff Hotel instead of going to the home I rented on Douglas Island overlooking the emerald green waters of the Gastineau Channel. For the first time in months, I actually felt emotion. I felt the weather on my skin and wanted instead to be in the ruggedness of wilderness. I drove to the Mendenhall Glacier about twelve miles out of town, on my way from the airport. Without regard to safety, I parked the car and started hiking. The expanse of the glacier and the orphaned ice mounds floating in the water moved me deeply. A few sea lions—animals that in my mind always seem to be smiling—were in the water, their whiskers barely breaking the surface, and a few others lay out on their backs, as though sunning, their black skin stark against the ice. I was mesmerized by the glacier and the blue tint—the color of windshield-washer fluid—coursing through the ice. It seemed to me to be like light blue blood, mostly hidden but flowing under the ice. I thought, that's me—*true colors hidden under ice.*

I was drawn to the stillness of the rust-colored grasses around the glacier and the several bald eagles that circled the sky. This, I thought of nature, is God. For the first time, I allowed myself to wonder about Penny in relationship to my move and her health. I put myself in her shoes. What was she feeling? She had asked me to stay, and I had said no. I wondered if she thought I didn't love her, or if she thought I betrayed her. How could I have left her alone during the hardest treatments of her life? Is that what God really would have wanted or required me to do? Maybe Reverend Harrod's story really was coincidence, or perhaps it wasn't intended as a sign for me to leave. Instead, maybe God simply wanted me to be near her and take care of her. Thinking of her in this way, I felt my emotions tingle, perhaps the burn of shame.

Later, after having checked into the hotel, I took a walk to a bookstore and thought it apropos to buy Jack London's *To Build a Fire.* The cold air stung. I loved having feeling again, any feeling, even if it was just cold air on my face. I felt free in that bold environment, and for the first time in a long time, I felt like I was emerging from an emotional fog, thinking and feeling clearly. Somehow, in that quiet night, truly alone in a town where I knew not one person, where I had no family or friends, I felt my own heart beat, and I felt like I owned myself. I was not beholden to anyone or anything. I was free of the stress of lying about my relationship with Penny, free of the stress of being involved with a source. I was free from the reasons I made a deal with God, free of my fear of my family's reaction to me being a lesbian. I was free of my reputation as a hard-nosed reporter and was free of my newly crowned reputation in Illinois as a recluse. All of these stressors, viewed against that rugged environment, seemed miniscule and meaningless in the opening moments of my stay in The Last Frontier.

There were more stars than I could count, and I loved looking at the sky and breathing the frigid snowy air into my lungs. In the best possible way, I felt insignificant here in this wilderness. I felt like Alaska was holding me, protecting me, and that there was plenty of room to move and breathe.

Mesmerized by this feeling of wholeness, I sat alone on a bench at the end of the docks and watched the movement of the sky. I could not believe the depth of darkness Alaska enjoyed without the light pollution of a city. For hours, I felt a sense of calm and stillness without the tether of another human being. I hadn't experienced that feeling before in my life, and perhaps I haven't had the courage to experience it since. Although I'd been in Alaska only about six hours at that point, I felt like my strength and my hope were returning. I wasn't completely numb any more. I certainly was not afraid. In a moment's time, without trying, the grace of clarity had arrived. I loved Penny. That much I knew. She loved me and needed me. I needed her. The God of this vastness could not be as limiting as I had convinced myself He was. I fleetingly also wondered, *Am I crazy? I really just flew 3,000 miles away from Penny and only now I am seeing that I should not have left?* I raced back to the hotel, and despite the three-hour time difference and knowing Penny needed what little sleep she was getting, I called her. "Hi, sweetheart," she said, perhaps knowing that nobody else would call her at midnight.

"I made a horrible mistake, love," I said, elated and knowing I had a chance to correct it without too much time lost. "I love you, and I don't want to be apart from you, even for one more day."

She burst out crying. "I'm so happy," she said. "I didn't want you to leave me, Terry, but I didn't want to stand in your way if this is what you wanted."

"I didn't really leave you, Penny, I just left you," I said, and we both started laughing at the nonsensical statement. "I'm coming home."

"Are there any flights out tonight?" she asked. All of the gaiety of our love was restored, and my ache for her was very deep.

"I can't do that, but I promise you this: If you win, I will quit next Tuesday and come to work for you. If you lose, we will plan on my return as soon as I can find a job or get into a law school."

"Terry," she asked seriously, opting for my full name instead of "T" or "sweetheart." "Why did you leave?"

"It doesn't matter," I said, still not ready to tell her, still not ready to drop into a deeply intimate conversation about my deal with God. "But I *am* coming home."

"I know, and I am happy. But why?" she persisted.

"Penny, I promise that someday I will explain it all, but I can't right now. I don't know how. Can you leave it be for a while? It's too complicated for a phone conversation anyway."

"Okay, but you're going to tell me someday," she declared. "I'll withhold sex."

"*That*," I overemphasized, "I'd have to see."

On November 8, 1994, Democrats around the country lost in a landslide. In Illinois, they took a particular thumping, with the Republican ticket collecting a two-to-one margin over the Netsch–Severns ticket and sweeping the constitutional offices. It was the year of the midterm elections where a Republican rout prompted President Clinton to declare at a press conference: "I'm still relevant." I watched Penny's very lengthy concession speech on WGN-TV. I could see how tired she really was. I ached that I was not near her, and yet, I knew that even if I had been there, I would have been hidden.

When we talked the night of the election, she sounded absolutely exhausted. I was worried about her—she was so tired she was almost slurring. She said to me, "I know we lost, but come home now anyway. We can talk about it tomorrow." she said. "You don't even have to have a job. We'll just be together."

The next day for Penny was filled with thank you calls to those that supported her, and we immediately planned for her to take a vacation and rest. Having just arrived in Alaska, there was no way I could take a two-week vacation. We decided that when she got back from resting, we would work out the details of my return to Illinois. I encouraged her to go out of the country to a very warm beach. "I don't want to do that without you," she said. Instead, she went to Florida. Someone on the campaign had a vacation home in Ft. Meyers and offered it to Penny, and she spent a few weeks there relaxing in the sun.

When she returned to Illinois, she was refreshed and refocused on our life together. She had wanted us to move from the house on Main Street and instead find something more out of town. We had finally decided to move one night the summer before, when at midnight, a man began pounding on our front door. He was yelling that he knew Penny was in there and he was not leaving until she came to talk him. He wanted a job, and she had promised in her election to the Senate to help people find jobs. She went to the window and told him, "I am not coming downstairs. It's midnight. Come to my office in the morning, and I will help you." He went away. And he wasn't the only one—people had stopped by at all hours of the day and night.

She said she wanted to start the house hunt in early December so that when I came home for Christmas, we could have a narrowed list of houses to look at and decide from. She began looking and took her brother Rod and his wife, Jane, to see her various choices. Amidst the house hunting, Penny ran into an old friend while she was at an event on the west side of Decatur, and she told Penny that she knew of a luxury house for sale, though not yet on the market, that Penny would love. Penny discovered that the builder, Ken Horve, had built this home for his wife of fifty-seven years, Peg, and him to retire. He said he had cut no corners on the house because it was to be theirs. He took time to customize the interior with handmade Amish cabinets and top-of-the-line features, details, and carpeting. When it came time to move in, his wife just couldn't leave the home they had raised their children in, she said. Now, Kenny was going to sell it.

Excited, Penny called me to say she had found a house. She hadn't even seen the inside yet. Later that night, she took Helen and Jane to see it, and when they got into the master bathroom with the Jacuzzi and skylight, Jane later told me that she had said to Penny, "You're going to have to have somebody special to share this with." Penny had replied, "I do, I just have to get them here."

Penny and I talked long and hard about the house. She was reluctant to purchase it without me having seen it. That didn't bother me—what bothered me was how we were going to buy it jointly and keep our relationship a secret. "The bank can't release details of our financing," she had said to me.

"No, but the deed will be public record," I said.

"We have to figure this out," she said, the first deflation of the joy of buying our first home together.

"Here's what we'll do: you handle the financing, and I will send you cash for the down payment," I said.

"But, T, it can't even be in your name," Penny said.

"One thing at a time, P," I said, feeling very in charge. "We can figure out the legal end of this later." Our spirits were dampened because we were denied the joy of having both our names on the deed, and I was thinking, *If my parents ever knew that I was putting money into a home and wasn't named on the deed, they would yell at me.* But I trusted Penny and didn't give this a second thought.

Later that month, we pooled our money, I sent her my half via Federal Express, and we bought the house. We could barely contain our excitement. I wanted Penny to take it easy through her last few chemotherapy treatments and wait until I got home to start packing for the move.

"Let's make the house our present to each other and not go big on presents this year," she said. We both agreed, although neither of us stuck to it. While she was in Florida, she had bought us both expensive jewelry, including matching Tag Heuer watches. We could only tell them apart by their serial numbers—mine started with a D and hers with a G—and so I gave them nicknames. Hers was "G for gorgeous" and mine was "D for darling."

Penny had a newspaper photo of Clinton and Hillary sharing a wonderful smile taped to the back of her Senate office door. An AP photographer had captured the shot, and I called him and asked if he would give me a large print of it and sign the back. Because we were colleagues, he sent it to me in Alaska, and I had it framed for her at a local gallery. I had also bought her a lapis necklace from the Rainsong Gallery, but I wanted to give her something handmade. I decided at that last minute to crochet her an afghan, which I did not finish before I returned to the Lower 48. When I arrived in Chicago's Midway Airport, I was being paged on loudspeaker. I was convinced that Penny was sick or that the chemo treatment had gone badly. I rushed to an agent, who printed out a message: "Terry, Penny is running about three hours late. She overslept. Please wait for her!" I laughed out loud, relieved, sat down, and finished crocheting the Connecticut blue and crème afghan. We spent the night in Chicago, shopping, eating, and drinking. We returned to Decatur the next day, and our first stop was our new empty house.

"Welcome home, T," she said. We stood in the empty foyer, and giddily, we kissed.

She showed me every detail of the house, She walked me into the empty bedroom and showed me where she thought the bed should go, and then we stepped into the bathroom. "It's got a skylight and a Jacuzzi. Can you believe that?" she said excitedly. She retrieved a canvas bag she had left by the door and returned with champagne and two glasses. Laughing, we popped the bottle and sat on the edge of the Jacuzzi tub, sipping champagne.

With the help of friends, we packed the house in Decatur and moved into our new home at Sims Drive, a renewed energy and life in our love. Despite Penny's best efforts to stay active, the cumulative effects of several months of chemotherapy were catching up with her. Instead of resting as she should have, she expended her energy on moving, shopping, and squeezing every moment from every day for work. On the day I was to return to Alaska, Penny became violently ill on the drive to St. Louis. We returned to Decatur. I cancelled my flight and stayed home for a few more days. We decided that Penny should take seriously the doctor's advice of resting more.

Doug drove me to the airport a few days later. When I returned to Alaska, I started to fully enjoy my time there, knowing it would be short-lived and I would be returning home to Penny soon. My plan was to work the legislative session through its ending in May, and by then, I would have received my law school admission results. Once I knew where I was going, I would simply tell the AP I was returning to school.

A month later, January 1995, Penny finished her treatments and her doctors declared that she was cancer free. When she called me with that news, I felt very humbled and small. I stepped outside of my house, wept, and prayed a prayer of deep thanks for her complete remission.

Penny joined me in Alaska in the beginning of February and told only her family that she was visiting me. When issues came up or reporters called, she did media interviews from my living room overlooking the Gastineau Channel with no one the wiser of her remote location. During our dinners and hikes in this rugged beauty, we talked about how happy we were that I was coming home.

"Even this short time apart was too much," I said to Penny.

Penny's trip to Alaska had brought an old freedom with it that we usually experienced only when we traveled internationally. We were happy and free, and yet there was still a sting to our secret. I introduced her to friends I had made in Alaska by saying, "This is my friend from Illinois." Each time I did that, I had two feelings: One, I felt cheap. She wasn't my friend; she was my spouse. And two, I felt confident that we were hiding our relationship well, being so nonchalant with friends. But one friend, Elizabeth Dronkert, a lawyer, later told me that she and her husband Gregory had thought Penny and I were lovers, "just by the way you looked at each other and sat next to each other."

And although we were thousands of miles from Illinois, we still had a close call, after snowshoeing in the Tongass National Forest. We stopped at the Baranoff Hotel for drinks. Penny spotted someone she knew from her first unsuccessful campaign for Congress. Since the naked-behind-the-furnace incident, the humor of these situations had faded, and we were both growing increasingly frustrated and angry. We strategized an exit. I knew the woman, who worked for Governor Knowles, so I would walk over and distract her while Penny walked out. Then, I paid the bill, and we met at the foot of the hill near the docks. We had been having fun, free of pressure and being known. Now, we were deflated and thrown back into hiding mode. After our quick exit, we decided to go home. We sat in front of the fireplace, sipping wine and talking.

"Sooner or later, we're going to have to disclose our relationship before somebody does it for us," Penny said. "I hated lying to Elizabeth and Gregory. I really could see all of us becoming lifelong friends and traveling together. How do we explain our lie later?"

We agreed that we couldn't go on with the elaborate, exhausting, and sometimes humiliating ruse we were perpetuating, and we wanted to be together without limitation. That afternoon, in front of the fire, we started to discuss in detail our transparency plans.

"I know that you have wanted to tell Sheryl about us for a long time. I feel the same way about Anita," I said of Anita Huslin, one of my dearest college friends who worked at *The Washington Post*.

"Yeah, but that's more complicated. She's a reporter," Penny said, and we both questioned whether Anita would be ethically bound to report this "breaking news."

We talked about disclosing our relationship to Patty. Penny was convinced Patty would be fine with it, but she had what I thought were unfounded concerns about how Patty's husband, Doug, would react. "Besides," she said, not for the first time, "I'm sure Patty knows. I mean, she has to. Why else would you be around me so much?"

I was still hesitant, but Penny seemed ready. "Terry, let's do this," she said. "If either of us feels the need to tell someone, let's just be sure we trust them. If you trust Anita, I'm okay with it."

Even this decision, while a relief in some ways, brought a heaviness with it. When was the most politically expedient time to disclose? Would Penny be able to accomplish her major goals on behalf of the people of Illinois if she came out as a lesbian? Would she be nudged out under some whipped-up pretense, or removed outright? Would I be fired, or just shunned so thoroughly that I'd resign? It seemed there was always some very good reason to delay coming out—I needed to get my career plans settled, Penny needed to get through the next initiative or the next health obstacle. As the month ended, our sadness grew at the thought of being apart again.

We gave each other cards the night before Penny was to return to Illinois. As we opened them, we both shook our heads and laughed. We bought each other the same card. It pictured a bald eagle soaring the skies, and the name on the back of the card was Master of the Wind.

"Sometimes," Penny said, "I think we have the same heart in two different bodies." We sat in front of the fire, reading the cards. "You are the love of my life," she wrote.

In April, I submitted my resignation to The Associated Press and returned to Illinois in May to the happiest reunion we had to date. Penny had flowers in every room and presents strewn everywhere in the house.

CHAPTER TWELVE

BONE MARROW TRANSPLANT, LAW SCHOOL, AND OTHER FORMS OF HELL

O nce I left journalism in May 1995, the next seven months before I started law school were glorious; Penny and I lived a daily existence in one home, with no cover apartment. Shortly after I returned, I traveled to see my parents in Pennsylvania, and then I returned to Illinois to settle in before joining the 1996 class of the John Marshall School of Law in Chicago. I decided I would get a copyediting job to supplement the money I saved while living in Alaska, but Penny didn't want me to work a regular job with a schedule that could potentially conflict with hers. "I want us to make up for lost time," she said. "Why don't you just work for me, and we can be together all the time?" She insisted that she needed a press secretary to gear up for her reelection campaign. I went on the campaign payroll as Penny's press secretary, which meant we could be seen in public together and work side by side on a daily basis—but this required even more exhausting vigilance to maintain our strictly professional personas in public, making sure we didn't slip and call each other sweetheart, darling, or babe. We both knew this arrangement couldn't continue indefinitely and often joked about what the neighbors thought when I pulled into the garage every night.

Our relationship seemed to become deeper every day, and that Fourth of July was the most memorable we ever shared. After the Blue Mound parade, we drove to Bement, a quaint, old town, where we met Patty, Doug, and the kids. We walked, laughed, and campaigned. Even the normally reserved Doug seemed expressively happy. As we approached large crowds on the sidewalks, Doug would ring a large school bell that he brought with him. When the Bement parade ended, we all sat in the shade of the maple trees near the high school and ate sandwiches and sipped cold drinks that Patty brought. "Patty," I said. "You make everything so nice."

I ran around playing with the kids, and then I sat and looked around, knowing even as the moment was happening that I was part of a small slice of Americana: the red, white, and blue buntings hanging from white Victorian porches, people walking by holding mini American flags and ice cream cones, high school bands wearing full parade dress, and staunchly proud but weathered military veterans in starched uniforms and highly shined patent leather shoes. "Someday, you will remember this as one of the greatest times of your life, and you'll be homesick for it," I said to the kids. Kristin, Weston, and Graham just looked at me as they would any other alien adult.

A week or so after the parade, Penny and I had dinner and decided to sit on our deck. As always, we waited until darkness fell to sit outside together in our Adirondack chairs. We were sipping sun tea with lemon wedges, enjoying the night.

"I want to talk to you about something that is bothering me," she said after a while.

"Okay," I said, not too worried, as we had been getting along very well and she was in complete remission and gaining her strength every day.

"I was thinking about how you are with the kids, and I was thinking you would be a terrific parent. We never finishing talking about whether you want to have kids," she said, referring to a conversation we had long ago when we lived on Main Street. At the time, she merely said, it seemed more a romantic sentiment than a potential reality.

"I always thought I would have kids, but after the cancer, I'm not physically able to," she said. "But you're young enough, and well, I think we should talk about this."

"Penny," I said, reaching over and touching her hand but quickly pulling away for fear that even in darkness, someone might see this gesture.

"That is lovely. But how would we do that? We are already maneuvering so much to hide our relationship," I said, genuinely surprised that she would even consider adding any more stress, complication, or complicity to a sometimes sadly comedic situation.

"We're going to figure that out at some point. And I just think having a kid could be a wonderful thing for us," she said.

"I make enough money for both of us, and if you wanted to work, you could work from home for the campaign and you could be with the baby," she said. "We could do this. Patty would help us too."

I didn't say anything for a while, thinking through the practical realities of having a child in an already deeply secret and closeted relationship.

"You know," she said, "I kind of had two kids once."

I was flabbergasted. "*Kind of had?!*" I said incredulously, not believing her.

"Well, when I was at the state department and I was in India, I identified these two kids, a boy and a girl, and I sponsored them. I have their pictures, and for years, I used to send them presents and money and write to them about going to school."

She told me their names and later showed me their pictures. "I did that for years, but they stopped writing, and I lost contact with them. I was always sad about that. Have you ever *thought* about having kids?" she asked, still pressing to continue the conversation.

"I always thought I would have kids. But you know, I am terrified of giving birth," I said.

"Really? Why?" she asked. "Millions of women do it."

"A lot of reasons," I said, suddenly feeling as though I was slipping into a dark emotional place and not wanting her to see that. I decided not to tell her that as a child I was sexually abused and that one of the "games" my abuser played was to pretend that we were having a family together. We would play act getting married, getting pregnant, and giving birth, and we'd use very large dolls that belonged to my sisters as pretend children. Instead of going into that hellish memory, I simply skimmed the surface of the truth and said matter-of-factly, "I've always had nightmares about it. I dream that I am pregnant and can't get out of it, and in the dream I know that I am going to die in childbirth."

"Wow," she said, "that's terrible, Terry. Tell me more about that."

Emotionally frozen, I replied off-handedly to stop the conversation. "There's nothing to tell. I have bad dreams," I said.

"You know," she said kindly and eagerly, "I would be there with you every step of the way, or we could adopt if you felt you didn't want to have the baby yourself."

I started thinking about Penny and me with a child. I had not thought about it before that night, but I liked the image in my head of the three of us as a little family. I had this image that we would have a very beautiful black-headed child and that we would dote on the baby and teach him or her the wonders of the world. Thinking about this with Penny by my side somehow brought a small sense of healing to my past and an ability, for the first time, to even consider having children.

"I think I could do that with you," I said, genuinely warming up to the idea. Then, instead of going deeper into the conversation, I diverted it. "Oh my god, what would the neighbors say?"

"Or Hawker, for that matter," she added with a low laugh.

"I can hear your old-lady constituents now at the coffee clutch," I said, and I started in a mock old-lady voice: "That Penny Severns is a saint. Taking in that unwed mother like that, opening her home, just a saint." Penny started laughing.

"You'd think that that young woman would have the decency to not take advantage of Penny. Where is her family? Trash. Just trash. I said it all along, Mable, that Penny Severns is too nice for her own good."

We laughed harder, and I can still see Penny leaning forward out of the Adirondack chairs, laughing so hard she couldn't breathe, wiping her eyes.

Eventually, we quieted down and sat for a while, looking at the stars.

"I'm serious," she said, trying to start the conversation again. "Terry, I love you in a way I never knew existed. I think we would be wonderful parents. I've always thought of Pat's kids as my kids, but when I met you, I started thinking about us having kids. And if you want kids, I don't want you to miss that opportunity because of me. I would do this."

In truth, while the sentiment was sweet and loving, I thought it was an insane idea given our living circumstances, and realized even in that moment that I was only humoring Penny with any discussion of us having children.

"Penny, we don't even have pictures of my family or of us together in our house. Do you really think this is realistic? I'd be a pregnant, unwed woman living in 'your' home. I'm not even on our deed."

"Terry, eventually we *are* going to reveal our relationship. I just want us to talk about this so we don't miss out on something with each other," she said. I sensed that she seemed hurt or discouraged that I was not engaging in the conversation in a real way.

"Let me think about it some more," I said. Even in that moment, I knew I would never agree to have children. I wasn't brave enough to think of us being parents. Being an out lesbian couple proved challenge enough. Somehow, though, just the fact that she wanted to do this felt like it could be enough for me, but we never spoke about it again in detail. After her death, I regretted greatly that I refused to explore having children more seriously.

We moved through the rest of the summer, taking our usual August vacation to Mexico, relaxing and soaking in much-needed sun and rest. That Thanksgiving, Penny's routine blood tests indicated something was amiss, and we learned that the cancer had come back in her lungs. After we had cried uncontrollably about the news, we kicked into a sort of desperate happy place, as if trying to convince ourselves everything would be all right. We decided to go all out at Christmas before her chemotherapy and my law school would start in January, and we embarked on a mission of retail therapy. We expended so much energy on Christmas, cooking pies and buying and wrapping presents. When we returned from Patty's house to our home very late on Christmas night, we turned on the heat and the fireplace and sat on the couch for a minute while we waited for the house to warm up.

"Penny," I said, very upset. "I can't believe this, but I didn't have a chance to wrap your Christmas presents."

She started laughing and said, "I didn't either. Let's just go to bed, and we'll do Christmas tomorrow."

"We have to do presents on Christmas," I said with new energy. "Let's close our eyes and pretend that our closed eyes *is* the wrapping paper." We both were so tired that all our emotions came out in laughter. We laughed so hard our sides hurt, and we couldn't stop.

"Okay," I said, turning this into a game. "The rule is that when we bring out the presents, we have to describe the wrapping paper to the person with her eyes closed, and then she can open her eyes," I continued. "I'll go first." I brought out the first present from the bedroom, a large Kanfer print of rolling fields. "This one is wrapped in red gingham cloth with a satin bow," I said, drawing on our first Christmas when I had actually hand-sewn the wrapping paper. The first present she gave to me was wrapped in silver and midnight blue foil. We played this game well into December 26 and decided it was not only fun, but that we would later tell people we did this for environmental reasons. "For your next campaign?" I said, eyebrows up.

That January, Penny started another year in the Senate and began yet another round of debilitating chemotherapy. I rented an apartment at the plush New York building on Lake Shore Drive in Chicago that boasted a gorgeous view of Lake Michigan to the right and a distant view of Wrigley Field to the left. For me, this time in our life began a routine of complete insanity. Twice a week, I would commute 200 miles from Decatur to Chicago for law school. I'd leave around 5:00 AM on Monday morning, stay two nights, come home Thursday for just a few hours, drive back to Chicago on Thursday night for Friday classes, and return to Decatur Friday night unless Penny was coming to Chicago for the weekend. My first weekend of law school, Penny and I got into a bitter argument. Her birthday was January 21, and she initially suggested I stay in Chicago and study that weekend, which irritated me. I wanted her to want to be with me on her birthday.

When I arrived in Decatur for Penny's birthday weekend, we were preparing to go to Patty's house for a small celebration, as the twins always liked to be together on their birthday. I started piling the presents in the car, Penny asked me if she could open some privately later instead of taking them all to Patty's. "Why?" I said, nearly tantrum like.

"I don't want Patty to feel bad. I don't think anybody splurges on Patty like you do on me, and I feel embarrassed," she said.

"I don't believe this," I said, feeling hurt. But instead of expressing sadness, I became enraged. I thought Penny didn't want me to come to the party because it would be difficult to explain why we were together yet again at another family function. This didn't even make sense, given that we had been inseparable over the last eight months, but I thought that now that she had had a break from me, she was feeling differently. In that moment, I became convinced that Penny was embarrassed of our relationship, which was not the explanation that Penny gave me. I felt rejected, edged-out, and angry.

"You know, why don't you just go yourself?" I said, and I retrieved the presents from the backseat of the car. "You didn't want me to go in the first place—that's why you *suggested* I stay in Chicago and study."

I stormed into the house, set the presents down on the counter, and grabbed my backpack. I walked into the guest bedroom, not wanting to be in our bedroom or the office, and pulled out my law books. I was confused and perhaps a bit paranoid about our relationship and how hidden it was. All my emotions converged. First, I focused on the fact that that my presence at family events was odd, since we told them I was only a press secretary or a friend. Second, I was also overwhelmed with the amount of reading I had to do for school, and I was unsure whether I would succeed. Furthermore, a low-grade guilt was bubbling up about being in school, given that Penny was fighting cancer again. Lastly, I had been excited about her birthday and had put great effort into getting her creative presents, which included an original voting ballot from the South African elections. I also got her a quality two-line phone for the house that had a speaker and a wireless headset because I had noticed that after she finished a telephone call at home, she would rub her neck or say that it hurt from cradling the phone.

"Great," Penny yelled from the living room. "Do what you usually do. Walk away without saying anything and then sulk in the rocking chair, not talking, instead of saying what's on your mind." Her ire was equal to mine. That little reaction was all I needed. I popped up from the rocking chair, strode back into the living room, threw my hands up, and pointed at her in an accusatory way.

"Okay, you want to know what's on my mind?" I said with such anger and verve that even in retrospect, thinking about that moment scares me because I was so volatile. "What's on my mind is that you didn't want me here this weekend for some reason. What's on my mind is that looking around this house: there's not one fucking picture of my family or us together. What's on my mind is that my art and antiques are in storage. Even though we buy art together, this is all 'your' art. We lie to everyone about this being your house. The Kanfer from Christmas—I bought that for *you*, and we simply tell people you bought it. We lie about why I'm around. We lie to my family; we lie to your family." My voice was now escalating to a fevered pitch, and it was clear this argument had nothing to do with the amount of presents in the car. "We lie about our vacations. Linda has a surprise birthday party for you, and I'm not even invited. I'm not invited as a staffer, let alone as your partner, and you can't even say anything to her. And I am sick of it," I was full-blown yelling, so enraged I was spitting.

"I am in the way here, Penny, and we both know it. Unless we do something different, I look like a fucking leach living in 'your home' or like a tagalong groupie at every event you go to. You pay the bills with a check, and I give you cash like we're in some greasy affair. I'm sick of it.

"And you not wanting me here this weekend just makes it worse," I continued, my voice shaking. I started crying. "I should have stayed in Chicago. *You* don't even want me around anymore. I put up with what everybody else thinks, but you didn't want me here this weekend, and it's fucking painful."

Penny looked shocked and deeply wounded, like a tornado had just blown over her without warning. We hadn't had a fight like this since she refused to go to the doctor when we found the lump in her breast two years ago. Her voice became very small, and she was poking her finger in to the corner of the couch, as though she were a child that had just been reprimanded and was trying to explain herself. Looking at her shocked reaction, I felt as though I had slapped her. I deeply regretted my outburst.

"I know how much work law school is," she said in a barely audible voice with no anger. "I didn't want you to feel like you had to be here for my birthday instead of studying your first weekend of law school. I wanted you here this weekend. I always want to be with you. I just didn't want to overwhelm you. You are driving so much. You are doing so much for the campaign, and you won't take a real salary, just some pittance, and I get tired of arguing about that. And, yeah, I guess I just worry about Pat, Terry. I want her to be as happy as I am, and I don't think she is. And you're right about the house. We have to figure this out. And we are both really exhausted. I know that. I'm sorry."

In a surge of energy, she stepped forward to hug me. I lunged toward her. We stood there crying and hugging tightly. I kept telling her I was sorry. When I stop and think about that moment, the sound of my yelling voice still pierces me all these years later, and I become nauseous. I marred her birthday with a paranoid, angry, and misplaced rant, triggered by both a misunderstanding and a growing frustration of hiding our love and our life together. We were so steeped in secrecy, I realized, that I started to doubt us, our own lies, and even our own truths.

"I want you to come to this party," she said, still hugging me. "I wish we could change it and go tomorrow, but the kids made a cake. Let's just go, and we can come home early."

We walked to the car with my arm around her shoulder, and I grabbed only one of the presents for her on the way out of the house. We didn't talk much, but we held hands, the argument and its volatileness having passed.

Before I returned to Chicago at the end of the weekend, Penny gave me a greeting card with Kanfer's art on the front. It was a print called "Prairie Grass," which was a photo of his that I always admired. Dated on her birthday, January 21, 1996, she wrote:

Dearest sweetheart,

You are the love of my life—in every way. Never have I loved like I love you—more deeply than I knew I could, more happy than I knew I could be, and more in love than I ever thought possible. You—and no other—make me feel things I've never felt. I hope you know how deeply I am in love with you—head over heels, almost giddy with laughter, joy, and love . . . more happy than I ever deserved to be.

And I hope you know how sorry I am for upsetting you this weekend. I'd never hurt you intentionally, and I truly am sad for hurting you at all—I love you so very much—you mean the world to me. Thank you for making this weekend so special for Patty and me. Your thoughtfulness, your smile, your humor, and the joy you bring everyone never cease to amaze me. The gifts—as always—were too much, too generous, but you always seem to know what to do—and what to get. I love the phone!!! And I cannot wait to have the ballot as a wonderful yet historic reminder of what our work is supposed to be about!! Thank you so very much for everything!!! I love you

more than my words can express. You make my heart sing and you make
my heart smile. You, my dear attorney-to-be, are the love of my life.

All my love, P.

Her card somehow made me feel worse. I felt as though she had to say those wonderful things about the presents now that I had made such a big deal of it. I didn't home come Wednesday so I could get some serious studying done. When I returned on Friday, I stopped to get Penny a bouquet of flowers, as I always did when I had been away even for a few days, and I pulled into a nearby church parking lot to brush my hair and apply some makeup. When I walked into the house, every piece of art was off of the walls and stacked in the center of the living room.

"You were right about the house," Penny said. "Well, you were right about a lot of things. I thought we should decide together how to decorate, and we should get your art from storage this weekend."

We never spoke about the argument. We just ordered a pizza from Del Carmen's, hung the art, and rearranged some furniture as though we had just moved in.

During that first semester of law school, I spearheaded Penny's media campaign for Senate reelection and conducted fundraising on her behalf. Besides the constant campaigning and her work in the Senate, Penny was also waging the continuing battle of her health, undergoing yet another round of chemotherapy.

Given that the doctors now deemed the cancer aggressive, they recommended an autologous bone marrow transplant, where the patient basically acts as their own donor. Penny's own bone marrow would be extracted from her body, treated and stored, and then reinjected into her system at a later date, after undergoing more chemotherapy. It was a long and painful procedure that required hospital isolation. We started to meet with various experts and hospitals in Chicago. Penny would come to Chicago the night before an appointment. I would go to law school the next morning, and then in the afternoon, we would visit various hospitals and doctors. After much research and review of Chicago hospitals, Penny decided to undergo this stem cell transplant procedure at Loyola University in Maywood. We made intensive preparations for the nearly two-month ordeal, virtually closing our house in Decatur. Penny's cat, Columbia, came to live with me in Chicago.

One of the more difficult conversations Penny had during this time was when she told her father that she did not want him to come to Chicago to visit her. I still didn't fully understand the disdain Penny held for her father. "Look," I said. "He probably needs to feel like he is doing something for you. So let him get your mail or check on the house or something. If nothing else, Penny, it will make it easier for Patty." She agreed and signed the paperwork at the post office, giving her father the authorization to pick up her mail. When we filled out the paperwork at the hospital, though, she insisted that he not be on the list.

The doctor recommended that only family members who often spent time around Penny be permitted to come into the isolated ward to see her because her immune system would be so intensely vulnerable. My stomach clenched with fear that I would not be able to see Penny, but to my surprise, before Penny or I could speak, Patty said kindly and lightly, "Oh, we claim Terry as part of the family."

"We sure do," Penny said.

Later that day, we learned that Penny had to have an emergency procedure and that her bone marrow transplant would have to be delayed. They had discovered that her bone marrow contained more cancer cells. They decided to do another round of chemotherapy and said that it would be easier if Penny simply had a port inserted into her chest.

While in the basement outside the operating room for that last-minute procedure, Patty, who was clearly bothered by Penny refusing to let her father visit, said to me, "Sometimes listening to Penny talk about Dad, Terry, I wonder if we grew up in the same household."

She also said to me that she was explaining to the kids that Penny would be in the hospital for a while and that Kristin seemed a little afraid. "Kristin told me that that if anything happened to me or Doug, and if Aunt Penny weren't around, she would want to come and live with you, Terry," Patty said. "I thought you'd like that."

I always cherished that notion. I loved those children.

Only Patty and I were permitted to see Penny, provided we scoured ourselves and then donned scrubs, booties, and hair nets to prevent exposing Penny to pathogens. Nothing could be brought into the ward or room that had not been thoroughly sanitized. Patty and I talked almost daily, as I was with Penny more often while Patty balanced a husband and three kids amid frequent trips to Chicago. I became a fixture at the hospital; I stayed overnight, often showered there, left for class, and returned in the afternoon. Did they really think I was simply a devoted press aide? Penny became terribly ill during these procedures, and all the books she bought to kill time were never even opened. For a while, I would read poetry to her, but after a few weeks, even that became very boring. Penny disliked sports, preferring books to ball games. I suggested that she consider just watching a little television, something she generally didn't like. Mostly bedridden and often stir crazy, we started watching the Chicago Bulls one night when there were no interesting movies to watch. We both became genuinely mesmerized with Michael Jordan's ability to fly, and soon we were planning our schedule around the Bulls games. It was a wonderful distraction, and I was always sorry when the final buzzer buzzed. At night, when I would sometimes go back to my apartment, we both would start crying. "I miss you when you leave, and sometimes I want to come after you, and then I wonder if you left the parking lot, or what," Penny said. "But I can't, I'm locked in. I'm behaving like a baby, aren't I?"

"Nope," I said. "Sometimes, I get in the car and wonder what you are doing and if you're sleeping or need me and whether I should walk back in. I guess that makes me a baby too because I start crying, and sometimes I cry all the way home."

"I hate that," she said. "Don't cry. I don't want you to cry."

"Well, you know," I said. "I park in the parking lot right below the large window in the hallway. When I get to my car, how about I flash the lights on and off, and you can wave to me?" It's eerie to think of those days when Penny would muster the energy to stand in the large floor-to-ceiling windows of the Cardinal Bernadin Cancer Center and wave to me. I would pull out on First Avenue, stop in the middle of the road, as there was never any traffic that late at night, and flash the lights on and off. Her black silhouette would wave to me, and then she would walk back to her room. I would often put on the sound track to the *Lion King*, a movie Penny and I watched with the kids and liked very much. It was the sound of a happier time, and it comforted me and inevitably made me cry as I drove those lonely Chicago streets back to Lake Shore Drive.

During those six terrible weeks, we had two major crises. Penny's mother, who suffered from emphysema, had been hospitalized several times that year. She had been in the hospital since mid-April. On May 2, Penny's father decided he was going to remove his wife from the ventilator. Penny, still very fragile and sick, begged her father to wait until she could at least see her mother again, or to at least wait a few days so she could digest the information. Penny's brother Rod, who was a fire captain on a twenty-four-hour shift and was unable to leave the firehouse, also wanted his father to wait. When Don wouldn't change the day or delay in any way, Rod quickly had to explain the situation to his superior so he could be at the hospital for the end of his mother's life.

Penny called me at the law school, and I could barely understand her. She was crying and asked me to come quickly. She didn't want to be alone. I rushed to the hospital, and when I walked in, Penny was sitting on the edge of her bed, looking more ashen than usual and weeping. She had been on a telephone hook-up to her mother's hospital room when they disconnected the life support. Penny stood up and hugged me, and I felt all of her weight, as though she could barely stand. "Will you say a prayer?" she said.

"Of course, Penny," I said. "Why don't you lie down and rest?" I said, shifting her to the hospital bed. I fluffed her pillow, covered her, held her hand, and said a prayer. Then she said, "You're a beautiful writer. Would you write mom's obituary?"

"It would be a privilege," I said, "but are you sure that's what your family wants?"

"Yes." She lay back, and I asked her questions about her mother's life. Answering them seemed to soothe her. I told her to rest while I wrote it, and finished it while she slept. I read it to her, and she cried. She then buzzed a nurse, told her that her mother had died, and said that she wanted to leave the hospital to go to the funeral. The doctor strongly advised against it for many reasons, not the least of which was that our home had not been sterilized. Penny insisted. They gave the senator a forty-eight-hour pass.

We made preparations to travel on Sunday for the viewing and return Monday morning after the funeral. Severe restrictions had been placed on

Penny. She had to wear a gown and a mask at all times, she could eat only certain foods, we had to take her temperature regularly, and she had to return to the hospital if she had a fever of any kind. I was instructed to wear a mask in the car and at the house.

The three-hour trip took more than six hours. Penny was throwing up, and had to lie in the back of the car. The roughness of the ride was difficult, forcing us to drive much more slowly. Because we were so late, we drove right to the packed funeral home. Patty and I tried to flank Penny to keep as many people away from her as possible and gently tell people not to her hug her. We were unsuccessful, either because some folks would say, "Oh, one little hug isn't going to hurt her," or because Penny, overcome with her own grief, would hug whomever she was speaking with. She didn't sleep all night and spent the hours moaning, still throwing up. Standing at the graveside the next day, Penny hung on my arm tightly and held my hand as though she didn't care who saw us; she later said she felt too weak and too tired and sick to care if anybody knew we loved each other. She was so sick that we couldn't travel immediately back to Chicago as we were supposed to. I kept trying to coax her to get in the car, believing she simply needed to be in the hospital if anything happened, but she said she just needed to sleep.

A few hours later, Linda Hawker and Cindy Davidsmeyer, a friend and press secretary for the Senate Democrats, came by to see her. I asked them to wait in the living room, and Penny said, "I'm just too sick." This deeply scared me. Penny was close to these women, and there hadn't yet been a circumstance in which she didn't want to see them. Awkwardly, because in essence I was just another staffer, I went back to the living room and explained that she was too sick but would see them soon. They said they understood, and I sat and talked with them for a while. Unusually, we mellowed into a real conversation, unvarnished of politics, about how sick Penny really was. I found their presence comforting, and I felt sad when they said they needed to leave. Penny and I returned to Chicago late that night, not arriving until well after midnight.

A week or so later, the second crisis hit. On the eve of my first final exam, I had left the hospital around 8:00 PM and was studying at my apartment. The hospital called me around 11:00 PM. Penny had a high fever—her temperature was 104—and she was delirious. It was a very dangerous situation because her immune system was compromised, the fever was perilously high, she was behaving erratically, and they decided to call her emergency contact. She had to be packed and bathed in ice, and they thought I should come. I rushed to the hospital, scrubbed, put on a gown, and walked in. By the time I arrived, her temperature had spiked to 106 degrees. A group of nurses were holding Penny, who was barely standing and seemed very agitated, while three other nurses quickly changed the sheets where Penny had thrown up. Penny was muttering, "Oh Terry. Terry, I'm so sick."

"It's okay, Penny, it's okay," I said, scared but trying to soothe her, and I leaned in to kiss her forehead. She threw up all over me, and then she started crying and apologizing. More nurses came to help, bringing ice and a needle of medicine. They gave me a set of blue scrubs, and I changed my clothes and returned in a few minutes. They had Penny back in her bed. She was not coherent and was mostly talking about nonsensical things. I had never seen her like this, and I was very scared. They said they were worried she would go into convulsions. A doctor came, examined her, and gave the nurses specific directions.

"Terry, Terry," she'd say, repeating my name throughout the night. Or, if she needed the nurse, she would say, "Nurse, nurse." Everything was doubled.

"I need to call Julie," she said of our friend Julie Curry. "Julie," she hollered as though Julie were just in the hallway. Julie had managed Penny's 1992 campaign and was elected to the House of Representatives serving Decatur. The three of us had become great friends, often traveling the district together for events.

"Okay, P, we can call her," I said, hoping this would placate her. "But it's pretty late, and Evan will be asleep," I said of Julie's young son. "You don't want to wake Evan."

"I have to talk to her, Terry," she said, and then she rambled on about some other topic. Then, she came back to Julie. "Instead of *walking* parades, I decided we should buy *mopeds*. I need to tell her that for the Fourth of July parade. I want to tell her that. If we order them now, we can use them for the parade," Penny said. I had this image of Penny and Julie circling one another on mopeds like clowns on bikes, and wanted to laugh.

Throughout the night, Penny would moan and talk about how cold she was and then drift off into sleep. I sat next to her, and as the nurse had told me to do, I kept washing her face with a cool cloth and alcohol and tried to rub her body and legs, which were packed in ice. The nurses came in every few minutes—they had administered some medicine into her port and were monitoring her closely. While I didn't understand everything that was happening, it was clear from the amount of staff and hurried nature of their work that Penny was in a dangerous crisis. I felt helpless, only able to sit near Penny and hold her hand or rub her head. Several hours later, she began moaning again. This time she was sweating heavily. The fever had broken, and thankfully, she fell asleep. It was nearly 6:00 AM. Now that Penny was out of immediate danger and resting, I left and went back to my apartment to change out of the scrubs before heading to the law school. I arrived just in time for my 9:00 AM first-year law school exam.

The next several weeks, Patty and I spent time at the hospital together. We tried to time our schedules so that she would be at the hospital in the morning while I was at class, and then I would arrive in the early afternoon so she could leave to be home with her children. I felt safer when Patty was there, particularly because she was a nurse. Once, while Penny was resting, we had decided to go to the cafeteria to get some drinks and take a break. As we stepped into the hallway to exit, nurses and doctors came rushing from both directions as a blue light began flashing in the adjacent room. "Dr. Cart," the intercom began. "Dr. Cart, please report to room twelve." Patty said that "Dr. Cart" is a hospital code word for calling in doctors or a cardiopulmonary arrest resuscitation team to respond to some life-threatening event. The patient in the next room had died. We looked at each other, clearly shaken, and Patty said, "Maybe we'd better just stay." We walked back to Penny's room, and I said simply, "Eh, we changed our minds."

As a patient nears the end of their bone marrow transplant, he or she is transitioned to a group home, a very sterilized halfway house of sorts. During those several weeks, doctors are able to monitor how the patient is doing, and the hospital is close if something goes wrong. They also recommend that the patient's home is thoroughly cleaned by a special team that will sterilize it as much as possible. Penny was impatient and wanted to be home instead of going to a group home. The doctors advised against it, but Penny insisted, and so she skipped that step and transitioned directly back to our home in Decatur. During this weeks-long ordeal before she was released, Dr. Patrick Stiff had told us, "You'll know if you're winners or losers within six months." I wished he hadn't used that language, but we understood that he meant we would know if this extensive procedure had cured Penny or not. The day she was released from the hospital, Patty and I were both there. We left the hospital, Patty and Penny in Patty's van, me following in the car. They pulled over in front of the Riverside Brookfield High School, and I immediately thought something must be wrong. I got out of the car and walked up. Penny said, "I am going to ride with you. Then Pat can just go down 55 and we can go down 57." We could have gone down 55 just as easily and then carried on to Decatur, but I didn't say anything.

Once Penny was situated in our car and we drove off, she said to me "I feel like we are starting our lives all over again, Terry, and I wanted to ride home with you." I felt a warm, graceful peace come over me. I too felt we had a new lease on life and that she had escaped death during the bone marrow transplant.

On the way home, Penny asked me to sing to her, something she had done on our first date. After I sang, we began to talk about the future, and we pledged that we would live healthier lives, exercising more, eating healthier, and getting more rest. This pledge also included coming out, which would stop the toll that so much hiding and lying was taking on both of us.

"We have to figure this out," became a mantra each time we ran into a secrecy hurdle, which now was almost daily.

CHAPTER THIRTEEN

BEHIND THE EIGHT BALL: RETELLING ALASKA

In November 1996, Penny won the state Senate reelection handily, she was still cancer free, and for a few brief moments, we were on top of the world. We decided to celebrate big. Tired of having to make excuses, even to our families, as to why the senator and her press secretary were spending yet another holiday season together in Decatur, we opted to travel and wanted to branch out from our regular excursions to Mexico, so we planned a trip to the Island of Margarita off the northern tip of Venezuela. As our departure approached, we went to the bookstore and picked up a pile of travel books and started marking restaurants and art galleries we wanted to visit and excursions we wanted to take. Our euphoria, however, was short lived. Everything came crashing down a few weeks later when Penny's doctor called and told her that the bone marrow transplant was not successful. *Clearly*, I remember thinking, in the doctor's own words, *we are not winners*. We decided to take the trip anyway and talk about what was next, politically and personally.

The day after Christmas, we flew to the Island of Margarita. We sat on the white-sand beaches and, given the most recent tiring health news, flirted with the idea of Penny leaving the Senate, me leaving law school, and just traveling. We spent many afternoons on the beach dreaming of how we would quit our respective roles and where we would travel. Pipe dreams, really.

One afternoon while sipping drinks and sunning on the beach, I said without forethought, "Penny, I want to tell you why I left to go to Alaska. I need to tell you that."

I told her how I felt when she told me that she had cancer, how scared I was, and that I was convinced that I had caused her cancer by introducing her to a lesbian lifestyle. "I made a deal with God that if he would make you well, I would leave you," I said. "That's why I went to Alaska."

"You *what*?" she asked.

I started to repeat what I had said.

"I heard you," she said. She seemed torn between anger and being deeply moved by this gesture. "Terry, I can't even . . . wait, you did what, now?" she said, still incredulous.

"I told God that if he would let you be well, I would leave you," I said, clearly forgetting that I had had two years to digest this and that Penny was hearing my rationale for leaving her for the first time. She didn't say anything for a long time. She got up, put on her shoes, slipped on her cover-up, and walked away. I sat there watching the waves break and the afternoon clouds roll in as they had each day, bringing a few hours of afternoon showers. I wondered what would happen. Penny hadn't asked me why I'd left for Alaska in many months. In retrospect, I think the news that the cancer had come back and that the bone marrow transplant hadn't worked stirred many things in me. Part of me wondered if Penny could really love me if she saw the real me, whatever that meant. I thought she deserved to see all of me so that she could decide, in what might be the final years of her life, whether she wanted to be with me.

A light rain started to fall, but I didn't want to leave the beach. I gathered our things and moved to a thatched umbrella and sat under it. I was convinced that I didn't deserve Penny, and I tricked my mind into believing that if she knew the real me, she would leave me. I stayed on the beach for a while, not sure if I should leave Penny alone or find her and talk. I opted to leave her alone. I was afraid to walk inside and find her.

Finally, I walked back inside the hotel. Penny was sitting in a chair in the expansive open-air lobby and seemed distracted. Perhaps in shock?

She got up, I followed, and we walked back outside and stood at the edge of the patio, watching the rain. We were standing side by side under an umbrella. The rain began to fall harder, and we were getting wet and chilly. Penny turned to face me, the emotional distance between us obvious.

"So you decided you would leave and go off to Alaska and not tell me why? You think that's okay?" she said with steam in her voice. "You made a major life decision, a crazy one, and you didn't think you should talk to me about that?"

I didn't know how to defend myself. I couldn't defend myself. I simply said, "I couldn't talk to you about it. I couldn't talk to anybody about it."

"You were going to tell me that day in the yard that the movers were coming, weren't you?" she asked, reflecting back to the day she came out of the house in jeans and bare feet.

"Yes, Penny, but how could I?"

"I knew something was going on. I *knew* it," she said, more to herself than me. "I just didn't know what it was or how to get to it."

We stood there for a long time. Her thinking, me waiting, anticipating a verdict about our future lives. A waiter walked over and asked us if we wanted anything. Penny ignored him, and I shook my head no. We stood there longer.

"Terry," she said calmly. "I'm really angry." Those words went through me like a hot poker.

"What do you want to do?" I asked, presuming she was so angry she would end this relationship. Whether she got my meaning, I don't know.

"Right now, I want to go take a shower and dry off," she said somewhat harshly. I felt like a reprimanded puppy as I followed her to our room. She walked into the bathroom and shut the door. I lay on the bed, looking out the window at the thick green palms and watching the rain drip down their leaves. When Penny came out of the bathroom, I showered. I stood under the shower regretting that I spoke on this trip, which was supposed to be restful. I felt selfish, sick, and scared. I was still in the shower when Penny cracked the door and said, "I'll meet you downstairs. Take your time."

I got out of the shower, got dressed, and went downstairs. Penny was sipping a beer with lime and eating a peanut mix from a bowl. I ordered the same and sat down. We still didn't speak.

We finished our drinks in silence, then got up and began to walk through the lobby, examining even the most mundane things as though we were in a museum. We walked down a level of steps and found a game room with pool tables. "Go get us a few more beers," she said. I did, and I came back to see Penny had racked the table and was shooting pool. I didn't even know she played.

"So, Terry, tell me about this," she said, holding her pool cue. "I want to know what you were thinking. Exactly what *were* you thinking?" This did not seem to be the environment for such an intimate conversation, and her anger was palpable. I couldn't tap into the real emotion I had felt when I had made the decision, so I just started talking.

"I'm not sure what happened," I said, feeling as though I were explaining an affair. It was a complicated discussion, now that I thought about it. I told her that I thought she was sick because of me. She wasn't a lesbian before she met me, and I had always been taught that homosexuality was a great sin, and I thought that if I hadn't fallen in love with her, she wouldn't have gotten ill. "I wanted you to live and be healthy, Penny, and if I was in the way of that, I was going to bow out. I knew that I would have to go far because I would never be able to keep my own promise," I said. Even as I said it, I heard for the first time how absurd it must have sounded to another human being. She stood there not moving from the pool cue, but her eyes were saying, "How could you do this?"

My monologue was devoid of emotions, stated matter-of-factly. I'm not even sure I was making sense. I could see, though, that when I spoke about the depth of my love for her, it momentarily pierced the armor of her anger. We half-heartedly played pool and walked back to the lobby, returning the empty beer bottles. It was as though the heart of our relationship was gone, like we were there on vacation but barely going through the motions. I realized the damage I had done—it seemed I had stolen our happiness.

The next days followed a hollowed-out routine, and I started to question whether I should simply say, "Let's go home." On one hand, I was convinced we would weather this. On the other, I was worried that we would become like any other couple who permitted the pulp of their love to slip through their fingers.

On New Year's Eve, we had reservations at an extravagant restaurant, but somehow it seemed too much under these new circumstances. We went to a small bar and sat a table in the corner. Penny made a joke at my expense about my having gone to Alaska, which I didn't catch at first. Then it dawned on me: she was trying to be funny and was mocking me at the same time. The warm wash of shame cascaded over me. I felt exposed and ridiculed. I had not gone to Alaska lightly, and I surely did not do it to hurt Penny. It had torn me apart. I understood that she was angry. If she wanted to talk, that was one thing, but I didn't feel I deserved this. Even she didn't understand the terrible struggle I felt. Stung and choking on shame, I picked up the napkin from my lap, pushed my chair back, and set the napkin on the table, preparing to leave. Penny put her hand on my forearm, stopping me.

"Terry," she said. "Don't ever do that again. You really hurt me. Not because you went, but because you didn't talk to me. We talk to each other about everything—or I thought we did."

"I just don't want you to be sick," I said, my voice cracking. I started to cry. "I would rather be sick than for you to be sick."

She shifted in her seat, her head tilted, and she opened her hands, as though unable to convey a thought. "Terry, I don't want *either* of us to be sick. But if you had talked to me, we could have talked it through and not have lost seven months together.

I didn't say anything. Then she opened up a little.

"I understand what you were feeling," she said, gently. "After Marsha died, I worried about me and Pat. I prayed for the same thing, that if one of us had to get sick, that I would be the one instead of her. I get it. But we're in this together, aren't we?" she said leaning forward, her face genuinely and earnestly asking me that question.

"Yes, Penny, we are—if you still want to be."

"I do. But I don't want you to make decisions without me," she said, leaning back.

As the night wore on, we were kinder and sweeter to each other but in a much more understated way than we had been previously. This revelation had changed us somehow. I didn't know how long this fragile feeling would last, but I felt as though our love was like hand-blown glass and I had dropped and cracked it. We glued it back together, but I always regretted that the hairline fissure remained through the rest of our lives. We rarely revisited that experience, but many months later, we talked again of my deal with God. This time, Penny was very soft and seemed humbled that I made that deal. She also seemed to feel sorry for my misguided love, but there was always a gossamer thread of anger woven into it as well.

The rest of the vacation, we genuinely rested, and when we returned to the states in mid-January 1997, I resumed my law school and press secretary routine, and Penny went back to more chemo and her Senate work. We spent much of March in Chicago on the weekends, visiting art galleries, buying art, and finding new restaurants to explore. We capped it off with our version of March Madness and bought tickets to see one of my favorite opera singers, mezzo-soprano Cecilia Bartoli, at the orchestra hall. Then I had to really hit the books hard, particularly since we were planning another trip to Mexico the next month. The night Penny was leaving Chicago to return to Decatur, she gave me a narrow card in a forest green envelope with the words *My Love* written on it. The quote in black letters read: "LOVE IS THE GREATEST REFRESHMENT IN LIFE." —PICASSO.

We left for Puerto Vallarta in April as planned, and the trip was wonderful and free from trouble and strife. The depth of our relationship, it seemed, had completely healed from the Christmas revelation. We continued to discuss coming out and living a "normal" life, but I was still afraid. Penny was nervous but more ready than me. We promised to solve this and come up with a plan when I came home that summer. Though we talked steadily about coming out, I believed it was something in the distance, not something imminent.

I realized just how much more ready Penny was, though, on a hot day near the end of July. She was doing yard work, and I was off golfing, our usual split routine so that we would not be seen together doing domestic chores around the house. On my way home from the Scoville Golf Club, I saw a sunset unlike any I had ever seen; it was more akin to a Western sunset than a Midwestern sunset: striking purple hues painted the entire western sky. I hurried home, jumped out of the car, and told Penny that she had to come with me; I had to show her something. She didn't hesitate or ask me what for—she just put her rake in the garage and closed the door. We drove to an overlook, pulled over to the side of the road, got out, and stood there watching in silent awe of the most unusual sky we'd ever seen. "That is magnificent," she said. Something happened between us while standing there in the middle of that country road. It felt as though that sunset solidified something within us. I can't explain it now anymore than I could then, but it felt as though by witnessing that sunset, we were united anew.

When we got back home, I pulled into the garage and was going to walk into the house while she finished her yard work. She said, "Don't go in. Show me how to golf." I was surprised for several reasons, primarily because she hated golf—preferring a good book to a green—but also because we would be standing in full view of the neighbors in the yard late on a Saturday afternoon. It was clear that something had shifted.

"Okay," I said. I grabbed a nine iron and a few golf balls from my bag. I dropped them in the yard. She chipped, and I retrieved the balls and gave her some basic pointers. It was nice to be in the yard with Penny and not care who might be watching us. When her half dozen golf balls were hit, we stood there talking. On occasion, Penny would take a yard tool and pull up crab grass. We were unpressured and, it seemed, normal—just standing in our yard, talking. "You know, you'll be done with law school soon, and I've been thinking about what we are going to do," she said.

"I guess I'll just get a 'show' apartment in Springfield and we'll do that routine again," I said.

"Terry," she said. "I don't want to do that anymore. I want us to live together, publically."

I am unsure what finally brought that notion fully into reality; somehow to me it is linked to that glorious sunset, which seemed to be confirmation that it was time—long past time. I agreed.

"Let's figure this out on our trip to North Carolina next week," she said. "I know we always say that, but let's finally do this." I agreed. I picked up the golf balls and the club.

The next week, we headed southeast. Instead of taking our annual summer trip to Mexico, we decided to spend our vacation in North Carolina, furniture shopping to redecorate our house. That in and of itself seemed to be an indication that we were moving toward coming out. Amid the hours spent driving and shopping, we talked at length about how we were going to go about telling people about our relationship, revisiting what people would think and who already knew. And we talked about the toll the secrecy was taking on our lives.

"I'm tired of what this does to both of us," Penny said. We concluded that we would not make any grand announcement and that our goal would be to remain private, but not secretive.

Our plan was simple, if not well thought out. We would have a picnic at the house. We would invite Christi Parsons, now a White House Correspondent for the *Los Angeles Times*, and her husband, Cody Moser, a pilot; and Jen Halperin and her then-husband Mike Hawthorne, both reporters. On Penny's side, it was going to be Ken and Sheryl Frye and Linda Hawker and her husband, Roger Ryan. Penny considered Patty a given. That I know of, Penny had never explicitly told Patty about the nature of our relationship, but she'd always felt her identical twin "just knew," and it certainly seemed she did. I was not sure it was a great plan, but I took comfort in the idea that we weren't going to overtly say anything, just get together and grill out and interact with our friends.

During our vacation, two things interceded. First, Penny started to feel really run-down and awful. She was done with the chemotherapy that she had started in January, and her quarterly tests continued to indicate that she was cancer free. Within days, though, she was in such terrible pain that we abandoned our vacation and came home. Penny was in so much pain that she couldn't sit in the front seat of the car and had to lay down in the backset for the entire twelve-hour trip home. And second, our beloved cat Columbia, who was very old and ill, started to die.

When we returned, Penny seemed to recuperate, but we let the picnic fall by the wayside. Penny was still in pain off and on. As fall approached, she rallied. The pain was less frequent, but it seemed that when it hit, it hit hard. By the end of September, Penny had been feeling well and hadn't had an episode for some weeks. When she said she wanted to talk to me about something, I presumed it was about reviving our party plan. Politics, not the picnic, was on her mind.

"I want to run for secretary of state," she said.

CHAPTER FOURTEEN

PLANS INTERRUPTED

I tried hard to convince Penny that the timing of this race was off. I wanted her to take a break from campaigning and focus on continuing to rebuild her full strength—not depleting it as one does while campaigning statewide. She would have no part of the conversation.

Perhaps I was tired of politics and the way it drained our lives. I knew that Penny wasn't fully healthy, and I wanted her to see that. She never could. I tried a different tactic. "At least," I suggested, "let's talk with a campaign-media expert," believing that an independent person would give Penny the same unvarnished advice. We met with President Obama's now-famous political architect, David Axelrod.

During that meeting in his Chicago office, Axelrod's advice was that the hard sell would be convincing voters that she was in fact healthy—and not just healthy, but healthy enough to handle a statewide office of this magnitude. She was certainly likeable, and people loved a fighter story, he said, but the sympathy vote would not be enough for this type of powerful position. He strongly advised that we conduct a poll, which we did with Penny's pollster, Celinda Lake, the Democratic Party's leading political pollster and strategist. We tested to see how Penny and her health were faring with voters and also to get a pulse of how her proposed campaign message, literacy, would play. The poll results were workable, and voters really liked her breed of personal-touch politician.

The night after we met with Axelrod, Penny was hyped. It was undeniable that politics was her lifeblood. She was happy just *talking* about running a race. I thought such devotion and happiness might also be medicinal, even if I knew that some components of the lifestyle were going to be poisonous. The state Democratic Party leaders weren't initially keen on Penny running for Secretary of State. They had pushed Penny very hard for months to run for a congressional seat, which was vacated by Congressman Glenn Poshard, who was now running as the Demcoratic candidate for Governor. Given her popularity, Penny would have been a shoo-in for that seat, but she rejected the opportunity.

"My life is different now than it used to be," she said. "We are apart too much as it is. I don't want to be commuting between D.C. and Decatur. I don't want to add more stress and travel. I want to be near you, without a show apartment. Secretary of State lets me do that. I can still have politics, and we can still be with each other daily when you are done." We talked about how to delicately spin to the press this decision to decline, as we couldn't disclose this particular reason for not running for the seat. We decided she would say that she didn't want to be away from Patty and the kids and that commuting was not attractive to her at this time in her life. It made sense.

For the next two months, she devoted her laser-like focus to preparing for this race. We started a full-time operation of garnering petitions, research, and background on the office of secretary of state, mission statements, campaign colors, and a media message. I had returned to the Decatur-Chicago commute for law school, working the campaign full time when I was not in class. Penny usually handled her own petitions to run for office. This year, because of her health, she delegated much of that responsibility. We had planned to announce her run in October, but everything was running behind, mostly because she didn't have the energy she once had. Unlike an uncontested bid for Congress, a candidate in this Democratic primary was not going to be given any gifts. She was going to have to earn every vote. The lineup for this lucrative office was formidable. In the primary was former–Chicago Cubs baseball player and now–Cook County Recorder of Deeds, Jesse White, who had focused a good deal of effort on inner-city youth and created the nationally famed Jesse White Tumblers. Also lined up at the door was Tim McCarthy, a former United States Secret Service agent and hero who took a bullet for President Ronald Reagan. After much preparation, we finally had everything in place.

On Tuesday, November 18, she announced her bid for secretary of state in a statewide fly-around of several cities that ended in Decatur. Despite her health concerns, even the low-grade headache she was experiencing that day, that fly-around was a highlight of my political life with Penny. We were at the height of our political partnership—the hours of planning, strategizing, picking colors, and creating a message were on full parade that day. On the plane, we would review the previous campaign stop, strategize, and refine the message for the next speech. I would make sure she had enough food and water to keep her going. The intimacy of the two of us being ferried around the state on a small plane, popping out at airports to talk politics and the health of Illinois, was energizing. Working the crowds on her behalf after each speech was simply fun for me. I was proud of her. At each stop, she was fiery about trying to curb the high school drop-out rate and wanted to work for legislation linking teens' driver's licenses to staying in school—no driver's license for a teen who dropped out of high school before the age of eighteen. The crowds loved that idea, and she brought the literacy message to life.

Neither of us, however, were prepared for what awaited her on the last campaign stop of the day in her hometown of Decatur. As we were descending over the airport, it looked like a large black ink stain was seeping onto the tarmac. As we landed, the visual became clear: hundreds of people gathered at the airport to welcome Penny home. People were there to honor her and encourage her in her race. She got to see friends she hadn't seen in a while. Hugs, laughter, and enthusiasm were given freely, and she gave as much back, reminiscing and thanking and telling her constituents that she couldn't do it without them. I can still see Penny alighting from the plane in her coat with the thick campaign notebook under arm. As we walked across the tarmac, I slipped the book from under her arm and said, "I'll make sure it gets to the podium." As we neared the crowd, I transitioned into the role of a senior campaign aide and simply said, "You should drink this in. They really love you, Senator." She squeezed my forearm and smiled. "Thank you for everything."

Penny was happy, and the race was off to a good start. The ensuing days and weekend turned to our personal lives. We planned to drive on Wednesday night to Indiana to spend Thanksgiving with my sister

Donna and her family. We decided it was time to move forward with our plan to tell our families. We'd start with Donna and her husband, Gary. Then Penny would tell her brother Rod and his wife, Jane. I asked why she was not telling Patty first. She said she was certain that Patty already knew. I didn't question it further. Early on in our relationship, Penny had confided to Jane that she had "met someone special." Rod and Jane had already made several moves to acknowledge our partnership by inviting us to dinner very early in our relationship and treating us very much like a couple. And when Penny's mom had been dying, Jane had made a point of pulling me aside at the hospital and saying, "Terry, Rod and I just want you to know we are 100 percent with you and Penny." We never spoke in more detail, but I knew what she had meant and was grateful.

I was a mix of nervous and happy that we had finally reached a point of disclosing our relationship on a limited basis. Perhaps because of that happiness, we both were ignoring the headaches that Penny was experiencing, writing them off on any given day to stress, not enough water, not enough sleep. Her migraines that she had suffered from for years. Again, fate was about to intervene, as it had with our picnic plans, and this time, it would interrupt more than our plans of disclosure.

Penny and I had wanted to get an early start on our five-hour drive to southern Indiana and leave Tuesday night. But between my own procrastination and handling campaign press calls, I didn't finish a law school assignment until early Wednesday morning. On Wednesday, Penny went to Champaign to have the car serviced and do some shopping. She would be back in Decatur by mid-afternoon and we would leave. I could tell she wasn't feeling well by the way she sounded. "You have another headache, don't you?" I said gently.

"Yes," she said. "But I'm okay. I think it's a migraine."

A few hours later, she called me from a Target store. She had gotten very dizzy and nauseous and had collapsed, and she wanted to know if I was close. I was not close. I had not even left Chicago. "Penny," I said. "I don't think you should drive. I think you should call the doctor right now."

"Damn it, Terry, it's the beginning of a migraine," she yelled. "I'm not calling Hoelzer every time I feel sick or get a twinge."

"Okay," I said. "How about calling Patty to come and get you? Will you please do that?"

"I just need to sit here and be still," she said.

I don't remember what she did to get home, but when I arrived later that night, she was in bed.

"Penny, we have got to call the doctor," I said.

"No. Please don't make me talk. It hurts. I just need to sleep. It gets better when I sleep. It's just a migraine, Terry," she said. I talked to Patty, who was on her way to Kansas to spend Thanksgiving with her in-laws. She thought Penny should go to the doctor as well, but Penny refused. She woke up around nine that night and said her back hurt terribly and was trying to rub it. "Let me do that for you, sweetheart," I said. She sat up on the side of the bed, and I got behind her and rubbed her back. It didn't help. We tried a heating pad, but it didn't help either.

"Penny, I am going to call Hoelzer," I said.

"Terry, I don't want to bother anybody during the holiday. It's a migraine."

"It's not a migraine in your back," I said gently, but I didn't push it further.

She went back to sleep. I called my sister and explained that Penny was sick, that we thought it was a migraine, and if she felt better the next morning, we would drive. She got up on Thursday morning but still felt horrible. I thought that maybe it was a migraine or the flu after all, since she was able to get out of bed. But within a few hours she was back in bed, terribly ill.

Penny woke up Friday afternoon and started throwing up, and she could barely walk the few steps to the bathroom. With any movement or light, she would nearly scream. She woke up again, crying, "My low back hurts, badly." Since massaging it didn't work, I thought we should try something else.

"It might feel better if I put some Icy Hot on it for the muscles," I said. Penny had gotten out of bed and ambled to the bathroom. As she was leaning on the bathroom sink, I rubbed the ointment into her low back. Nearly immediately, she started to scream and cry. "Oh, Terry, get it off, get it off. It burns. Get it off, get it off," she wailed. Quickly, I grabbed a washcloth and wiped it off of her, but she was absolutely inconsolable. The pain was too much. She was literally screaming as she tumbled into bed.

"That's it, Penny," I said, realizing how sick she really was. "I'm calling Hoelzer."

"Please don't, Terry. I just need to sleep," she said, cradling her head in pain.

"Then Hoelzer can tell me you need to sleep," I said. I was angry with myself that I had waited as long as I had. I called the doctor, apologizing for bothering her on Thanksgiving weekend, explaining Penny's two-day symptoms that now escalated into throwing up and severe sensitivity.

"She needs an MRI, Terry," Hoelzer said.

"She doesn't want to go to the hospital," I said.

"Start heading toward Springfield, and I will call you back," she said.

"Penny," I said, now taking charge, but not mentioning the hospital. "Honey, I have to get you up. Hoelzer said she needs to see you."

"T, I just need rest," she said.

"You're right, sweetheart, you do. And as soon as I get you to Hoelzer's, I promise I will bring you back and you can rest," I said.

"Okay, Terry," she said, and I was surprised that she acquiesced.

Penny at that point was virtually dead weight. She could barely stand, let alone walk. "I'm going to call 911," I said.

"Please don't. I can make it," she said. I didn't want to force her, and Hoelzer hadn't said to call 911.

"I'm going to try *one* thing," I said, putting my index finger up for emphasis. "If that doesn't work, I am calling 911."

"Okay, Terry," she said, still laying in bed and holding her head, trying to shield her eyes from any light. First, as she lay back, I slipped on her sweats and then a shirt. I grabbed a few things to put in a bag. "If you're bringing me back, I don't need those," she said.

Still as sharp as ever, I thought, but I ignored her remark. I walked into our den and rolled out the Levenger office chair and turned it around next to the bed. Very gently, I said, "Honey, I am going to put you in the chair and wheel you to the car. All you have to do is sit up on the edge of the bed."

It took every ounce of my physical strength to hoist her into the chair. She kept her head down and her eyes closed. I rolled her through the living room, out the front door, and onto the sidewalk that looped around the front of the house. We had to cross a lip down to the second piece of sidewalk, which caused her to scream, and then I rolled her to the garage. I backed the car out, turned it around, and hoisted Penny into the driver's side.

On the forty-five-minute trip to Springfield, Hoelzer called and gave us the location of a MRI facility near the hospital. We got there, and they helped me get Penny out of the car and into a wheelchair. They took us right into the examination room. Penny asked me to stay with her, and the technicians didn't protest or make me wait outside. I sat next to Penny in a chair while they slid her into the MRI machine. I tried to talk to Penny during the test, but the machine sounded like a jackhammer and she couldn't hear me. We weren't there for long when two technicians, a man and a woman, came out and handed me Penny's films in an envelope. "You need to go to the hospital right now," the man said.

We called Patty on the way to the hospital. A team of doctors was waiting at the emergency room entrance. Penny was out of my hands. They rushed her away on a gurney for tests. A little while later, they pushed her back into the hallway. She slept. Shortly after, they said they had a private room for her. Hoelzer came into the room. "Hi, Terry," she said, greeting me warmly. "Penny has a tumor, and we need to do emergency surgery. That's what's causing the headaches. I have called Brian Russell, he's a neurosurgeon, and he's on his way here now," she said.

I went to Penny's bedside and pulled up a chair, holding her hand. "P, sweetheart," I said, not really wanting to wake her. "Honey, Dr. Hoelzer's here, and she said that you need to have some surgery tonight." My voice started to crack. I wanted to be strong for this.

"You have a tumor," I said, grimacing, glad her eyes were closed and that she couldn't see me. I started to cry. I could see tears forming in the corner of her eye.

"How bad?" she asked, squinting her eyes open.

"I honestly don't know," I said. "The surgeon is on his way in. They are going to do this tonight, so it must be pretty urgent."

"Do you think we can wait for Pat?" she asked, but she didn't wait for my answer. "Terry, I want to wait for Pat."

"I'll ask. I'll tell them that's what you want," I said.

A few minutes later, Dr. Russell appeared at the door.

"Is there anybody from Penny's family?" he asked. Hoelzer, Russell, and I stepped into the hall. "Dr. Russell, this is Terry Mutchler," Hoelzer said. "She is Penny's long-term friend." She added that he could feel free to talk to me. At a different time, under different circumstances, I may have thanked Hoelzer, or may have even contested the introduction or been embarrassed. Now, I simply moved into the reality of that graceful introduction, grateful for it. The three of us walked to a lighted X-ray display machine on the wall. Russell showed me the picture of the tumor in Penny's head. "We have to get that out as soon as possible."

"She wants to wait for her twin sister to travel back from Kansas. She's on her way here now, but she probably won't arrive until tomorrow."

"Terry, I don't know about that," he said.

"Dr. Russell, it's really important to her," I said. "Please. She'll feel safer."

It was nearly 11:00 PM anyway. The three of us walked back into Penny's room. Dr. Russell woke her up and explained the delicacy of the situation and the operation. He said that he thought they should do the surgery that night. "I want to wait for my sister, if I can," she said. Russell said that as long as she remained stable, he would wait the few hours until Saturday morning. The minute something changed, though, he would have no choice but to go in. Although Penny was in a precarious situation, I felt relieved to be at the hospital, where she would be attended to. I tried to stay away from the feelings of guilt for not forcing Penny to the hospital sooner.

I stayed in the room with her that night, and she seemed to sleep. Patty arrived and we walked with Penny as she was wheeled to the operating room doors. We each said goodbye and reassured her that everything would be all right. We went to the waiting room and nervously waited. Four and half hours later, Dr. Russell emerged through the operating room doors. He said the surgery was successful; they removed all of the tumor, although it was malignant. They would talk to us later about another chemotherapy regimen. They prepared us by saying that she would look a little "beat up" and that her head would be heavily bandaged. I excused myself to make a call and walked away to a pay phone.

Instead of picking up the phone, I leaned in so I would not be seen and wept in relief that she had pulled through such a serious surgery.

The press dimension was always part of our lives, and now more than ever I could not ignore it given that Penny was a statewide candidate, although she needed rest. The same questions that arose each time the cancer came back were facing us again: how, when, and what to tell the public. This time, I had to make these decisions on my own. I decided I would disclose this news on Monday, and hopefully by then Penny would be able to be part of those discussions and I could honestly say she had been part of preparing the news release. I had flirted with the idea of announcing her withdrawal from the race, but knew I would not do that. Unbelievably, she rebounded from the surgery quickly. Even I was surprised that she had any semblance of strength let alone humor.

"Penny," one of the doctors asked Saturday night during their routine neurological checks for a patient who just had brain surgery. "Who is the governor?"

"Glenn Poshard," she said without missing a beat. He looked very alarmed. Glenn Poshard was the Democratic candidate for Governor, but he was not the governor. Then, Penny laughed at her little political joke. "Jim Edgar. I was just fast-forwarding." The doctor laughed nervously.

On Sunday, Penny seemed more like her old self, still weak but definitely stronger than she had been. She was talking about the race and was impatient to leave the hospital. Later that day, I broached her departure from the race. "Penny," I said. "Don't you think you should withdraw and regain your strength?"

"No," she said. "What should we tell them?" Keeping the details as light as possible, I simply said, "I am going to brief the press tomorrow morning." I stayed in the hospital room and wrote a short news release explaining the situation. I knew that the press would want details. So when Dr. Russell came in to examine Penny, I asked if he could tell me a little bit about the tumor. For example, I said, "is it the size of a quarter or a dime?" Or, could he describe it? Perhaps not understanding the press and political campaigns, I think he thought my questions were crass and distasteful.

"Well," I pushed, "could I say it was the size of a nickel? Would that be accurate?"

"Yes," he said.

I knew that no amount of spin could mask this truth; that Penny's cancer had spread again, the third time in three years despite several rounds of chemotherapy, radiation, and a bone marrow transplant. Armed with details and a positive attitude, I held a press conference on Monday, December 4, 1997, in the state capitol. I informed the public that Penny's cancer spread. Still spinning, I told the press: "There's no way to soft-shoe a tumor. But the good news is that it was the size of a nickel and was not a brain tumor." I said this as though a malignant tumor on the skull was some how minor, less serious than it really was. As they should have been, the reporters were brutal in their questions, tough and unsparing with more than a little measure of disbelief when I told them that Penny had said hello while being wheeled back from surgery. Unbelievable as it sounded, that was true.

At the end of that press conference, I had a scare of a different sort. A reporter for the Decatur paper, Tony Man, asked me, "How do you want me to identify you for the story?" I sensed danger but played it cool. I said, "What do you mean? I'm her press secretary." He was a gay man and was partnered, and his question was a coded message that he understood our relationship.

"Yes, but do you also want to be identified as a family member?" he pressed. I was on the verge of being outed. I didn't want to overtly lie, and yet there was no time to calculate a response. The Senate press secretary, Cindy Davidsmeyer, was standing near. She interjected, "How about you also say she's a close friend." Cindy and I never talked about Tony's question. From then on, in most articles and news broadcasts, whether national or local, I was identified as spokeswoman and "close friend" of Penny Severns.

Despite her rapidly failing health, Penny had no intention of walking away from this Secretary of State race. I came back to the hospital and told Penny that the news conference went well, but that she had to understand this from their perspective. A statewide candidate for a lucrative office that controlled thousands of jobs in the state had brain surgery less than a week after announcing her candidacy. They had a right to ask tough questions and to question whether she should be in the race at all. By afternoon, the

Senate press secretary told us that the press wasn't taking the news conference all that well, demanding more answers, wanting further clarifica-
tions, and asking if we would make her doctors available, and if not, why. I
knew this story of surgery and ill health couldn't stand for more than one
news cycle without deeply affecting the campaign. I suggested two things:
I would do a walk-through of the pressroom and answer any other questions they had, and Penny should consider letting me arrange a bedside
interview. "In their minds, you are comatose and out of it," I said. "They
think we are lying about how well you are doing. We need to give them
some evidence. You're strong enough that we could do an interview and let
people know you really are doing okay."

She was reluctant given that her head was thickly wrapped in bandages, but she agreed.

I arranged a short bedside interview with a *Chicago Tribune* reporter
so we could at least try and get the image of "strength" into the public arena,
with Penny listening to the Senate floor debate from a phone hookup to
her hospital bed. The interview went well, and the article talked about how
Penny wanted to talk politics, not cancer, and how Penny was craving news
from the Capitol about whether the education package would pass and
about her upcoming race for Secretary of State. As any good article would,
though, the *Tribune* declared that despite Penny's optimism, "hard facts
remain." The report painstakingly detailed Penny's family history of the
disease and how Marsha died, and she compared the size of Patty's tumors
versus Penny's. I even came to understand something for the first time in a
meaningful way when I read the article out loud to Penny.

Politics, Penny had told her, is how she gets through difficult things,
copes with them. Being able to focus on something else that's important
to her, and not her own health, made things bearable. That struck me, and
it had both a good effect and a bad effect. When Penny and I would argue
about whether she was healthy enough to do something, I usually focused
on the sentiment of "this is what she wants to be doing." Doing what you
want is a medicine not to be underestimated, even though at times, I had
let it go too far.

Sometime during that hospital stay, the doctors had told us that the
bone scans showed that Penny's cancer was also in her spine and that she

had a spot on her ribs. Perhaps unable to absorb any more bad news, perhaps in serious denial, we simply did not discuss this part in detail and instead focused on the fact that they had successfully removed the cancer from her skull. "The chemo will zap the rest of it," Penny said, as though cancer on her ribs and in her spine were an afterthought.

CHAPTER FIFTEEN

GIBSON GIRLS

While Penny was in the hospital, staff of the Democratic gubernatorial candidate had called Penny with get-well wishes and a request. Would Penny speak at a fundraising event the next week? In fairness to his team, the *Tribune* article had talked about how well Penny was doing and outlined Penny's drive and desire to focus on the political health of the state and not her own. When I hung up the phone with them, I said in disgust, "Can you believe this? They want you to come to a fundraiser."

I swallowed the rage I was feeling, both that they had asked but more that she was entertaining the thought. "Let's just talk about this when we get home and you get some strength," I said, delaying what I knew would be an inevitable argument. Later we did have a gentle but terse argument, and I said, "Penny, your head still isn't even healed. You do not want to be there shaking hands, being around all those germs, literally with a hole in your head."

"I'm going," she said.

A few days after her release, I drove Penny, with her head swaddled in bandages, to a fundraiser at the Crowne Plaza Hotel in Springfield to appear on behalf of gubernatorial candidate Glenn Poshard, now president of Southern Illinois University. I was terrified. I simply wanted her to stay home and rest. Normally, we would be very careful of any physical contact in public. When we got out of the car, it was clear she was exhausted. She walked in on my arm, she was frail, and perhaps for the first time, I thought that she was going to die. I felt angry and disgusted by the politics that brought her to this fundraiser that night. Once inside the vast hotel, I handed her off to a campaign handler and tried to explain that they needed to stay right next to her. "I'll be okay," she said. I just could not bring myself to go into the room and watch her. I could hear the uproarious applaud when the master of ceremonies announced that Penny Severns was in the house.

If they really cared about her, I thought, *they wouldn't have asked her to do this.*

By mid-December, Penny was on oxygen and was very depressed. She was frustrated that she couldn't participate in the usual Christmas festivities—trimming the tree, shopping, wrapping presents. Still, she had not come to terms with how sick she was and she refused to rest.

"I'll sleep when I'm dead," she would say flatly when I would try and get her to rest. She insisted that the doctors give her traveling oxygen canisters instead of a full-blown machine at the house because she was not going to stay home. When she was at home, she became frustrated and angry at being so ill. She was more ambling than walking.

With the campaign, Penny's health, and law school, housework was last on the list, and it was starting to show. Our cleaning lady had quit, and there just wasn't time to keep up with it all. Every time we swore we were going to clean up, Penny would say, "Oh forget it, come and talk to me," and I would. Or, I'd say, "Hell, let's watch a movie." We were both exhausted. She was exhausted and dying. Because a neat house gave us a measure of peace and we had no more room to handle it, we came up with the grand plan of throwing everything into our bedroom closet to keep the house orderly.

On December 19, 1997, Penny was in lots of pain and slept for most of the day. She got up in the late afternoon, feeling better. We started talking about what we wanted for Christmas, the obvious gift of health aside.

"You know what I want, Terry?" Penny said quietly. Then she became angry and began rapidly ticking off a wish list: "I want us to be in Chicago, shopping and having one of our old weekend romps in the city. I want to stay at our apartment. I want to go to Tower Records and look at books at Rizzoli. I want to have a drink at Philanders. I want to go to Bobbi Brown and buy makeup. I want to go to Atlas. I want to buy a Dalí. I DO NOT WANT TO BE SICK."

She paused and then quietly declared, "I really want a steak from Gibsons, their thin French fries, and a beer."

"Penny, if you want a steak," I interrupted, focusing on the only attainable thing from her wish list, "I'll run to Pete's and we'll grill a steak."

"No, Terry, I want to *go* to Gibsons. I *really* do."

I knew she was serious. I looked at the clock. It was 8:00 PM. I called Gibsons. The dining room closed at 10:00, but they served food till 2:00 AM in the bar.

"Are you sure?"

"Damn sure."

Euphoria seemed to kick in. I was on a mission and was dashing around the house like a crazy woman. I checked the oxygen tanks' gauges, a little uncertain if she had enough to be away over night. "Besides, they have hospitals in Chicago," she said dryly. I stepped into the knee-deep mess of our clothes closet. I packed for us. I gave Penny a quick cat bath, helped her get dressed, went and gassed up the car, and put two Diet Cokes in the drink holders. In the dark, we pulled out of Decatur around 8:45 PM and hopped on I-72. I was flying. It seemed like we were on an adventure or escaping. We listened to music—Chris Isaak, Dylan, Sting. We laughed and talked about Christmas in limited spurts.

We finally arrived, Chicago was decorated for Christmas, and we were ecstatic! We got to Gibsons around 12:30 AM. Penny ordered a New York Strip; I ordered a filet; we split the fries. She ordered a beer and I ordered white wine. She really wasn't supposed to be drinking with the medicine she was taking, but said, "What the hell." We sat at a table in the bar near a window watching people and the lights. "Remember the convention and coming here?" she said of the 1996 Democratic Convention. We had stayed at the Drake and went to Gibsons nearly every night to talk politics and drink beer after the sessions ended.

We didn't eat much but kept drinking. When we finished, we went to C's North. Penny was struggling to breathe after walking from the basement garage to our apartment. She couldn't stop coughing. We got inside, turned on the lights to the tree, and sat on the couch. It was nearly 3:00 AM. We went to bed, her coughing got worse. It was the first time she slept all night with the oxygen on.

The next morning, Penny said, "We're here. Let's do it all." We went to Wishbone for breakfast and Bloody Marys. After that, we headed to Tower Records, where we bought a few dozen CDs, many in triplicate: one for our house in Decatur, one for our house in Chicago, and one for Patty. We went to the Nike store, Burberry, and Atlas Galleries. We both, I think, were trying to buy our way back to health. Finally, in the late afternoon, we made our way out of the City. "Let's drive along the lake," Penny said. And so I hopped on Lake Shore Drive and drove north just so that we could turn around, have a better view of the City, and see the neon-pink sign of the Drake Hotel.

The next week, Penny lay on the couch while I wrapped Christmas presents. We drove to Patty's on Christmas Eve around noon. We spent most of the afternoon reading, napping, and playing games with the kids while Doug and Patty finished last-minute stuff. Later that night, sitting in the living room, we noticed the kids giggling as though they knew something we didn't. Then they all disappeared and turned out the lights. They came into the living room, singing with a candlelit cake for my thirty-second birthday. As she always did when Penny and I stayed at her house, Patty gave us Kristin's room, without discussion, and Kristin slept on the pullout couch. This time, though, we both protested that Kristin should be in her own bed on Christmas Eve, but Patty wouldn't hear of it.

The house was quiet, but every time *we* tried to be quiet, we failed. I tripped on the edge of the bed while turning out the light; Penny dropped a full glass of water on the floor. Finally, nestled in the small, twin bed, we started laughing, unable to sleep. "Let's open our presents now," Penny said. We had brought a few presents with us to Bloomington and decided to open our other gifts when we returned to Decatur on Christmas night. Penny had bought me two hand-sewn leather journals from Italy. The next morning, as our rule of no picture taking together ended long ago, we took dozens of Christmas morning pictures. We drove home and turned on our tree.

"I love Christmas with you," Penny said. "I'm glad you got me back into it after Marsha died, Terry."

CHAPTER SIXTEEN

RACE TO THE FINISH

As we went into January, Penny was fighting two wars; one of them I could help her with, the other she had to fight alone. She was fighting the spreading breast cancer, and I was trying to keep her a viable candidate in the Secretary of State campaign because she wanted it so badly. The media attention was now constant, making our personal lives all the more tense—we continued to ensure we kept our relationship a secret although I was in plain view as her campaign press secretary. This particular primary race was shaping up to be a textbook example of bare-knuckle politics. Orland Park Police Chief Tim McCarthy, the former secret service agent, was a Republican-turned-Democrat. He and his camp were anything but statesmen. Unheard of for professionals, McCarthy's press secretary publically heckled me during a speech I gave on Penny's behalf to an endorsement session of the Independent Voters of Illinois, interrupting me from the audience as I stood on stage addressing the committee.

Furthermore, our camp was getting constant reports of campaign workers being harassed. Despite being sick, Penny insisted on holding a news conference, her last public appearance, to denounce McCarthy's "thug-like" tactics and to ask the Cook County State's Attorney to investigate the allegations. She explained that an unmarked Chicago Police Department car had been following our campaign workers. The car would park outside of a voter's house, and after our campaign worker would leave, a McCarthy operative would approach the house and interrogate the voter about his or her signature and whether or not he or she was a

Severns' supporter. Eventually, an employee in the city law department was suspended for improper use of a city vehicle. In looking back at the video of the press conference, I don't know how I, the media, or anyone else could have missed how close she was to dying.

As Penny's health continued to diminish, we should have conserved all her energy. Instead, our life was getting more hectic. We were not taking care of ourselves in any sense of the word. The race continued to escalate, and Penny continued to meet those challenges. I was handling Penny's media campaign and taking care of Penny, but thankfully one component of my life had idled—I had a long Christmas break from law school until mid-January. By early January, Penny could barely walk. Her travel oxygen canisters gave way to a large oxygen machine. I was administering shots and giving her medicine in three-hour increments. Exhausted, I awoke and Penny was not in bed. I followed the oxygen cord to both Penny—looking exhausted sitting on a barstool—and the kitchen covered in flour. "What are you doing?" I gently asked.

"I really wanted to make you a pie, Terry," she said on the verge of tears. Somehow, I knew she needed to do this, so I didn't protest or try to fix it but rather sat down on the opposite side of the counter and, fighting back tears, asked if she needed a hand. "No, I want to do this myself," she said.

Another significant sign that her death was close came the weekend of January 10. One of my nephews, Dave, was being sworn in as a police officer in Louisville, Kentucky, about five hours away. Patty said she would stay with Penny, and Penny sent Dave a handwritten congratulations. I went on Saturday and returned on Sunday, though I frequently called and talked to Penny. While I was away, I had a dream that Penny had died on a Saturday at 4:02 AM. I felt sick when I awoke and called Penny to tell her I would be home early that afternoon. "I had a visitor while you were away," she said. I was angry, failing to hear how peaceful she had sounded for the first time in weeks. "Who?" I demanded.

"Terry, it was a good visitor, but I will tell you when you get home."

Penny told me that sometime Saturday night, Patty was on the couch in the living room, and Penny was in our bed. Penny said she woke up and saw an angel above the bed. She said that the angel told her it was sent from God to give her a message. She said that she and the angel spoke, and when it left, she bolted into the living room, looking out the window and saying, "Where did that angel thing go?" I looked at Patty. Was Penny hallucinating?

"Well, what was the message?" I asked eagerly.

"I don't remember," she said.

Then Patty said, "The weird thing was that I was asleep on the couch, and I woke up and heard voices. Penny was talking to somebody." She said that she could not have been fully wake, and she lay back down. "A few minutes later, Penny came walking very fast into the living room asking me where that angel thing went."

I told them that I thought it was a spiritual sign. An angel of healing was about to deliver Penny's good health or, I said reluctantly, that the angel was sent to prepare Penny to die. I, of course, believed that it was the former.

Later that day, while retrieving something from the basement, I confided my weekend dream to Patty. "I wanted to talk to you about something," Patty said kindly. She told me that Dr. Hoelzer had told her, "Penny wouldn't be with us at Christmas." After that revelation, I dismissed the dream and the doctor's warnings, holding out for a miracle and believing that this visitation was a sign that Penny would get well. When Penny lived, it would be a bigger miracle. I refused to consider that the angel's visit was yet another manifestation of just how sick Penny was.

Law school was starting again, but I knew I needed and wanted desperately to be with Penny. Over Penny's objections, I dropped to part-time classes so I could care for her, now only needing to be at school for a few hours a couple of days a week. Studying was another matter. I had bad dreams about Penny, and even when there was a pocket of time to sleep, I couldn't. Every aspect of our lives was becoming more complicated. Around-the-clock care had begun. I loved being with Penny, and we would often chuckle at the many creative ways we learned to take care of her under this new reality of her health and limitations. I learned how to physically maneuver her from the bed to the commode as though we were dancing; I learned that putting corn-starch on the toilet seat protected her fragile skin, which was starting to tear; I learned you can't keep a spoon in a bowl of soup during long rest periods between sips because it would burn her mouth; I learned to microwave a washcloth to sooth her face or freeze a washcloth when her fever would spike; I learned that putting Vaseline on the tip of the oxygen tube kept it from irritating her nose; I learned that root beer floats were a great conduit for masking medicine; I learned that preparing several needle injections in advance rather than drawing the medicine before each shot saves time. I was thankful that Patty was often there, helping Penny and taking on the tasks of doing laundry, cleaning, and bringing food. We tried to cover for each other's schedules. One morning before dawn, I was leaving the house to go to Chicago and Patty called to say she was just a few minutes away. In what seems a sad and eerie scene to me, I remember Patty and I waving out the window to each other as I was entering the highway she just exited. I felt as though we were the Three Musketeers.

During this hectic and sad time, I became very close with Rod and Jane. One late afternoon during this time period, I was handling media interviews and had to be at WAND television in Decatur. Patty had left, and Rod and Jane had come to have dinner with us and were there before I got home. When I arrived, I was surprised to see Penny dressed in a pressed shirt and wearing makeup. Penny had told Jane she wanted to look nice for me and had asked her to help her get ready. And Penny wanted to have dinner in the dining room. We set the table, using our fine china and linen napkins. Rod made homemade chicken and dumplings, and we decided to open a bottle of wine. We laughed and talked, and I told Penny a few pranks from my college days that I had never told her before. It seemed so natural to be there with Rod, Jane, and Penny. I wondered why we were so afraid of coming out. Later, Penny said to me, "That was so much fun, T. Let's do this regularly when I get better." I agreed.

To be sure, not all the caregiving went smoothly. While I always found myself patient and very soft with Penny, not everybody I interacted with got the same tender treatment. Because Penny was ill, I took over the bills, both personal and for the campaign. Personal finance is definitely not one of my strengths. I was trying to solve a credit card problem of Penny's— they had put a hold on her card for failure to pay in the last few months. Because I was not her spouse, the agent told me, they could not even speak to me. For the next two hours, I spoke to two agents and then tracked down the company's legal counsel, eventually solving the problem. When I hung up, my emotions erupted—our secrecy, my financial inabilities, Penny's sickness, and the invisibility: the combination had worn me thin. I threw the cell phone against the wall, smashing it.

I was scared, tired, and angry. Penny was not doing well at all. Her size-seven feet had swollen to a size twelve. Her blood counts were dropping, but she didn't want to go the hospital. We arranged for her home health care nurses to give her a blood transfusion at home. But the nurse missed the port in Penny's chest, and the blood was pumped under her skin instead of into the port in her vein. Penny's brother Don Jr., who was at the house on a visit, noticed that Penny's skin was swelling and bruising. Penny was in tremendous pain. Instead of remaining the mellifluous campaign spokeswoman, I lost my temper and spewed an expletive-driven tirade at the nurse.

The frustration of Penny being so ill and us being closeted and not being able to explain who we really were to each other was bearing down. Even holding her hand in our own home was difficult. We would arrange the blanket so that it was covering our hands. We had sneak-in kisses when we were momentarily alone in the room together. I felt like I was splitting into two people, and I started to wonder who this other rageful person was that was emerging.

Penny was far too ill to continue campaigning, but she wouldn't give up no matter how much cajoling or convincing many of us tried to do. And now the primary was dirtier than usual, even by Chicago standards. The McCarthy camp had challenged the validity of Penny's nominating petitions, attempting to get her thrown off the ballot and depriving voters of a chance to vote for her at all. In Illinois, a political candidate needed to file 5,000 valid signatures of registered voters to be on the ballot. Penny had filed 7,194 signatures, but McCarthy alleged that not all of them were valid. Penny always knew, and the public later learned, that the powerful long-time Democratic House Speaker Michael Madigan was behind that underhanded maneuver of challenging the veracity of a voter's signature on a petition.

Madigan initially denied being involved but later threw his support behind McCarthy, at least acknowledging that his help on the ballot challenge had been minimal. Political observers and reporters alike conjectured that Madigan needed the former secret service agent on the November ballot because he was popular in Chicago's southwest suburbs, where Democrats had to win key legislative races in order to maintain Democratic control of the House. If Penny remained, Madigan feared, Penny and McCarthy would split the white vote, paving the way for Jesse, an African American, to win, and risking other south-side seats necessary to maintain the Democratic majority and keep Madigan in the Speaker's chair. Penny didn't hesitate to blast the powerful Speaker publically. Privately, though, she was pragmatic about the art of politics. "Terry, it was a smart move for him to keep control of the House."

The Board of Elections found "no general pattern of fraud and false swearing," but Penny still fell 176 signatures short of the necessary number for her to be on the ballot. The handwriting was on the wall in large neon letters, but Penny could not be convinced. She still refused to quit the race. Two days later, though, the State Board of Elections would make that decision for her. On Wednesday, February 11, the Board voted 6-0 to remove Penny from the ballot amid her opponent's claims of fraud. The removal sent shockwaves through the political world, particularly given that Penny was an experienced politician with a sterling reputation.

Penny was too sick to attend that very important meeting in Chicago, so I went on her behalf. When the meeting adjourned, I was surrounded by reporters. I faced intense and brutal questions from the press, including whether the Senator realized that fraud was a jailable offense. I defended Penny's integrity and reminded them of whom they were speaking. I could sense my impassioned, personal defense was not making a dent, particularly with the blustery broadcast reporters. I made a battlefield decision to give an aggressive quote—borderline in bad taste—that would turn the tables a bit on McCarthy. I decided to portray this hero as a coward. It was a risk to be sure. He, after all, took a bullet for the president of the United States, and a beloved one at that. What I was about to do could have backfired on Penny, but at that point, I needed a tectonic shift. I was strategizing this all while answering questions, and my calculations could have been off.

"He wasn't afraid of a bullet. Why should he be afraid of a ballot?" I said. I had said it once to Penny as a joke, and she had used it a few times.

Saying that to reporters was like throwing raw meat to a dog, and their questions turned to McCarthy's character, enabling me to then talk about campaign issues, not the fact that Penny was just kicked off the ballot. It wouldn't change the overall coverage, but it would give me a means of escape and hopefully let me get a few knocks in against him, which would be particularly important if Penny challenged this decision in court.

After the questioning, I went to class numb, having battled Chicago's toughest political reporters. I had by no means won, but I at least hoped I had maintained a status quo for Penny and her integrity. The Chicago scribblers were a much tougher crowd than the downstate journalists. When I arrived home, Penny and I stayed up all night. It choked her to walk away from a fight she believed in. She talked amid broken breaths, and I listened. And then she said, "What do *you* think?" I paused for a long time before speaking a truth I knew she did not want to hear. It was long past the time for her to focus 100 percent on her health. There would be other elections. Other fights. She needed complete rest and needed to get better. If she really wanted to help Illinois, to serve Illinois, she had to help herself. She said she wanted to think about it more through the weekend and talk to Pat.

We both tried to rest, Penny in the bed and me in our white chaise lounge. I left for Chicago around 6:00 AM. For some reason, Patty could not be there that morning. Her father would fill in, and if something happened, I could return that night.

I was just finishing class and heading to a late lunch when Penny called to say she was short of breath. "Penny, you have to go to the hospital. Right now," I insisted. Surprisingly, she didn't resist. Although I had only been in Chicago for about four hours, I got back in the Volvo and met her at the hospital. I handled press calls, explaining that Penny had become short of breath while having lunch and went to the hospital as a precaution. I told them that I had seen her (although I was standing right with her) and that she was now stable and had been watching *Seinfeld*, a true tidbit that the press had used and Penny thought was funny.

On Friday, instead of staying at the hospital, I went to our home to thoroughly clean the house for Penny's return. I washed the windows, cleaned the floorboards, waxed the floor, and undid the weeks of neglect. I had lost track of time, and Penny called me around 11:00 PM, wanting to know where I was. "I stopped at the house to get some clothes and decided to clean it for your arrival home," I said.

"Don't worry about the house. I'd rather have you with me than cleaning. I don't care about the house. And besides, in about an hour, it's Valentine's Day, so come over."

CHAPTER SEVENTEEN

VALENTINE'S DAY WILL

For our fifth and final Valentine's Day, Penny and I shared hospital food on a scratched aqua blue plastic tray. A silver tin lid with a hole in the middle covered the plate of vegetables and a dinner roll. The small cup of chocolate pudding and a small bowl of canned fruit were a stark difference from the gourmet meals that usually accompanied our romantic celebrations. How, I don't know, but Penny managed to get me a Valentine's Day card. "I didn't have a way to get you a gift, T," she said, handing me the card. "I'm sorry. When we go to Puerto Vallarta in April, we will celebrate everything."

"Sweetheart, I want *you*, not a present. Don't worry about it," I said, and I added, "I didn't have time to do what I really wanted to do either. But I did get you something small on my way home from Chicago the other day. I didn't even have time to wrap it."

I gave her a book of love poems. She removed the Saran Wrap covering her glass of milk and clinked it against my can of Diet Coke.

"I love you," she said.

"I love you too, but let's never do *this* again," I said, waving my hand at the expanse of the hospital room and then toasting our love.

We laid the book and cards aside that Saturday and started planning. We turned the hospital room into a makeshift war room to talk about the ballot challenge and her health. Politics and end-of-life preparations, odd bedfellows. Our conversations threaded through both topics, back and forth, diving into the political—should she try and stay on the ballot?— and seemingly stumbling over the personal—what would happen if Penny died? Shellacked over it all, when we couldn't bear the shorthand of what we were talking about, we either focused on the upcoming Easter trip we had planned, or we rested, eyes closed and still. Even now, trying to tease these conversations apart is difficult. They were not full, linear conversations. They were too painful for that. Rather, they were conversations and portions of conversations that I remember like a needle over a scratched vinyl record: words and static. I play and replay these memories trying to rehear it all, identify the missing words; I search for the courage to put it down on paper the way it happened, or the way I remember it happening. Even today terror comes over me at the keyboard. Writing this now, as talking about it with Penny had then, I feel as though my bones are vibrating under my skin. I feel like an imaginary bolt in my knees is loosening, my legs are wobbling, and I am falling apart. Penny's death terrified me. Her absence terrified me more. Telling the truth about it now scares me still because every day of my life since Penny died, I have tried to interpret what it means that we could not grip tightly onto the reality that she was dying and that we did not cleanly handle the end-of-life preparations and make straightforward declarations. Sometimes, I feel as though I am looking at a structure in a heavy fog, and at any given moment, either the fog obfuscates the structure, or the winds of time move the fog and I can see clearly.

I moved the food tray from in front of Penny, walked it into the hallway, and slid it into the rolling rack of discarded trays. Then, on the narrow over-the-bed table in front of Penny, we spread campaign papers, her challenged ballots, and newspaper articles. She picked up the yellow hospital menu. On the front, it listed her vegetarian choices for the next day's dinner. On the back, I had written the names of fifteen reporters who had called earlier that day, wanting interviews on various topics. Even today, as I look at the list of familiar names, my notes, and their questions, I am exhausted at the amount of work involved in running a statewide campaign, let alone while the candidate is dying, let alone while the chief aide is in her third year of law school 200 miles away from campaign headquarters.

"Did you get back to all of them?" Penny asked, scanning the list of names and then fidgeting with the oxygen tube feeding her nose.

"Yeah. That was from Wednesday. There were a couple of them I had to leave messages for, and they haven't called back yet."

"Most about being in the hospital?" she asked.

"No, some were about the race."

"What did you say?" she asked.

"I stuck to the message: You know, minor setback. Wanted to be cautious. You've been on the phone non-stop with supporters and fundraisers and in constant contact with the office."

"I *have*," she said, quick and defensive.

"I know, honey," I said soothingly. "I'm just saying what I told them." I knew I needed to switch from my role as partner and ease into the role of handler. Penny needed some political handholding, some reassurances. I needed to keep her spirits up, and I knew that given everything that was happening, less was more.

"I know," she said apologetically. "Terry, I'm tired," she seemed to almost confess. "I'll be glad when all this is over."

I didn't ask what she meant.

"The *Sun Times* photographer isn't letting up. They really want to do a photo spread at the house. They've done something with Jesse, and I think they are doing something with McCarthy," I said.

"We can't do it, I don't think. Not now. Do you?" she asked.

Again, our unspoken language, conveyed in a look, held it all: that she was too sick, that we were lovers, that we lived together, all of it. And what a risk it would be to open the doors to our house to a news photographer. The pressure of that kind of uncontrolled setting was too much for both of us to handle. Those situations are stressful when you are being completely honest, let alone when you're trying to create a platonic facade.

"I'm trying to figure that out," I said, thinking through all the angles. "The problem is, what we run into, is that if you don't do this, it looks odd. All the other candidates have agreed, why not you? What are you hiding?"

"You mean other than you?" she said, tossing her head at me.

I smiled but inhaled sharp air. In that moment, I felt like I was a hindrance to Penny, and it was a reminder of my not keeping my deal with God—that she could have been better off without me. Even the hint that our relationship would be revealed to non-family, or in a way that we didn't control, scared me. She laid her head back on the pillow and tried to fluff it by raising her hands behind her head.

"In a few more weeks, we'll be on a beach. This bullshit ballot challenge will be over. I'll have won the primary, and we can rest for a few weeks before we get going on the general, maybe even go away again this summer."

How did I miss that she was dying? How did she miss that she was dying?

I rubbed her head.

"Café de Artistes," she said, her eyes closed.

"That place was great, wasn't it?" I said, remembering the first restaurant where I had eaten duck. How odd to remember the duck, or that Penny liked that dish, here now in the hospital room. We rested for a while, and I jotted some notes on different reporters and messages that I wanted to tailor for particular areas of the state. Penny fell asleep. She looked dead, really. I stepped out of the room for a minute. A nurse asked me if the senator needed anything.

"A miracle," I muttered under my breath, tiredly.

"Excuse me?" she said.

"No, she's sleeping," I reported. " If she wakes up, will you tell her I just went to the waiting room to get some coffee?"

"Out of the machine?" She laughed and came around the nurse's station as if I had said something crazy. "Honey, have some of this." She walked into what looked like a small closet. She pulled a mug off a short refrigerator and poured me coffee from a regular coffee pot.

"The good stuff," she said.

"The good stuff," I repeated in a meaningless way. I thanked her.

I walked back into the room and sat on the windowsill, sipping coffee. The room was quiet, but the ward was not. Machines beeping, nurses talking, and the intercom calling for various doctors. I shut the door and returned to the windowsill and looked at the pile of work for the campaign and also at my law books stacked next to the chair. I looked at Penny and thought how beautiful she was to me, even with no eyebrows or hair. Her hands rested on top of the sheet over her belly. She had on her wedding ring, and I replayed her marriage proposal to me. I longed for those happy days again, our romps to Chicago or St. Louis, buying art, spending countless hours in bookstores. I knew she shouldn't be in this race. From a press perspective, I think I was surprised nobody had called for Penny to leave the race. I think all of us—press, public, and even family—were caught up in the charm of Penny Severns. If this had been a candidate that wasn't loved or who hadn't given so much personally over the years in so many small and big ways, we would have never let her continue. This was a woman who once, unable to resolve an elderly constituent's Medicaid payment issue on a Friday night, bought the constituent's medicine on her own credit card; this woman was a lawmaker that gave her constituents twenty-four-hour access to her. They knew that Penny had put her constituents first, her family second, and herself last, and I think that's why they decided to stick with her.

"This is who I am, Terry," she would say when I would broach the subject about her bowing out of the race. Part of me wondered how much of her drive for politics resulted at this point from her fear of having nothing standing between her and the stark reality of her medical situation.

I looked out the window at the grey sky and remembered the first time I flew over this snow-covered prairie in February 1993. Looking down on the harvested corn stalks jutting through the snow, below a sky that seemed to cover these endless acres like a cake dish, I felt an immediate kinship with this small Midwestern town, which was steeped in the history and lore of Lincoln. Springfield was to give me the greatest love I had yet known. It dawned on me, sitting in that hospital room, that I had been in Springfield five years this month, and I thought to myself, *Happy anniversary, Terry.* I moved to the chair nearer Penny's bed. I should have been studying for class, but the idea of opening dense, pictureless law books made me more tired. I put a pillow behind my back, closed my eyes, and dozed.

Penny woke with a start a little while later and wiped drool from her chin.

"I hate this whole thing, Terry," she said with utter disgust.

"I know, sweetheart. I know. Feel better?"

"Hungry, but not hungry," she said, trying to reposition her clearly uncomfortable body.

I walked into the bathroom and returned, laying a warm washcloth on her face.

"You really spoil me, Terry," she said.

ABOVE: Senator Penny Severns skiing in a 1980s downhill race; Terry Mutchler on a boat in Canada 1992, the summer before meeting Penny. BELOW: Senator Penny Severns, U.S. Senator Paul Simon, and state Rep. John Dunn at a meeting.

ABOVE: Penny Severns briefing the Speaker of the United States House of Representatives Thomas Phillip "Tip" O'Neill, Jr. BELOW: Senator Severns in a 1993 campaign photo; Terry in Alaska.

ABOVE: Terry and Penny on the steps of their hotel in Venezuela in 1996.
BELOW: Penny's Valentine's Day card to Terry, 1997; Terry and Penny, New Years, 1996.

Dearest Sweetheart,
All my love on
Valentine's Day.

You are — and always
will be — the love of my
life. And I thank the
dear Lord for ya.

All my love. //.

Dearest Sweetheart —
  I've never been in
love — as I have told
you many times — like

I'm in love with you.
You give a wonderful
new meaning to those
words — and to everything
else — I love you with all my heart.
                              Placy

Dearest Sweetheart,
  You are the love of
my life —— and you make
me so very happy!

    Thank you for your sweetness and
your many acts of kindness — All my love, P.

Dearest Sweetheart,

You make my life so much sweeter and so wonderful...

I loved our time this week(end) and love you dearly for your sweetness and gentle love. All my love, D.

Dearest Sweetheart,

I love you more than words can express. Our combined hearts will diminish any challenge...

Along with our faith in Him.

You are the love of my life - always.

Ray

LOVE
NOTES

ABOVE: Penny's father, Don Severns; Penny; Carmel Settles, Penny's Executive Assistant; Penny's twin, Patty Love; Patty's husband, Doug Love; and Terry at Penny's Senate swearing in in her Senate Office, 1997. RIGHT: Terry and Penny, Louisville, KY, at her niece Rachels Parker's wedding reception.

ABOVE: Penny asleep on Terry's couch in Alaska, February 1995. BELOW: Terry announcing Penny's death, flanked by Penny's executive assistant Carmel Settles (left) and Linda Hawker, Secretary of the Senate and Penny's former campaign manager (right).

PENNY L. SEVERNS
· 1952 · 1998 ·

Penny in our thoughts

Reflecting on a political career that spanned more than 25 years

Herald & Review file photos

NOV. 7, 1994: U.S. Rep. Glenn Poshard marches with Severns during a torchlight parade through downtown Decatur the day before the 1994 general election.

Goodbye to a public servant, tough but tender

SPRINGFIELD — When the

Through the years

April 12, 1983:

On the night she was elected to the Decatur City Council, Severns spoke with then-Mayor Elmer Walton as they awaited returns at the Macon County Building.

Nov. 4, 1986:

A jubilant Severns celebrates her election to the 51st District State Senate seat with her twin sister, Patty Severns Love.

ABOVE: Newspaper coverage of Penny's death. BELOW: Penny's funeral: Decatur Fire Lt. Jerry Sullivan presenting an American flag to Terry, Penny's two brothers Rod and Don Jr.; Penny's father, Don; and to Penny's twin, Patty Love.

"I don't spoil you enough," I said. "When I make my millions, I really will spoil you."

She couldn't seem to get comfortable. A nurse came and helped us position her and remake the bed. Penny stopped shifting and sipped some water. She seemed to be in deep thought, looking out the window.

"Terry, unless you get hit by a bus first," she began, and I immediately knew where this conversation was going, as this was a phrase that she had employed when she wanted to talk about her death. I sighed and shook my head, unable to let her speak about this.

"Unless you get hit by a bus," she persisted, "I'm probably going to go first. I believe I am going to be all right, but I think we should do a living will and a will."

"Okay," I said, as if I were a child that was reprimanded and was now giving in. I became aware of each joint in my body. It felt like my body was coming unhinged. We had had this conversation several times over the years. The first time we ever had talked about Penny's death, she wasn't even sick. It was our first winter together. We were downstairs in the living room wrapping Christmas presents, and we got to talking about Marsha's death. Penny told me about Marsha's husband, Chris Hamilton, and how much she thought they had loved each other, although they had gotten divorced. Penny and Chris had spent some time together before Marsha died. "You know, Terry," Penny said to me at that time, "I'm fourteen years older than you are, and so unless something bizarre happens to you, or you get hit by a bus, I'm probably going to die first. If that happens, I want you to know I want you to be happy. And I don't want you to be alone." At twenty-seven, I couldn't handle that conversation at all. I was not mature enough to see the depth of her love in that remark, that offering. I didn't have the foresight to know how much those words would come to help me many years after Penny died. At that time, though, I became angry and unable to fathom being with anyone else. "Stop saying that," I said. Instead of hearing Penny's kindness for what it was, I twisted it, and a very old feeling of rejection was rising within me as though she were giving me away. Because Penny was healthy, I couldn't fathom a discussion about death. Also, in my household growing up, it seemed everyone was always speaking in code, or never said what they really meant. In retrospect, I wasn't looking at the face value of her words and instead was trying to figure out what she "really" meant.

"I know you can't hear it now, and it's not like I want you to be with someone else, that's not what I mean," she explained. "But I love you with all my heart. You really are spectacular and kind, and I wouldn't want you to be alone, Terry. I would want you to be with someone who loves you and treats you well."

Despite her reassurance, I just fumed, unable to absorb any of the kindness or characterization of myself she was expressing. Eventually, she just gave up.

"Okay, okay, I'll just stay healthy," she said. I often think now how tiring and lonely it must have been for Penny to try to talk to a partner who on one level was not listening. I was so trapped in my own self-hating image, which was wrapped tightly in inexperienced youth, that it was unfathomable to me that I could be so loved, let alone by someone like her. Her tender words, that years later would echo permission for me to deeply love again, fell like rain on concrete instead of on the rich fertile soil of equal partnership.

At the hospital years later, with death more of a foregone conclusion than a mere possibility, I still couldn't handle the conversation.

"We can do a living will today at least, and then you can write the other will," she said. "I want you to handle this, and then you can take care of Patty so she won't have to worry about this stuff." Penny had asked me to write the will many months before, when the cancer had spread to her spine and ribs. She had asked me again in December when doctors removed the tumor in her skull. I didn't want to do it, and yet, I didn't want to let her down. She had asked me to write many things—speeches, press releases, campaign material, a personal letter to a minister that meant so much to her, her mother's obituary. Without reservation, I had said yes to them all. But this was different. I felt confused about this. I believed Penny was going to live. She believed she was going to live. Why was this so different than the wills we would scribble before traveling internationally? Young, indestructible, and not yet touched by death's hand, I never did a will of my own. If Penny and I died together, I said, I didn't much care what happened. Penny, though, having experienced the rough aftermath of her sister's estate, would type out a document leaving everything to Patty before we would fly. Then, when we would stop to see Patty in Bloomington before departure, she would give Patty the document and the usual one or two thousand dollars that we gave before each trip.

Once she also said, "If we die, I don't care if you back a U-haul up to the door and take everything."

Another aspect of writing a will troubled me. If I wrote this will, wasn't I in effect saying I didn't have faith? That I didn't believe she would live? I felt strange inside when I thought in depth about writing Penny's will. My stomach would feel uneasy, the early queasiness of throwing up, just thinking about picking up a pen to write her will. Then, if I started to write it in my head, I would get a searing jolt of pain, like the same type of twinge one gets when you put a fork to a tooth with a cavity, or the sensation you get when you step on a tack barefooted. I would become heavy and laden with that mental effort. I could not face it, or endure it, even for her.

"Penny," I said again, rebuffing her suggestion that I write the will. "Maybe we should have John Keith do the will. I'm not even a lawyer." John Keith was a former judge-turned-attorney. He was an election specialist who was handling Penny's campaign's legal issues, and he was also an incredible divorce lawyer. The running joke around town was, if you were getting a divorce, hire Keith before your spouse does.

"But I trust *you*," she said. "Terry, I don't want Patty to be stressed, and I don't want my dad to have anything," she said, ignoring what I had just said and giving me directions of her last wishes. That she wanted to omit her father didn't surprise me given their rocky history. "And I am thinking that Donnie and Rod can take care of themselves," she said.

"Penny, this will is going to be public," I said.

"What do you mean?" she asked.

"It's a public record. The newspapers will write about it."

"Really?" she said. Her political prowess aside, I was shocked that she didn't understand that her will was a public record and, yes, it would be newsworthy.

"It'll be news, Penny." With just enough law school to be dangerous, I told her about a case I had read where if you leave an immediate family member out of a will, without stating that you did it directly or overtly, the court will presume you forgot them, and it gives them room to contest the will.

"Well, okay, I'll leave them $250," she said.

I didn't think that was a good idea, and I said so. "Penny, look. Patty is going to be in an awkward situation with your family. I think you should rethink that part of it and leave them something more substantial.

"Okay, what about the executor?" she asked.

"What do you think?" I said. Penny initially wanted me to be executor. I was a soon-to-be lawyer, and she didn't want Patty to have to be stressed with the pressures of being an executor. I had not completed my classes in estates and wills in law school and mistakenly told Penny that I didn't think an executor could also receive anything under the will unless they were a family member, confusing the general provision of law that precludes a person from witnessing the will if they are named in it. A witness cannot take in the will, an executor can. "Maybe you should just name Patty."

"What about co-executors?" Penny asked. "You could do it together."

"It'd be the same thing," I said, adding, "Let's just make Patty executor, and if she can't serve or doesn't want to, I will do it."

I expressed the fear and shame of being outed that was on the prowl inside of me again, and I reminded Penny that the will would be public and that the newspapers would write about it, and however we did this, the public was going to know. The public would wonder why a senator left her estate or part of it to her press secretary. To write me in the will would be to confirm that we were partners.

"Then we'll write one for the public, and you and me and Patty can talk about what to do. We really need to get this done, and I want you to handle it," she said earnestly and matter-of-factly.

We were interrupted by a call from a reporter. I was happy to be away from the conversation. It was like having a constant hangover. When Patty and her family came to the hospital later that day, the kids spent time with Penny. They gave her homemade Valentine's Day cards and then went off to the waiting room with their father.

Penny was determined to get the will and the living will done.

"We need to talk about the will," Penny said when Doug and the kids had left, leaving the three of us alone. Immediately, more sadness filled the room.

Penny and I took turns filling Patty in on what we had discussed. She asked me to explain to Patty that the will would be public. "Tell her what you told me about this being in the paper," she said. I explained to Patty that as a public official, Penny's last will and testament would be a public record and would be written about, particularly since she was a statewide official.

"Can you believe that?" Penny said to her twin.

Penny told her that we decided to write a public will that wouldn't raise any eyebrows, not explicitly stating that it was because our relationship would be public.

"I'm so glad that you will have each other to get through this," Penny said, a sentiment she would often repeat.

I thought Patty seemed distracted and pained by this discussion. She didn't say much. She would fluff Penny's pillow, organize the bedside table. She seemed to be doing the same thing I was: *anything* but facing the reality that her sister was dying and we needed to do a will. Penny started telling Patty what we had talked about less than an hour earlier: That she believed she was going to live. That she didn't want her father to have anything. That if she died without a will that the law would give Don fifty percent and then Patty, Rod, and Donnie would share the other fifty percent. Penny said that she knew Donnie and Rod could take care of themselves and didn't need to leave them much. We talked again about leaving her brothers something. Penny wanted it to be $250. I said that $250 seemed a meager amount, and I suggested that she leave them more, in no way less than $1,000. She thought that was a good idea.

"Penny, Patty is going to be left to deal with your family," I said. "Leaving your brothers less than a thousand will cause her some stress, I think."

Then, Penny simply said, "Terry will write the will to avoid any questions, and we can figure things out after that."

The unspoken language was in play again. We were agreeing to write a public will, but we had a private understanding that Patty and I would sift through this nightmare together. We were doing this to avoid "any questions," but we didn't finish the sentence to say we were avoiding any questions about whether we were romantically involved.

I simply did not want to have this conversation on any level. None of us did. This wasn't the perfect solution, but at least under this temporary plan, we would divert public attention from our relationship and have time to deal with whatever we needed to.

In some ways, I felt relief that we were done with the conversation for the time being and that I wouldn't have to deal with questions about who I was to Penny. I was also relieved because I trusted Patty implicitly and knew she loved Penny. I loved Patty. Patty had only ever treated me kindly. We often, it seemed, tried to "out give" each other, picking up restaurant checks or buying presents or sending notes of support. Patty had even tried to help convince me to accept a portion of a health insurance policy that Penny had collected on. Years before Penny had been diagnosed with cancer, she took out a life insurance policy for $10,000. She had done this after Marsha died and after Patty was diagnosed with cancer. She would receive $10,000 if she were to get cancer. When she was diagnosed in 1994, the insurance company sent her a check. Penny wanted to give me $5,000. My misplaced anger again took over, and I told her I didn't want a dime of that money. It was blood money, and I wasn't taking it, I had said.

"Terry," she said to me. "It's free money for us. We can take a trip or redecorate. The campaign doesn't pay you nearly as much as you are worth, so this is like a bonus."

"No," I said. "Period. You and Patty split it."

"Terry, it won't be any fun if you don't take some of this."

I wouldn't budge. "How about this," she tried. "How about you, Patty, and I divide it among the three of us.

"Penny, I don't want the money," I said flatly.

I figured Penny must have called Patty because shortly thereafter, as I was sitting on the living room floor writing an extensive nominating application for Penny to receive the Profile In Courage award from the Kennedy Library, Patty called me.

We chatted, and she said, "Terry, we really want you to take some of this money." I was gentler with Patty but stood firm, encouraging her to split it with Penny.

"Penny's right," she said. "It won't be any fun if you don't take it. Besides, if you don't take some of this insurance money, I am not going to either."

I called Penny and laid down my own new rules: I would not split this three ways. She and Patty could take $4,500 each, and I would agree to take $1,000. In the end, Penny divided it at $4,000 for her and her sister, and she gave me $2,000.

At the hospital, Penny took Patty by the hand. "I'm so glad you two have each other to get through this," she said again.

Then, with the semblance of a plan shaping up, we called a nurse and asked if she would bring the paperwork for a living will to be executed. When the nurse carried the document in, I felt like she was carrying a corpse. We filled it out, the nurse witnessed it, and it was filed with the hospital. I felt sick and wanted to flee.

"Okay, well, that's done," Penny said, somewhat exhausted. She continued, "Terry, you really need to make quick work of the will."

I said I would get to it, but I felt like was walking and thinking through quicksand. I could not get it done that day. We shifted the conversation to happier things. The kids came in again and gave Penny and me Valentine's candy, and we talked with them. They stayed for a few more hours and then left. I tried again to write that night but didn't have the heart.

On Sunday, I was able to create a file on the computer and label it "Penny's Will," but I couldn't get any further. Monday brought with it more political campaign work, and then Penny had a visitor. A nurse came into the room and told Penny that Gwenn Klingler was in the hallway and wanted to see Penny if that would be all right.

Penny liked Gwenn, who was a member of the Illinois House of Representatives. Although in opposite parties, they were friends and were supportive of each other's legislative agendas when they could be. Most recently, the Democrat and Republican had worked together on a move to impeach Chief Justice Heiple of the Illinois Supreme Court for obstruction of justice. He had been stopped for a traffic offense, had resisted arrest, and had flashed his court credentials to avoid the arrest. Penny was the first lawmaker to call for his impeachment, something that had not happened in Illinois since the 1840s. Klingler was the first House member to draft the impeachment resolution. The lawmakers were criticized as being on a witch hunt because Heiple also happened to be the deciding justice in the infamous "Baby Richard case," where a young infant was removed from his adoptive home and returned to his father. Many characterized the impeachment move as retribution for the flawed decision. He was not impeached but stepped down from his role as chief justice.

"Terry, I look terrible," Penny said. "I think I should say another day."

"No, you don't look terrible. I'd say hello, Penny," I advised. "You'll be glad you did." In retrospect, I felt a pressure that I didn't understand at the time. I wanted not to be on this ride of death alone; anyone we could bring in to join us brought a measure of relief to me, made me less scared.

"Tell her to wait a minute," Penny said.

I stepped out to speak to Gwenn, slipping back into press secretary mode. "Hello, Representative," I said, shaking her hand. "The senator would love to see you. She just needs a few minutes."

"Please tell her to take her time," Gwenn said. I walked back in to the room. Penny was still embarrassed at how she looked. I tried to soothe her and told her that even if she didn't look her best, Gwenn wasn't going to care.

"Help me, Terry," she said. "This hospital gown looks terrible." She was too weak to get dressed, so I rolled the blue hospital gown down to her waist and helped her put on a white shirt and a blue hat. Penny insisted on putting on a little lipstick and using the pop-up mirror in the sliding tray. Even that effort exhausted her.

Usually, in a situation when someone wanted to see Penny, particularly if it was another member of the legislature, I would excuse myself from the meeting, checking back to be sure it didn't go too long. This time, Penny asked me to stay in the room. I went and got Gwen. She walked in, and I could tell she was startled at Penny's appearance. I think Penny picked up on it too because in true Penny fashion, she worked hard to ease Gwenn's initial shock and discomfort. "Oh, Gwenn," Penny said. "It's so nice to see you. I love that skirt. Where did you get it?" Both women seemed relieved to have something else to focus on other than the reality of Penny's health. Gwenn pulled at the side of her plaid skirt, looked down, and said, "I think I got this at Talbots." Then they laughed about one of them saying something about the store's "red phone sales."

"I didn't want to bother you," Gwenn said. "I just stopped to say hello."

They chatted politics for a moment. "Penny, I'm going to let you rest," she said. "I hope to see you back at the Capitol soon."

I walked Gwenn to the hall, and she was choked up and sad. "Terry, I . . ." she started. I was afraid she was going to be kind and tender. I couldn't bear it. I knew if Gwenn spoke one more word, I would weep. "Thank you, Representative Klingler," I said firmly, trying to keep things professional, not personal. "I know it meant a great deal to the senator." Our eyes caught each other, and while my voice was firm, my eyes were moist and darting in fear. She didn't push. She just smiled gently and nodded.

"Keep me posted, Terry," she said.

She stepped off the ward, and I leaned against the wall in relief that I had escaped an emotional breakdown. I sometimes wonder that if she had stayed one more moment, I may have told her the truth of my relationship with Penny, how scared I was, and that I feared Penny was dying.

"That was nice," Penny said, genuinely happy to have seen Gwenn. She slept most of the rest of the day, and I tried to study. On occasion, I would open the "Penny's Will" file and try to add something. Later that day, or perhaps early in the week, Dr. Hoelzer delivered the very difficult news that nothing more could be done for Penny medically; that a third round of chemotherapy would not be helpful. Penny took that news very hard. She seemed to be thinking deeply about what Hoelzer had said but not talking with me about it in depth. When she did talk, she would say to me, "I believe I am healed. I believe that. I just wish we could see something turn here pretty quickly."

The next morning around 4:00 AM, still awake, Penny wanted me to ask the doctor to stop being "negative" about dying. "I believe that I am healed and will recover," Penny said defiantly. When Hoelzer came in a few hours later for rounds, I broached the subject and tried to convey what Penny had asked me to. Finally, Penny herself spoke. "I just don't want you to give up on me," Penny said, near tears. Hoelzer put her hand on Penny's shoulder and reassured her that she was not giving up on her and that she was reading every medical journal she could and exploring other options. That Hoelzer was still studying and searching for a result calmed Penny very much. Hoelzer told Penny that she, too, had faith, but that she had to look at things from a medical standpoint, and that "this is where we are."

On Tuesday, Penny seemed both agitated about being in the hospital and pensive about her health. She refused to talk about her health or the fact that Hoelzer basically told us she was dying, although I don't recall her using that word. Instead, she focused on her Senate work. The City of Decatur was experiencing an outbreak of a mysterious and deadly strain of Group A Streptococcus. Constituents were concerned and calling Penny's office. She insisted on returning calls to those constituents and writing a letter from her hospital bed to the Macon County Health Department. She dictated a draft of the letter, and we faxed it to Director of Nursing Debbie Durbin, urging her to release more public information. Working on the health of her district, as opposed to her own health, seemed to cheer her up. However, when the letter was done and we finished with media related calls. Penny seemed to fall back into a depression.

I still hadn't absorbed the reality that she was dying. I left Wednesday morning to go to class. Penny called me later that day to say that the hospital was releasing her to go home that afternoon, not the next day as we had planned. But Penny had insisted that she wanted to go home with me, and she said she would wait.

"T, I want you to bring me home. I don't care if I have to wait." I had left Springfield for class that morning and planned to sleep in Oak Park for a few hours before returning later that night.

"Penny, you should go home as soon as they will let you," I said to her.

"I'm gonna wait for you, T," she said. On one hand, I loved this. On the other hand, I wanted her home as quickly as possible and I knew it would create questions—who would want to stay in the hospital a second longer, no matter who took them home? I knew this wasn't going to be lost on Patty, since she would be at the hospital. I didn't want Patty to be hurt. So I created a cover for this desire of Penny's and spun it: I told people that Penny really wanted to ride home in her Volvo; that she loved that car.

When I hung up, exhaustion and nausea hit me hard. I knew I couldn't safely drive back to Springfield, get Penny from the hospital, and drive another forty-five minutes home to Decatur. But I had to get there. I asked a close law school pal, Ed Kennedy, to come with me, so he could drive and I could sleep. I dropped him at the Hilton, arranged for the Hilton to bill the campaign, and asked some reporting pals to entertain him that night. I then went to the hospital to retrieve Penny for our last ride home together.

We got home, and Penny's brother Rod and some of his firefighter colleagues helped get Penny into the house. Penny was in a great deal of pain, and when they lifted her, she cried out. "Don't you do this for a living?" she said, in the only moment of curtness that I witnessed in her entire illness. "I'm so sorry," she immediately said to the firefighters. "I just don't feel too good."

As we had with the hospital room, we turned our living room into a double war zone: one part for the health battle, one part for the political fight—or finishing up the race and withdrawing. Caring for Penny, campaigning, and studying were too much for me to do alone. I knew I needed help with her physical care. The firefighters and I stood there talking logistics—where the hospital bed would go and whether to keep the wheelchair she refused to use. Penny, perhaps not wanting to admit how sick she was, said, "Terry, you and I can keep doing this. Let's do it ourselves. I don't want anybody else helping me go to the bathroom or seeing me without my hair."

We had a gentle conversation about the main focus being Penny getting the most comfort and care, and we decided that we needed some professional help. Penny acquiesced to letting me call her friend Sheryl Frye, a physical therapist, to help us get her situated comfortably in bed. I shouldered the primary caregiver responsibility, as did Patty when I could not be there, which prompted Patty to raise an important concern when she was there alone with Penny. When I was taking care of Penny, I was physically able to move her. But Patty, as slight as her twin, didn't have the physical strength to move her. For the hours I couldn't be at the house with Penny, we needed professional help. Penny reluctantly agreed to hospice nurses.

At this point, Penny was bedridden, and I spent most of my time by her side. She was very weak, and sometimes I had to lean close to her mouth to hear what she was saying. During her hospital stay, she told the doctor she believed that she was healed because she was prayed for, and we were simply waiting for that healing to manifest. Caught up in her confidence and the shared belief that she would live, we continued to plan our trip to Puerto Vallarta. We kept saying she "just had to gain a little strength."

On the first evening back at home, most everyone had left except Patty,

Sheryl, and me. I stayed up most of the night composing a statement that Penny had asked me to write. She wanted it to be personal but to the point. Patty was doing laundry, preparing food and medicine, and talking with Penny. Sheryl was helping Penny stay comfortable. Both of them would listen to drafts of the statement and make suggestions. Penny wanted to have a copy in her hand, and so I printed each draft for her and we would make suggestions and edits. The last set of edits came from Sheryl, which added a reference to St. Augustine about belief versus understanding. Penny really liked it, and so did I. The final version was completed around 5:00 AM.

The next morning, the house was bustling with people. Patty was still there preparing to leave for Bloomington to get her kids off to school. Rod came by after his shift ended, and Sheryl had returned. To my embarrassment, Penny kept fawning over me. "Doesn't Terry look beautiful?" she asked Rod. And she would say to us simultaneously, "You are such a beautiful writer. She's such a beautiful writer and eloquent speaker, this is going to be very good. It's a good statement. It's what I want to say."

I wondered if they thought all bosses said this stuff to press secretaries. In a moment alone, I kissed Penny goodbye, and she told me to be very careful and to let Ed drive as I had not had much sleep and she knew I was exhausted.

On the morning drive to Springfield, I was tired and I couldn't stop crying. I retrieved Ed, and we went to the Capitol. In Penny's office, I asked the Lord for strength to read this statement well. During that news conference, I was unable to read the statement without weeping. Afterward, I went to Penny's office, shut her door, and called her, crying, saying that I had let her down. She had seen the news conference, as the local television played it.

"You could never let me down, Terry," she said. "You did great. You were real."

CHAPTER EIGHTEEN

LOOKING AT THE ART

While I was in Chicago for school that day, Patty had stayed with Penny, but she needed to leave to be home for her children by midafternoon. Don and Audine, a woman Don had married a few months after Penny's mother died, had come to the house around 4:00 PM to be with Penny until I arrived. When I arrived, Penny was very tired and weak. She really had to think about what she wanted to say and had to muster the energy to get it out. It helped to lean in and put my ear nearer her lips. I was in the kitchen talking to Audine, and Penny said something to her father. He couldn't quite hear what she'd said and asked her to repeat it. After his second request for her to repeat it, I walked into the living room to see if I could help.

"Uh, I think she wants you to leave and for us to stay with her," he said.

I almost wanted to laugh at this absurd notion. But then the thought popped into my head that maybe Penny had some things she wanted to say to her father in private, given their troubled relationship. I glanced at Penny to check this out. Frustrated, Penny waved her hand and shook her head as if to say no. It seemed that not being able to communicate well made her want to cry.

Don walked into the kitchen with his wife.

"Honey," I said. "Take your time here. What do you want?" I bent down and put my ear to her lips, waiting. "As long as I'm this close," I laughed, "I might as well have a kiss."

I pecked her lips and then her cheek and then just waited.

"I want Dad to leave," she whispered haltingly.

I walked into the kitchen and thanked both Don and Audine for all their help and for all the food they brought.

"It's getting late," I said, "and you guys have the drive back to Bement. Penny and I are fine now. You really helped. Thanks."

That gentle hint didn't work.

"Well, we'll just stay, and you can go do whatever you need to do," Don said.

I didn't want to hurt his feelings. "Penny would like for you guys to go home and rest, and you can come back tomorrow," I said, trying to force an upbeat conclusion.

"Well, I think we'll just stay on the couch," he persisted.

I remember taking a deep breath and trying to be both diplomatic and firm. I needed a break from the tangled web of why Penny's press secretary would be staying with her.

"Don, really, thanks. This is what Penny wants." I put it off on her, which made me feel bad.

Gracefully, Audine cut in as Don began to protest again, "That's fine. You two rest."

They walked into the living room and said goodbye to Penny. I walked them to the door.

Back in the living room, I put the bedrail down on the bed, kneeled on the floor, and held Penny's hand for a while.

"Sorry about that," she more mouthed than said.

Although the house was hot, Penny was shivering. I kissed her head and told her to relax, and I got a blanket to put on her. It didn't seem to help. We were quiet for a long time, and I couldn't stand not being able to at least get her warm. *Surely I can fix at least that, right?* I thought. I walked to the linen closet and got two sets of flannel sheets, went to the dryer, threw one set in for fifteen minutes, and walked back to be near Penny until the buzzer rang. I retrieved the warm sheets and walked back to Penny. I pulled off the sheets that were on her and piled the warm sheets against her body, putting the blanket back on top. She exhaled a satisfied "hmmm." I then took the less-warm sheets and put those back in the dryer, and I kept this cycle going. I felt like a jack-in-the-box with this routine.

"You don't have to do that," Penny whispered very slowly, her eyes closed. "I want you to rest. But it *is* warm."

For the next few hours, I rotated the sheets while she slept. If only motion could have kept her alive. She woke around 10:00 PM. We held hands with one hand, and I used my other hand to rub and scratch her head—something she had always told me felt good because her black stubbly scalp itched.

"Do me a favor?" she asked haltingly.

"Anything," I said, perking up.

"Get in bed with me. Lay down with me."

She was hooked to wires and a catheter, and after the ordeal with the firefighters and Sheryl getting her arranged comfortably, I was afraid I would hurt her. I put the bed rail closest to the wall down. Gingerly, I climbed in bed, lying on my side, talking nearly nonstop from nervousness: "Are you okay? Does this hurt? I'm not hurting you, am I?"

"Rest," she said. And for just a few minutes, we lay there, holding hands under warm sheets. I was thinking that just a few weeks before, we had made love in the chaise lounge. And now Penny was so sick she could barely talk. I couldn't rest and I rolled off the back of the bed and got up.

"Stay," she pleaded. Looking back, it causes me great pain that I could not be still enough to lay down next to her like she wanted while she was dying, and that I peppered her with questions of whether she was all right. Instead of lying with her, I kneeled on the floor and rested my head on the bed next to her, holding her hand.

"Do something else for me, will you? I want to see our art," she said.

"Okay," I said, unsure what exactly she meant. "Should I take pieces down and bring them?"

"No, I want to walk around and look at the art."

I knew that was impossible; she wouldn't be able to stand.

"P," I said. "I can get you out of bed, but I can't get you back in bed."

"I want to see it, Terry."

Her pleading eyes trumped my nervousness. If I couldn't lie in bed next to her, I could surely do this for her. I walked into the dining room and unfolded the blue and silver wheelchair, grateful we had kept it against Penny's wishes. I moved it to the edge of the bed and told her that we were going to have to move her very slowly. I lowered the bed rail and helped her sit up. Her body was connected to so many things, so I took some time studying the tubes so that I wouldn't get her tangled up. I swung her legs to the side of the bed and then got behind her to try and help her scoot to the edge. Just getting ready to get her in the wheelchair probably took forty-five minutes. It was not a frustrating effort in any away; it was slow and gentle.

"Can you believe this shit?" she said, barely audible, somewhat disgusted at the state of her body. "I am so sick of this."

"It's okay, P, you just need to gain your strength." I truly thought that was all that it would take.

We had established a routine that seemed to work well. It was what we called our "swing thing." I would put my hands under her arms and clasp them behind her back. She would drape her hands around my neck. I would lift and turn her in one swoop to wherever we were going. I had put pillows and a round of warm sheets on the chair, but I was certain they were cool by now because of how long this process took us. As I prepared to count the one-two-three of preparation, I was praying mightily that I wouldn't drop her or hurt her.

"Okay, here we go. One, two, three."

She swung around and landed in the chair, thank God.

"Let's just sit for a minute," she said.

For the next hour we both caught our breath. Mostly, she sat with her eyes closed as I held her hand. She would open them and smile. We would smile but not speak.

I wanted to make sure that nothing was in the way of the wheelchair. We had never maneuvered it around the house. I moved a wooden chair that was near the foot of the bed and took a final walk through the house to be sure nothing would be in the way during the art tour. I pulled fresh warm sheets from the dryer and put them on her back and legs and wrapped a third around her shoulders and chest. I put a blanket over her and then laid the blue and cream afghan I crocheted for her while I was in Alaska over her legs. She picked it up, rubbed it against her face, and smiled.

I couldn't figure out how to hold her hand and push her at the same time. She was too weak to keep her hand up near mine, so I just pushed her to the right of the fireplace. The first piece of art she studied was a charcoal etching by Jean-Francois Raffaelli. She loved that piece. It reminded her, she had always said, of Decatur and the Staley smokestacks. In the scene, workers walked the streets as smokestacks plumed in the distance. It hung above the brown leather chair we bought in North Carolina.

"Do you want me to take it down?" I asked.

"No," she shook her head. "I . . . just . . . want . . . to look."

I stood with my hands on the handles of the wheelchair, and she sat admiring the piece. I remembered the day we bought it like it was yesterday. "That was quite the day, wasn't it, P?" I said. She nodded. Was she thinking of how we headed for breakfast at Wishbone, across from Oprah's studios? Was she thinking of the salty Tabasco taste of the Bloody Marys that we were certain wouldn't affect our art-bidding ability? Was she thinking that she would never see the Staley smokestacks again?

I turned the chair to the left, and we looked at the Altman pastel above the mantel. "The Three Chairs." A Pennsylvania artist, Harold Altman had a studio outside of State College, where I attended undergraduate school. Atlman had an art opening in Chicago, and we had our picture taken with him. We rolled into the dining room.

"The kids," she said of the pieces of art hanging in the dining room. Alexandra Nechita was an eleven-year-old Romanian artist, a child prod-igy known as the "Petite Picasso." Penny loved the paintings and always thought those pieces were a great investment. Penny looked at Larry Kanfer's "Winter Morning" that was in the dining room as well. We rolled past the walnut table with the papier-mâché grapes in the center bowl and up to the pieces on either side of the dining room window. We had loved and bought the vivid and vibrant work "Bodegon en Rojo" by Spanish artist Manel Anoro from Merrill Chase Galleries. It reminded us of the picnic we kept promising to have but never did.

I pushed Penny under the arch from the dining room into the kitchen. The archway held two little watercolors we had purchased in Puerta Vallarta at a street fair, and as we were rolling into the kitchen, she said, "I want a Diet Coke and some peanuts."

I was stunned and still hadn't grasped what was happening, that she was dying. The only thing she had eaten in days were root beer floats. "P, do you think that's a good idea? I mean, peanuts are pretty bad on your system, and the Diet Coke will burn your mouth."

She looked at me with those big brown eyes and laughed a little.

"What's it going to do, Terry?" she sputtered out of breath. "Kill me?"

I stopped our rolling art tour and pushed her wheelchair up to the cherry table we had made in Arthur, Illinois, a piece that I sometimes long for because of its story as well as its looks. I had played hooky from law school on a fine September day a year or so earlier, and we had made a day of it. We traveled to Champaign, hitting bookstores and restaurants. We stopped at Kanfer's gallery and made our way home through the district. Then we stopped in Arthur and visited some of the Amish woodshops. Penny spotted a pair of cherry ladder-back chairs. She loved them. They were in perfect shape, and we couldn't understand why they were in the sale warehouse. The craftsman explained that someone had ordered them but wanted the wider slat to be on the bottom. He had built them with the wider slat on the top, and the buyer refused the order.

Penny and I decided that it would be cool to take those chairs and to have a little table made to match. We decided to buy the chairs then but to design a table and have this man make it. The gas jets were burning as the day was getting dark. He pulled a pen from his white shirt pocket and pulled out a piece of paper. "Let me get your name," he said.

"Penny Severns," she said.

He wrote the name, but something seemed to trouble him.

"Severns," he said. "Don't I know that name?"

"Well, I'm your neighbor from Decatur," she said.

"Yeah, but I know that name from somewhere."

I just watched, seeing how this would play out.

"Well, actually, I'm your senator."

"That's right," he said, pumping her hand and smiling. "I remember back in '87 or '88 you held a town meeting at the grain elevator when we were concerned about new regulations on buggies."

I almost fell down. She held a town meeting for the Amish, who didn't vote and shunned political activity.

"That was a good night, and we got a lot done," she said.

He finished writing the receipt, gave her a yellow copy, and said, "I'll wait for that table design."

I remember falling in love with her again that day. We walked back to the car, and I said, "You actually held a town meeting for people who couldn't vote?"

"They are my constituents," she said. "Plus, they probably need more of my help than anybody."

We drove back to Decatur, laughing and talking and trying to figure out what the table should look like. We agreed on mission style with slats on the side and square feet. That night, we pulled out the orange tape measure and sat on barstools while tracing out the design and writing measurements. I loved that table and the memory of the day connected with it. And now a more potent memory would forever be stained in the grain of wood: Our last lengthy conversation alone was breathed over that table in front of the kitchen window with cold moonlight standing guard.

Instead of going to the refrigerator, I walked through the laundry room to the garage and got two Diet Cokes from there. On the way back in, I saw in the laundry room the "Tree of Life," a ceramic tiled piece she bought in Israel that hung on the wall. I asked if she wanted to see it knowing she liked it. "No," she said, and she continued very slowly. "You know, we need to put that in C's North. The blues will look good with the couch."

"We'll do it when we fly to Puerto Vallarta. We are leaving from Chicago," I said.

The peanuts were already on the counter, and I grabbed those as well. I sat down and popped open the silver and red cans of Coke and pulled a piece of mail over to use a coaster. I opened the jar of peanuts. She closed her eyes and inhaled as though I had put filet mignon under her nose. I set the peanuts down. She never sipped the soda and never ate one peanut. Neither did I. Our voices were quiet as we sat at the table and the moonlight spilled in.

"I know we talked about this, but I am sorry about the news conference today. I just couldn't get through it," I was choking up. In retrospect, I think my body knew what was happening, but as with everything in our lives, our private truth got woven into a public reality.

"It's okay," she said, making every effort to put her hand on mine. I scooched closer to the wheelchair and held her hand.

"I couldn't," she paused, trying to catch her breath. "Have gotten . . . through it either . . . and you were the one who had to read it."

It took so much effort for her to speak at that time that I didn't want to make her talk, and yet, I wanted to tell her what was in my heart and know what was in hers.

"But I feel like I let you down."

"Sweetheart, it's fine. That suit looked great too," she said.

She seemed to be looking at something outside the window. I looked and couldn't help but laugh.

"You're thinking about that car, aren't you?" I asked. She nodded.

Sitting in front of the house was a beat-up blue car with a license plate that read, COACH.

"I hate that car," she said. It belonged to a neighbor who parked in front of our house instead of his.

I really looked at her. Her face was swollen, her lips were pasty. Her eyes were half shut. And yet, I still felt giddy about being near her. We sat there for a while holding hands. The holiday Diet Coke cans looked like red and silver castle guards.

"I'm worried," she said.

I leaned in intensely, for Penny rarely expressed these types of thoughts these days.

"Tell me, honey," I said, sure that she was going to talk about her health, about dying, about living.

"I'm worried about all the classes you're missing to be here," she said. "Pat and I both talk about it."

I felt a surge of anger in that moment, but I kept calm.

"Penny, please don't worry about that. It's fine. This is where I want to be."

"That was my dream too, you know," she said of law school.

Another long pause.

"I can't wait for Puerto Vallarta," she said, her voice slow and trailing off.

"Me either," I said. "It's only a few weeks away." I smiled. "Oh man, can't you just taste the food at Café de Artises?" I said, remembering our previous trips.

She nodded, which was really more like her chin falling to her chest, and she seemed to be falling asleep.

"The sunset," she muttered, and I knew she was talking about the afternoon cocktail we shared at an overlook of the Bay of Banderas. The blood-red sunset amid the cotton candy blues and pinks was something we talked about often.

"I'm going to get you back in bed," I said.

I wheeled her to the kitchen, and we stopped there so she could see a still life of pears in a bowl we bought together. It was an expensive little piece but one we loved deeply for its simplicity. We rolled into the living room, but instead of making a right to take her to the bed, I said, "Do you want to see the Chagall's?" She nodded her head. I wheeled her to the front door where the Chagall's were on either side, and she looked at "Michael Saving David." Clearly worn out, she ignored the other Chagall, "The Wedding," for a moment. The sheer beauty of these pieces aside, we had chosen these two for our living room, as they represented to us a coded message. "The Wedding" was of course chosen to represent our marriage. "Michael Saving David," while we bought it for the colors, also looked like a couple escaping in a Romeo and Juliet moment. "That's us, escaping to our own wedding," Penny had said once, and we laughed, enjoying our shared secret.

"Menpes," Penny said in a whisper. I rolled her over to see the Menpes in the hallway.

Our art tour ended, and Penny slept in the wheelchair. I lay in the hospital bed holding her hand. Rod stopped by and helped get Penny into bed, and she fell asleep that Friday morning just before dawn.

CHAPTER NINETEEN

"YOU BE STRONG"

On the morning of February 20, the steely grey light crept into the bare windows in our living room, where Penny lay in a hospital bed facing the fireplace. Paradoxically for a house of secrets, none of the windows in our home, except for our bedroom, had curtains or blinds. Penny was weak but talking. I remember looking at the burning flames in the fireplace and thinking they seemed stronger and more full of life than she did. A faint milky circle began to seep into the edges of her usually glassy brown irises. The Volvo was scheduled for routine maintenance that morning, and I picked up the phone to cancel. Penny asked me to keep the appointment, but I didn't want to leave her, particularly since the car dealership was forty-five minutes away.

At a convenience store parking lot a few nights before, a politically savvy Oak Park policeman saw the Senate license plates and our darkened headlight and said, "I'd get that headlight fixed. The high-profile owner doesn't need a ticket a few weeks before the primary."

So despite my reluctance that morning, Penny asked me to keep the appointment.

I left around 7:00 AM, hoping to be home by noon. Don and Audine had come to be with Penny until I could return. While the car was being serviced, I stopped in one of our favorite art galleries, The Larry Kanfer Gallery. I saw a small tabletop picture of sunflowers I knew that Penny would like, and I took it to the counter and purchased it. As the clerk wrapped it, I decided that I also wanted to buy Penny a more significant piece of art. I noticed Larry setting up some large prints in his showroom of various Midwestern nature scenes that he called "Prairiescapes," and I was walking toward him to take a look when my phone rang. I could barely hear Penny. "Come home, Terry," she said. "Everything seems so far away."

I could hear in Penny's voice that something was different—different than any other time she had been frail. And she had never asked me to come home or to hurry before. I silently prayed she wouldn't die before I got home.

I grabbed the sunflower picture, rushed back to the car dealer, and told them I didn't care how far along they were, I had a family emergency and needed the car right that minute. I raced home at ninety miles an hour on I-72, which years later the legislature renamed the Penny Severns Highway.

When I arrived, Penny was in great pain. I was extremely angry at Don, who was not in the living room with Penny but rather eating in the kitchen. If he had been with her, I thought, he would have seen how much pain she was in. And she was so weak, she couldn't have called to him for help. *I'll deal with him later*, I thought. I called her doctor, who said that she would call hospice and have them come to the house to administer a morphine drip.

Earlier that week, Dr. Hoelzer had prescribed the narcotic, but when I went to pick up the liquid, the pharmacist refused to release it, as I "was not family." My rage had surged, and even now, I am embarrassed at the string of profanity I spewed to Hoelzer's staff about not being able to get Penny's medicine, that she needed it right that minute and should not have to suffer. Hoelzer's nurse had then intervened with the pharmacist, vouching for me as Penny's "personal assistant," and the medicine was released.

On the phone with Dr. Hoelzer that morning, I started crying and told her that I didn't want Penny to suffer and asked if she could hurry with the order. Less than half an hour later, Hoelzer called me back to say that everything was arranged. "Terry," Hoelzer said, focusing on me. "How are *you* doing?" But I pressed my thumb and index finger into my eyes and fought back tears, not accepting her offer of kindness, which I couldn't bear.

"I'm okay, thanks." She didn't push.

"Would it be alright if I came by the house tomorrow to see Penny?" Hoelzer asked. I knew that a visit from her would cheer Penny up. Penny liked and respected Hoelzer. She used to say that she found it endearing that someone so smart was so demure.

"She would like that," I said, adding that midmorning or early afternoon would be better, as early morning was a tough time of day for Penny.

The hospice nurse arrived shortly thereafter, and he began to gently tend to Penny, starting with her very torn and broken skin on her bottom. I stepped out of the living room and walked into our garage, sitting on the steps for a moment to catch my breath. I remember looking around and seeing our ladder; our tools; Penny's bike; the bulk rolls of paper towels, toilet paper, and tissues; cases of Diet Coke; our lawn mower; and Penny's green gardening gloves. I could not bear the ordinariness of these things. I felt an inexplicable surge of anger. *How can we have normal everyday items in our garage while Penny lies dying in the other room*? I also couldn't understand how I could simultaneously believe that she would live and yet also speak truthfully about what was happening—this was a phenomenon that a psychotherapist, years later, told me was called living a parallel reality.

I stood up from the steps, reached for the cordless phone, and called my mother. "She's going," I declared. I could hear my voice breaking, and I pushed my thumb and index finger over my eyes again to forcibly stop the tears. My body felt very light, and I was almost dizzy, as though if not for my skin, I would float away; as if I were a collection of molecules and air, not a physical being. Like Penny, I felt very far from myself.

"She's going?" my mother repeated, gently.

"Yes," I said, and my voice finally broke.

"You have to be strong for her, Terry. Don't cry now."

I caught my breath and stopped crying. "You're right," I said, inhaling deeply with a renewed resolution to not cry in front of Penny.

My mother then said, "Listen to this old woman. Make sure you sit right next to her and hold her hand and don't let anybody take you away. Get a chair, Terry, and pull it right up next to Penny's bed, and don't move, no matter what anybody says." She added, "And kiss her and tell her we love her."

My father got on the phone for a moment and simply said, "Take it easy. Everything is going to be all right."

The hospice nurse had finished caring for Penny, and I heard him say to Don, "Where's Terry? I need to talk to her for a moment."

"Uh, what do you want her for?" Don said to him from the table.

I told my mother I needed to go, hung up the phone, and stepped in from the garage. Perhaps it was my own interpretation, but Don's voice seemed filled with resentment. I tried hard to keep my temper in check.

"Oh, there you are," the nurse said as I stepped into the kitchen. I had no idea what he was going to say to me, but I wanted him to say it as far away as possible from Don, who always seemed to be hovering. I asked the nurse to step outside with me. "Sure," he said, and we walked out into the driveway. "I want to give you some tips on how to make Penny more comfortable while she is lying down." He explained that relieving pressure off of Penny's very torn skin was important for her comfort. He walked me through positioning a foam egg crate under her bottom. Then he handed me a card with his home number on the back if I needed anything.

I was frustrated and scared. Unable to really express the sadness I was feeling, I said to him sternly, "Look, I need to know what's happening. She has family out of town, and there are people that want to see her. I need to know if she is dying."

He hesitated, saying that no one can predict when someone will die, which caused my frustration to nearly boil over.

"I would call them," he relented. My lawyer-journalist mind spun even that plainly spoken information. I thought it was meaningful that he never used the word "dying," and I bizarrely focused on that omission. *It must mean that she is going to live, but that she is just really sick right now,* I rapidly reasoned. How the mind can betray the heart. I went back to the living room and sat with Penny and said I was going to call Patty. Don was in the kitchen, sitting at the small table under the window.

"Wait for a minute and sit with me, Terry," Penny said. I sat in the chair next to her, holding her hand. "Here," she said, patting the left side of the bed, heavily and slowly. "Everything seems so far away," she said, repeating what she had told me on the phone.

"What do you mean, P?" I asked hesitantly, afraid that I knew exactly what she meant: that she was leaving this life.

"I feel like I am on the horizon out there," she said, looking out the window to the right of the mantle. "I don't feel like I'm here. Stay close to me."

I was terrified. Deep down, I knew what that meant, but in that moment, I refused to accept what she was saying. Up until that day, I had no experience with death. I didn't know then, as I do now, that witnessing death, looking at it directly, is a powerful, rare, privileged experience. I was unable then, as I have been able to since with friends and family who have died, to drop down into that serious and quiet space and explore the magnitude of leaving this life; to let Penny talk about it, let her speak or say what she needed or wanted in the closing moments of her time on this planet. Instead, I became falsely chipper.

"I got you a present," I said with faux enthusiasm, nearly singsong in tone. She smiled faintly.

"I stopped to see Kanfer," I reported. "He told me to tell you hello and that he was sending you good wishes for a speedy recovery. He told me that when you are ready and feeling better, he has a picture for you that he thinks you will like."

I pulled out the framed sunflower field and showed it to her.

"You don't even like sunflowers," she wheezed, and I could see the effort it took her to lift her hand to fix the oxygen tube. Instead, I adjusted it for her.

"I know. But you do, and they look so happy, don't they?"

"Put it on the mantle. I want to be able to see it," she said, and I set it on the right side of the mantle.

I felt as though the air in my body was being displaced with terror. Death's rising waters swirled at my feet, filling my legs. I was panicking. I stepped out of the room and called Patty. I said, "I think you better come now," and I relayed what the hospice nurse had said. She said she would be right there. I called Rod and Jane as well. While I was waiting for them to arrive, I stayed close to Penny, who couldn't get warm. "So cold," she would say. "Lie with me." Not being able to comfort or warm her pained me. I knew from the night before that I wouldn't be able to overcome my own fear of hurting her if I lay with her.

"I have a better idea," I said, although clearly the best idea would have been to lie with her, as she wanted. As I did the night before, I retrieved two sets of sheets from the closet and put them in the drier, bundling her in warmth every fifteen minutes. I also took a washcloth and put it in the microwave for twenty seconds until it warmed. I would lay it over her face, and she would exhale an "oh" of comfort.

"Want some music?" I asked. She slowly nodded yes. "Rojo?" I suggested.

"Perfect," she mouthed. Some point later in the evening she asked me to put on a recorded sermon, but to have it on where we couldn't hear it, just so we'd have the presence of the minister's voice in the house.

"Will you make me a root beet float?" she asked. "I like yours best," she added, closing her eyes and waiting. I swelled with the pride of a crafts-man, my secret was that I went heavy on the ice cream, light on the liquid. I made the drink quickly and returned to the living room. I got on my knees, leaned over the bed, and slowly fed her a spoonful at a time. A sense of calm came over me when I fed Penny with a spoon. Perhaps this sensation came because feeding her was a small, doable task that happened slowly and at which I was always successful. I found that my breathing slowed with the rhythm of putting the spoon to her mouth and holding it until she would sip. Being that close to Penny, it seemed there was much about her face that I had never noticed in the five years we were together. Leaning over the bed on my elbows, I learned to be patient in a way I had never been before.

Shortly after Penny finished her root beer float, Rod and Jane arrived. Penny seemed to relax more. She tried to talk to Jane about her garden but was breathless. She seemed to cut short what she wanted to say and simply said to me, as she had many times before, that Jane's garden reminded her of Monet's.

Patty arrived and hugged Penny. I consulted with Patty about who to call and who not to call. We debated about whether to call particular friends, or keep this evening to a very small group, which we were both in favor of. I asked Penny if there was anybody she wanted to see. She wanted to see her beloved and loyal secretary, Carmel Settles, who had been ask-ing to visit Penny for days. I called Carmel and said she should come that night. I asked Penny if she wanted me to call any one else. She asked me to call Donna just to say "so-long." I had been encouraging her to see people, thinking it would cheer her up and also because I knew that many of her friends would want to see her. Again, I ran through a list of the names of various friends, even very close ones. She just shook her head no. "Not right now," she said. "I'll see them next week." Perhaps she, too, couldn't face those goodbyes.

Doug had arrived with his two young sons, Weston and Graham. Patty said that Kristen had a school musical event that night and so decided it would be best for her to keep to the normal routine and visit on Saturday instead. We all, it seems, were in denial of Penny's impending death. The boys, somewhat frightened, came into the living room to see their aunt. Penny smiled and gave them a big exaggerated wink, turning her head and opening her mouth. They smiled. She talked to them for a minute. They kissed her and then went outside to play. I was convinced that although they were frightened, the boys knew what was happening in a way that all kids know the truth on some level. It made me think of a time when all of us were at a Mexican restaurant in Decatur, and Graham, who was perhaps four, sat on Penny's lap. While he was playing with a necklace she had on, he asked his favorite aunt, "Are you two married?" The discomfort among the adults was palpable. "Well, Graham, only a man and a woman can be married," Penny said. She later said to me, "Kids don't miss a trick."

I smiled as I remembered that story, and I looked over at Penny, whose eyes were closed. I realized that Penny looked old. I, too, was in denial of how close Penny's death was. I believed that Penny would live, and so I made room for each family member to have their own moments alone with her. I thought she and I would be alone later that night, as we had been the night before. The boys were clearly scared, and I wanted to be sure they were okay. I went outside and tossed a football with them in the side yard. Was this an act of generosity? Or perhaps I, too, felt like a child and was simply afraid to face the reality that my spouse was dying in the living room. My knees were jumping the same way they had on the day that Penny got the call that the cancer had returned.

Even though I had only been outside for five minutes, Jane came quickly to the sliding glass door on the deck, waved me in, and told me that Penny was asking for me to come. I quickly went to her side; Jane stood nearest to me. Everyone else—Don, Audine, Rod, Jane, Patty, and Doug—stood in a large semicircle around the bed, waiting. Penny reached her left hand out, took my hand, and pulled me down to her. I thought she was going to whisper something to me or ask me to do something. Instead, in front of her family, she put her hand behind my neck and pulled me to her. She kissed me full and long on the lips. She looked up at me and said, "You be strong." I was stunned at the public display, and I couldn't accept or hold this notion or the power of that gesture, the undeniable truth of what it meant. When I announced her death, I gave that phrase away; I told the press that Penny told *her family,* "You be strong," when in truth she had kissed me and given me that admonition.

There was a silence in the room when Penny kissed me, and then Jane cried out. Wiping her tears, she said, "Aw, she wanted you to have a kiss."

Penny's kiss stilled me on the inside, but in front of her family it made me outwardly nervous. I blurted out, "Ooh, hey, lucky me." I wanted to weep at my immaturity and trivialization of her last loving gesture, and of my own inability to listen as Penny wanted to share with me her feelings about crossing the chasm of this life into the next.

Jane, sensitive and perceptive, said quietly to the group, "I think we should give Terry and Penny some time alone." To this day, Jane's words remain one of the greatest gifts I have ever received.

Penny's father was reluctant to leave. He kept trying to walk back into the living room. Rod, somewhat frustrated, stood guard at the kitchen door. His father would pace and look in. "Give 'em a minute," Rod said firmly.

I knelt down next to the bed and took Penny's left hand in both of mine.

"I love you," she said. I put her hand next to my cheek and wept openly. She tried to reach and put her other hand on my head, but she was too weak to keep it there.

"Penny, what can I do for you?" I sobbed.

"You already have," she said.

"Penny, I don't know what to do," I said, clearly unable to just be; instead I desperately wanted to take some action, any action.

"I am so happy that you and Patty have each other to get through this," she said. She continued, "I believe I am going to live, Terry. I just need to get a little strength."

"I do to," I said, genuinely feeling relieved and safer that she believed she wasn't going to die then. "But you know, Penny, if you don't live, you are going to see your mom and Marsha and Brother Branham."

"How will I know him?" Penny asked of the minister whose recorded sermons she had been listening to but whom she had never met.

"You'll know his voice," I said. "When you see him, will you tell him what an awesome job his son is doing?"

"I'll find him for you," she said. "Will you do *me* a favor?" she asked.

"Anything," I said.

"Will you call Brother Joseph?" she said of Brother Branham's son.

"Absolutely. What do you want me to tell him?" I asked, thinking she was going to ask him to pray for her, or to ask when she would see the manifestation of her healing, or ask for help in general.

"Tell him thank you for everything." I wanted her to ask more of him. She said, "No, just tell him thank you." She was quiet for a minute, and then she said, "Terry, I have to tell you something." She spoke slowly and breathlessly.

"Penny, I have something to tell you too," I said. I let her speak first.

"Remember that time when you were sick and went to the hospital?" she started. We had had dinner at Bianco's Supper Club in Springfield, a 1960s landmark, with staffer Donna Ginther, Linda Hawker, and her husband, Roger. As usual, Penny and I pretended to go our separate ways after dinner. That night back in Decatur, I became terribly ill. I woke Penny around 1:00 AM. I had pain in my chest and was very nauseous. I thought I was having a heart attack, but surely at twenty-seven, I was too young. Penny got up with me, and we went down to the living room. I sipped water, hoping to sooth the pain. Nothing worked. I started sweating terribly, and I felt as though I were having contractions in my chest. Penny put a cool washcloth on my head. About an hour later, I finally said, "I think I need to go to the hospital."

We debated calling an ambulance, but knew we couldn't be seen together at this hour. In the end, I took myself and was in the hospital for two days. Penny didn't come to see me. When I was released, I was too sick to drive to my apartment in Springfield. Feeling angry and defiant of our circumstances, I drove to Penny's house in the daylight and parked only two blocks away, as I did not feel strong enough to walk several miles home.

Penny came home early, around 3:00 PM. I was asleep. Later, she came up stairs with an extremely large bouquet of colorful flowers. I was sitting on the edge of the bed. She crouched in front of me, crying.

"Terry, I will never do this again. I feel like a heel. I can't believe I didn't take you to the hospital. I can't believe I let fear get a hold of me that way. I am so glad you are all right."

"It's okay, sweetheart," I said, now crying more at the sad condition of our lives. "We can't be seen together, Penny. But this is dangerous. What if something really terrible had happened? I was hurt that you didn't come, and I understood that you couldn't come. Honestly, I wanted you there and I didn't want you there."

"You deserve better than this, Terry," she said.

"So do you," I said.

"It's like I said in del Valle's office—all we want to do is love," she said, recalling our one-hour breakup a few months before. "I am really, really sorry. I don't want to lose you. Will you forgive me?"

Now, five years later, as she lay dying, that experience was on her mind.

"I am sorry, Terry, that I didn't go with you to the hospital that day and didn't come see you. I never got over that." She was crying again. I wiped her tears and kissed her forehead and face repeatedly, as though the kisses would heal her, and I reassured her. "Penny, it's all right, it's okay," I said, continuously kissing her. "We got through it. Don't waste your energy on that."

"I love you, Terry," she said. "I have never loved anybody like I love you. You are the love of my life. You know that, right?" she said, but before I could answer, she said, "I am so sick."

"I know, Penny," I said, rubbing her head. "I know."

I felt that I had to *do* something, not knowing that being with her was enough. I laid my hands on her and started to pray aloud.

"Make it short, will you?" she said, and I remember just asking the Lord to be with her as she crossed the river of life and death. After the prayer, still holding Penny's hand, I said to her, "There's something that I have to tell *you*. I am so sorry that I left you and went to Alaska. I'm sorry I did that, and I am sorry that I didn't talk to you about it before I did it," I cried through every word. "Forgive me for that, will you? I didn't mean to leave you."

"I understand," she said. "You went because you loved me. It's okay. We didn't lose each other, and we're together."

"Penny, there is something else too," I said, still believing I was a spiritual liability to her. "If my relationship with you made you sick," I said, "then this relationship was wrong, and I want you and the Lord to forgive me."

She became very agitated. "DON'T SAY THAT," she said so emphatically that she started to cough. "Terry, we are so far past that. I love you. Period."

We sat for a moment, then she gently said to me, "Hold me." I hugged her very tightly. The scratchy agitation of my remark dissipated, and a quiet tenderness emerged between us.

Don was trying to get into the living room, and Rod held him at bay for a while longer. I heard Don say, "Well, what are they doing?"

Rod said, "They're talking, Dad."

Don said, "I know, about what?"

I tuned him out.

"Terry, let's do the will right now," Penny said.

"Penny, if we do the will right now and your dad sees it, he is going to contest it and say that you were under emotional distress," I explained.

"I don't want him to have one damn dime," she said. "Can you make sure that doesn't happen?"

"Honey," I said gingerly. "I know how you feel, but you can't do that. You can't do that to Patty. You have to leave something to him and to your brothers. Patty has to live with this."

"Okay. Will you take care of it?" she asked.

"Yes, but I don't think we should do it tonight. I'll do it later."

"Okay. I could sign it now or you could auto-pen it. Just date it the day we talked about it in the hospital," she said.

"Valentine's Day?" I said with incredulity and sorrow.

My emotions were raw. I didn't want to write the will. I wanted a lawyer to do it. I again suggested that we have John Keith draft the will. Had she agreed, I would have ignored my own concerns about her father challenging the will and asked John to come that night. She would not agree.

"There isn't time. And I trust *you*," she said. "Let's talk to Patty." In retrospect, her request that I write the will was unfair. It was too much pressure for a partner. I was too emotional to think clearly, and I was not a lawyer yet. We should have left this to a professional.

I was crying very hard now. She was crying but catching her breath. Her nose was running. I removed the oxygen tube to wipe her nose with a tissue. She started coughing and struggling for breath. I put the oxygen back in her nose and she calmed. We let the topic of the will drop. I figured that we would revisit it again when Patty arrived. We were still for a moment. I kissed her softly. She lay with her eyes closed and smiled. We were quiet for a few moments. When I noticed her little smile, I said, "What are you thinking?"

"About how we made love a few days ago and I wish we could make love again."

A few days before Penny went into the hospital, she had wanted to move from the couch to her white chair, a classic chaise that was her first purchase in her first apartment. She wanted to sit upright in the chair because she said she could breath easier than when lying down. We had been sitting in the chair together, watching a movie, and I had my arm around her. She nestled in to me closer and then started kissing my forearm and worked her way up to my lips. We didn't speak; I didn't worry that I was hurting her, or ask if she was all right. I simply gave way to making love and working around the intravenous drip hooked to the port in her chest and the oxygen cord feeding her nose. "My breathing must not be as bad as I thought," she said afterward, with a mischievous smile.

"I don't know how I got so lucky to have you, Terry," she now said softly. "You really are the love of my life. Promise me, Terry, that you will always be happy."

"I am happy right now, with you," I said. I couldn't stop crying, and I surely couldn't think of my life without her.

The night was disjointed and confused, yet still and calm all at the same time. Someone was always with Penny, while others were straightening things, folding laundry, or cooking. Carmel had arrived, and at some point in the night, Patty, Sheryl, Carmel, and I had another conversation with Penny about the will and how it still wasn't written.

I felt terrible. Penny had been asking me to do this for so long. Sheryl suggested we do it right then and there and offered to serve as a witness. Penny shook her head. I said, "She doesn't want to do it with her father here."

Penny said, "You'll just have to make quick work of it and auto-pen it." The Governor and most members of the legislature have an auto-pen. It is calibrated to the author's signature and is designed for signing a high volume of letters.

"Good idea," I said, almost absentmindedly. With Penny so sick, though, using the auto-pen instead of having her sign legal documents on her death bed in the presence of her father made some sense.

When Patty and I were alone at Penny's bedside, we spoke again as we did in the hospital on Valentine's Day about how the will would be a public record and how our relationship would be exposed if I were named in it. I gave up trying to figure out how to do this and keep our relationship secret. I told Penny that I thought the best thing to do was to leave everything in the will to Patty for public perception, and then Patty and I would privately deal with separating personal property and handling the estate. We all agreed that was a good plan. Penny took both of us by the hand and said she was glad we had each other to get through this. Then she said, "Be generous. Not too generous, but generous." She could have been talking to Patty alone, or to both of us. I assumed she meant that Patty and I should be generous when bequeathing things to her brothers and friends.

A few hours later, everyone went home but Patty. I was on one side of the bed holding Penny's hand and she was on the other, holding her other hand. I got up to use our bathroom in the master bedroom. When I was returning to the living room, Patty met me in the hallway between the den and the bedroom. "Just because you are not in the will—" she started. I stopped her with a raised hand.

"Patty, let's not even go there," I said with implicit trust. She continued.

"Terry, I want you to know that I consider this your house as much as Penny's."

"Thank you, Patty. Let's not even go there," I said again.

"How are we going to do all this? I have no idea what Penny wants," she said, overwhelmed.

"Patty, don't worry. We'll figure it out together. I know what she wants." Patty asked me to show her what Penny wanted to do with the art, and I started to run through the pieces that Penny wanted to give to Graham, Kristin, and Weston. Then I felt strange standing there talking about things while Penny was laying alone in the other room, dying. I didn't want to be away from Penny for even a moment longer. I think Patty felt the same way. "We can talk about this later," I said, and we both walked back into the living room. Penny was asleep. It was about 8:00 PM.

"Terry," Patty said gently before we returned to Penny's bedside. "You know, she might not wake up."

"What do you mean?" I said, shocked.

"She might go in her sleep, Terry."

I had not planned for that. I rushed to her bedside and started crying. I looked at my sleeping darling. My stomach hurt terribly, as though it were contracting. I held her hand and wept over her. Not wanting to wake her, I went into our guest room, closed the door, got down on my knees, and leaned over our rocking chair. "Father," I begged, sobbing. "I know that I didn't keep my promise to leave her. I just couldn't. Please Lord, don't let her die. I love her. But if it's your will that she die, don't let that be it. If she has to die, I am begging you, Father, please let her wake up just one more time." I went back to her bedside, where I remained. I kept rubbing Penny's head and hand. Stroking her body. I kept whispering, "I love you, Penny," and I kept my head rested against her. I kept telling her everything was okay. In my heart, I kept asking the Lord to let her wake up one more time. Patty was on the other side of the bed holding her other hand and also telling her how much she loved her. "It's okay to let go," Patty said. I didn't want her to suffer. And yet I didn't want to let her go.

"It is okay to go if you have to go, Penny," I said, not really meaning it. Selfish as it was, Penny sick was better than Penny dead.

Around midnight, Patty and I had moved to the end of the bed, trying to keep Penny warm, tucking the sheets around her tighter and rubbing her feet. And Penny woke up.

"What are you doing?" she said, grimacing and irritated. I was so happy that she had woken up and spoken to us. *Thank you, God,* I said to myself. Patty and I chuckled a little at her ever-present presence of mind. Penny reached for my hand, and I walked back to the side of the bed. She squeezed my hand and went back to sleep. I laid my head on her. A quiet yelp intermittently came from my throat, but I was not crying. Sometimes, I buried my head against her arm; sometimes I just watched the fire and thought of the fun we had together. I longed for her to be well. The night was still and ready. And so was she. Around 2:15 AM, Penny's breathing became very labored. I can still hear the thickened, struggling noise, like a severe pneumonia, coming from her throat. We held her. She was in her last moments of life. I was crying and bracing myself. My body stiffened. A few minutes later, around 2:35 or so, the back door opened and Donnie came in. "Hurry, Donnie, hurry," Patty said, calling over her shoulder. He took off his jacket and in the same motion knelt down next to Patty, and they held Penny's right hand. I cradled her left hand in both of my hands. "I'm here. Donnie's here," he said gently to his younger sister.

The noise coming from her throat stopped. Her chest stopped moving. Patty felt for Penny's pulse in her neck. Then she said, "I'm calling it at 2:40 AM." She and Donnie got up and hugged each other. Quietly, Patty walked to the fireplace and turned off the gas burner. I couldn't move. I kissed her lips. I laid my head back down on her chest and closed my eyes. Then I opened my eyes and looked at her, hoping she would wake. I did this several times. Finally, I laid my head on her chest and quietly wept. I wanted to go with her. Patty walked over, and we hugged each other. She said we should pray. I didn't want to, but we did. I don't remember the prayer other than thanking God for Penny's life and asking him to be with us. Donnie and I sat by Penny while Patty called her father and brother and a few close friends. Linda Hawker wanted to come to the house. We decided to wait for a few hours to call the coroner.

The house was very quiet and somber. People spoke in whispers, like a wake. I knew that this news would travel quickly, but I still couldn't move. As friends and family came, I felt I needed to make room for them; I didn't want to leave her, but I felt I should give them their space. I went into the kitchen and sat at our table. I decided to call my friend Anita Huslin, but I couldn't remember her home number. I dialed *The Washington Post*, knowing that the newspaper had a policy of connecting any source at any time of day or night. The receptionist did ask me, however, if I knew what time it was. "Yes," I said. I remember none of my conversation with Anita except that the sound of her voice comforted me. She later told me I had said only, "She's gone, Anita. Penny's gone." I called my sister Donna, and then I called Tony Man, the reporter for the Decatur paper. I didn't notice at the time, but the column he wrote on her death started with saying he had received the call "from a family member." I remember Patty and Linda separately wanted to know who it was that Tony was referring to, whether it was Patty or Rod. I said in complete candor, "I honestly don't know." Even though I knew that I called him at seven thirty, which he reported, I couldn't figure out who he meant. I didn't make the link that I was a member of the family in the eyes of this reporter. Years later, rereading his column, it dawned on me that he was writing about me. I was stunned that I had missed that connection.

Around 8:00 AM or so, we called the coroner, Michael Day. He and another man, I presumed a funeral director, arrived dressed in black suits. He greeted each of us and said we should say our good-byes to Penny. When these men arrived, something inside of me shifted. I felt as though I had to take care of the details for Penny. I had a sense of quiet steadiness and of being in control, directing and handling things as I did on the campaign trail. Michael told us that we might not want to remain in the room as they prepared Penny's body, as it can be unpleasant and startling. Patty looked distraught. I put my hand on her shoulder to comfort her. "Patty, you did everything you could for Penny while she was alive. That's when it was important. You don't need to watch this. It's really okay to wait in the other room." Patty had been comforting me earlier, being steadier than me. Now that Penny had died, Patty seemed to slip into a pained confusion. I wanted to help her and Penny. She stood by the doorway of the kitchen. "I'm going to stay with her," I said to the men who slipped on latex gloves. I held Penny's hand as they lifted the sheets. The smell was strong, yet I didn't flinch or resist it. It just was. They removed the catheter and lifted her to clean her skin where her bodily fluids had oozed from her when she died. They removed the sheets. They had rolled in a gurney with fresh sheets, and they gently lifted Penny's body onto it, and then they dismantled the hospital bed. While they were gentle and slow, treating her body as though she were alive, it seemed like everything was moving too fast. I did not want them to take her out of the house. They removed their gloves, and I asked for a moment with her before they rolled her out. I don't remember if they left the room.

I remember rubbing her head and saying, "That feels good, doesn't it, P?" I vaguely remember Patty and I talking about Penny not wanting to go out of the house with a bald head, and I got a tam. I remember wanting her to wake up. I remember looking at her face. I gently and quickly kissed her lips that were pasty and sticky. "I love you, Penny," I said to her corpse.

I stood up and said to the funeral director, "Can I ask you a couple of favors? Could you take her out the front door between our Chagall's? And when you leave, would you drive out Sims, under the cottonwoods? Penny loved them."

For a moment, I thought he was going to cry. "Sure, Terry," he said.

Patty stood in the corner near the living room closet adjacent to the front door, looking stricken and small. We hugged. Then the coroner draped Penny's body in a red velvet cloth. I kept my hand on her body as they wheeled her through the front door. Everybody in the house seemed frozen in place, crying. I walked next to her as they pushed her down the sidewalk. I flinched each time the gurney would hit a bump or crack, jostling her. Patty watched out the window. I saw neighbors looking out of their windows. One of the men opened the back door to the hearse. I couldn't bear it. I couldn't bear to say good-bye. "Could I just have a minute?" I genuinely asked again, as though he might say no.

"Take all the time you need," Mike said. The men stepped up on the sidewalk, their hands clasped in front of them, and stood waiting. I stood in the street next to Penny, who lay on the gurney waiting to be loaded into the van. I was trying hard to focus and absorb my last moment with her as I stood on her right side, my back to the house. I ignored the neighbors in the windows and resented the neighbor who had walked outside at that moment to lower his American flag to half-staff, although I knew this was a sweet and respectful gesture. The air was cold, yet I did not want to let Penny go. I wanted to pick her up and run away—from them, from death—I wanted to steal her just to be with her. At the same time, I wanted to climb in the back of the hearse and ride with her as if we were on an ambulance ride, as if she would wake up. With both hands, one on each side of her head, I folded back the velvet cloth covering her face and bent over the gurney. I leaned down and kissed her, one of only a handful of times we kissed in public in the United States.

"I love you, Penny Severns. I loved you the moment I saw you," I said, now bent over her and weeping hard. I knew that if I didn't step away from her that very moment, my emotions would give way and I would sit down on the curb and weep uncontrollably. I did not want to make a scene. I didn't want this to be about me. "Good-bye, darling," I said, and I gently lifted the red cloth over her head. I stepped back and stood there in the street while they collapsed the wheels of the gurney and slid Penny into the back of the van, headfirst. "We'll be very careful with her, Terry," Mike said. I wanted to jump in and give her one more kiss. I wanted to scream. I wanted to fall down and pound on the pavement, demanding her return. Instead, I stood and watched as he slowly closed the doors and drove around the sloping curve of the road and she passed under her cottonwoods. I felt as though a retractable tether was stretching between us, and that at any moment it would snap and break, severing the intense pain and tightening in my chest. But it never did, and it never has. I exhaled deeply, perhaps bracing myself, and walked back into the house. I stepped over the threshold and started preparing to hold a news conference and announce my partner's death to the public, slipping once again in to the role of Senator Penny Severns's spokeswoman and close friend.

CHAPTER TWENTY

ANNOUNCING HER DEATH

I walked back into the house and into our bedroom and shut the door. I wanted everyone to leave. I wanted to be alone. I wanted to sleep. I wanted there to be quiet and stillness in the house, not the frenetic movement that was overtaking it as we turned the den into yet another war room of preparation: this one for her funeral. I sat down on the bed, on Penny's side. I lay back against her pillow. I could hear the clanging of pots. I could hear the phone ringing. I couldn't stand the noise, even though it was somewhat muted. I got up and walked back into the living room. Linda said something about reporters beginning to call.

"We have to announce her death formally," I said, knowing the depth of reaction that the death of this senator and statewide candidate would draw. Penny deserved dignified closure. There was some discussion among family about where to make this announcement. Should it be at our home? At the Capitol? I knew that Penny would want this to be in her district and said so.

"How about city hall?" Luanne said. Luanne Jacobs was previously married to Don Jr. and was also a city councilwoman.

Instinctively that made sense. It would be poignant and meaningful to Penny to announce her death in the place she first won public office—on the Decatur City Council—with the largest number of votes in city history. Luanne said she would open the council chambers and get the room ready. I sat down for a few moments with Patty, Doug, Rod, Jane, and Don Jr. I said that I would simply be announcing her death, give the time, and say that she passed away of metastatic breast cancer. I wouldn't be taking questions, although I knew the press would ask. Was there anything in particular that they wanted me to say? Patty said to me that it was important to say that Penny "had died" and not that she "had passed away." I agreed with that candor.

I took a shower and stood under the warm water for a very long time. I remembered how Penny and I would often shower together before work, and once, although in a great hurry, we dawdled and both ended up being very late for a campaign event. "From now on," she directed, "when we are in a hurry, it's just a business shower." And I thought of that oft-repeated joke when one of us wanted to take a business shower and one of us didn't. Again, as with standing outside the hearse, I felt if I didn't move in that moment, I would never leave the shower or the bathroom. I dressed in black and took a black paisley scarf of Penny's and draped it around my neck. I stood at the mirror applying makeup and jotting notes on a leather pad. Carmel helped me. I tried to rehearse my speech, afraid that I would break down and cry as I did a few days ago announcing she would no longer seek the office of secretary of state.

I walked into the living room, ready to go. Jane put her hands on my shoulders and said, "Don't you look nice?"

Rod said to me, "We don't want you to do this alone. Do you want us to come?"

"No, Rod, it's okay," I said. They didn't really know how to deal with the press, and I thought it better for them, and for Penny, if they didn't come. I told him I viewed it as a gift to them. Linda and Carmel decided to come with me. As I prepared to leave the house, I froze. I didn't want to leave Penny. I wanted to be in the safety of our home, where we were together last. I remember Rod, Jane, and Luanne stepping away to have a discussion, and then Luanne said she would drive me.

Before I left the living room, Rod took me aside privately and said, "You won't understand this really, but if things get out of hand with my family, if you need me to come over here and keep my father in line, call me." By then, I loved Rod and Jane, but I was scared and couldn't shake the nagging question of who to trust. I had always trusted Patty. I instinctively felt that I could trust Rod and Jane, but I was grieving and didn't embrace that feeling immediately. His bold statement made me want to tell them everything.

I remember getting to city hall and seeing a line of reporters and cameras. I saw the cameramen hoist their cameras to their shoulders and train the lenses on me as I walked across the pavement into the building. I inhaled sharply and kept walking. One of them asked me if they could grab me for a moment. I said I would talk with them afterward. They were very somber. I shook hands with several people who said how sorry they were. I braced myself and asked for some warm water for my throat. I waited for the WAND-TV cameraman to white-balance his shot, and then I moved to the podium. I remember seeing the same reporters in the audience that had covered the campaign; the same reporters I had worked with years earlier.

I felt jittery, and I could see my hands shaking, which was unusual for me. As a press expert, I rarely get nervous in front of the press. I cleared my throat and said, "Thank you for coming. I am going to make a short statement. I am not going to take any questions, and the family would ask that you respect their privacy at this very difficult time." I felt like I was watching myself both as Penny's press secretary and her partner, speaking to this crowd.

I looked to the back of the room and felt as though I was looking way into the distance, as though I were not in this room at all, but on that horizon that Penny spoke of just yesterday. A sense of a calm and a feeling of control came over me. It was similar to the sensation that I get in my mind and body when I am praying or when I am standing in front of a jury—I feel as though I am in sheer command of the moment. I knew I would not cry. I knew I would get through the moment. I reported that Senator Severns died in her sleep at 2:40 AM from complications of metastatic breast cancer. She was peaceful and surrounded by her family. And then, not strong enough to hold the gift Penny gave to me, I continued: "Penny shared a thought with her family last night that they thought would be appropriate to share with her Illinois family. She told them, 'You be strong.'"

"Terry," I heard someone say, "do you have funeral arrangements?"

"Funeral arrangements will be forthcoming. Thank you." I think I wanted them to ask me questions—I wanted to stand there and keep talking about Penny—but they did what I asked and did not ask another question.

I turned around and hugged Carmel and Linda. Carmel said something very kind to me about how Penny would have been proud of me for getting through such a hard press conference. I hugged her again. Then I approached Luanne.

"Luanne," I said, hugging her tightly, "Get me the fuck out of here, will you?"

"You bet," she said. We walked outside, and I did an interview with a reporter. I got in Luanne's truck. She said, "Terry, can I do anything for you? Do you need anything?"

"Yeah, I want some Scotch," I said. That was the beginning of my daily odyssey of alcohol abuse for the next eight months.

Luanne was a businesswoman who owned a gourmet restaurant and deli, and she called her manager. "I want you to close the upstairs room and get it set for about ten people," she said. "And send somebody to get some Scotch." We walked into the restaurant and went directly upstairs. I didn't want anything to eat, but just wanted the Scotch and soda. Luanne, Ann McElroy, Sheryl, Carmel, and a few other people who I do not remember sat there telling stories about Penny. I started to tell them a revised version of the first time Penny came to my house, framing it as though we were just friends. "She knew I liked Scotch," I told them. "And she came to my door with a bottle of twenty-four-year-old Scotch and said, 'Is the bar still open?' But I couldn't tell them how we fell in love and how that weekend was filled with such happiness.

We sat there for about an hour, and I became very, very upset at being away from the house. I felt panicked, as though Penny were at our home waiting for me and I was not there. "Luanne, take me home, will you?" I asked.

We got back to the house. Rod and Jane had gone home. Don and Audine were there. Don said he was going to the funeral home to make the arrangements. Penny would have never wanted that, and I was irritated that he simply announced he was going to do it. I pulled Patty aside and said, "You know Penny wouldn't want your dad to do this, Patty."

"We'll go too," she said.

Carmel was getting ready to return to Springfield, and I felt overwhelming love and gratitude for her. Because she had admired the sunflower picture that I had given to Penny the day before and kept telling

Penny how much she liked it, I decided to give it to her. I had hoped that the magnitude of the emotional value of this gift—the last present I gave to Penny—would show her how much her presence and kindness meant to me, and how much her kindnesses to Penny meant to me.

At the funeral home, I started to take the lead on making decisions about cremation versus burial. The funeral director asked some questions, and as I started to answer, he said, not unkindly, "This has to come from the family." He asked the questions again, and I looked to Patty. She said nothing. Don started answering the questions. In my head, I just whispered to myself what I would say to Penny, who I knew would never have wanted her father to be involved. "It's okay, Penny, they are just questions."

When he was told he could choose a coffin for the cremation and the urn, Don said, "Uh, we don't want anything too expensive, just what the state requires."

"Patty," I said, exasperated. Still, she said nothing. I felt sick. I wanted to smash every urn in the funeral home. I wanted to kick over every coffin in the showroom. I wanted to scream. I wanted Patty to do something. I couldn't. Legally, I was nothing. The funeral director had just made that clear. Instead, I clenched my teeth and asked, in anger, for the Lord to keep my temper in check. Then the funeral director asked who would be verifying her death and signing the death certificate. I stood from my chair and said that I wanted to do that. Don said, "No, I'll do that." He signed the paper.

I said, "I would like a copy of that, please." The funeral director said that in the state of Illinois, only family members can receive a copy of the death certificate. Today, I still do not have a copy of it.

I returned to the house. My sister had arrived, and I was grateful for her steady presence. I introduced her to everyone, and we sat talking. I remember Doug and Patty being there, as well as Don Jr., Luanne, Rod, Jane, and a friend of the family. Around six, we turned on the evening news. The entire thirty-minute broadcast was devoted to Penny's death. There were many stories of remembrances, political fights, and victories spanning the entirety of her short life. One of the stories began with a heavy focus on me and my relationship with Penny as press sectary and close friend. The news story ran clips of previous interviews I had done over the years, speaking for Penny about various issues in her district. The reporter said that when Penny ran for office, I spoke for her. When Penny was sick, I stepped in for her. And, the reporter continued, when Penny died, it was me again who stepped up for her. They ran the clip of me announcing her death. Patty looked at me oddly—she seemed upset or bothered with the reporter's focus on my role and me. I shrugged my shoulders and quickly said defensively, "I had nothing to do with it. I am really sorry they did that." Why was I apologizing? I was her press secretary.

Patty, Doug, Rod, Jane, Luanne, Don Jr., and I gathered in the dining room to speak about the funeral arrangements and the music and sermon choices. Much of that is a blur to me, as it was more of a briefing of what would happen, rather than a discussion. I thought that something was bothering Patty, but I had lost all sense of discernment, as everything was covered with the pall of Penny's death. I tried to talk to Patty. She was bothered that people were drinking at the house. As we sat around watching the television news coverage, a few people had a beer, and someone had a glass of wine. It wasn't riotous or distasteful. Penny and I had alcohol in the house.

Everyone was leaving. I felt a deep kinship with Rod and Jane and walked them to their truck, and we lingered and talked for a while before they left. I stood waving. They started to pull away, and then I saw the brake lights. Rod backed up. They waved me over. They were worried about me. They didn't want to leave me at the house alone, they said. I don't remember his exact words, but Rod said something like, "Things might get rough." He looked pained and tense, almost as if he was holding his breath or was afraid to ask the next question. And then he said, "Please tell us you guys had a will."

I drew in the sharp February air. I didn't want to lie to Rod and Jane. They had been nothing but helpful and loving to me. And it was clear they were worried about me and obviously knew that trouble might be brewing with Penny's family. Given that Rod and Penny shared a similar view of their father, I knew his concern was centered on Don. I didn't want them to worry: Penny and Patty and I had an agreement, and everything was taken care of. I knew what Penny had wanted, and so, I convinced myself, I wasn't really lying if I said yes. "Nothing to worry about," I said. "There's a will."

Their relief was visible and palpable. As soon as I said there had been a will, they both exhaled with relief. I think Jane put her hand over her chest and said, "Oh, thank God."

Everyone left. Don Jr. was returning to his home in Iowa and said he would be back on Sunday night. He asked if he and his friend could stay at the house when they returned. I was hesitant at first. I wanted my space, but I was also fearful and knew his presence would be helpful. Of course he could stay, I had said, but I said I thought it would be better if it was just the two of us. That night, my sister Donna stayed with me, but I don't remember any of our conversations. I remember her straightening up the house, but I don't remember anything she said to me until the next morning.

CHAPTER TWENTY-ONE

SILENT EULOGY

I didn't sleep at all; I just tossed and turned and cried. The next morning, Donna came in and asked me if I wanted some tea. She was already up and dressed and was tidying up around the house. She went to the kitchen and returned almost immediately.

"Terry," she said. "I don't want to tell you this." She looked pained.

"What?" I asked, panicked and insistent.

"It's starting."

"What do you mean?" I said.

"When I walked into the kitchen, Don took Penny's purse off the counter and took it to his car," she said.

After the funeral home debacle, this was too much. I threw on a shirt and pants. "Do you want me to come with you?" Donna asked gently.

"No." I strode to the kitchen. The purse was gone. I had specifically not moved it because Penny had put it there herself.

"Don," I said. "Penny's purse was right here. Where is it?"

"I put it in the trunk of my car," he said.

I became hysterical. "Don, I want that purse brought back in," I said, surprised that I could be so stern with him.

"There's checks and credit cards in there," he said. I unsuccessfully demanded that he return the purse and not touch anything in the house. "Don," I pleaded, "at least put it back until Patty gets here. Please."

"I can't do that," he said.

In my mind I had two options: the first was violence—I could just smash his car window—or second, I could try to find a more creative way to get that purse back into the house. I went to his wife, weeping uncontrollably. "Audine, please. I don't want to move anything that Penny touched. Please, at least until Patty gets here, would you tell him to return the purse?" Every fiber of my being was on edge. I felt as though I was going to pass out from the expenditure of energy. I was desperate and starting shaking. "Please, Audine, I am begging you."

Her eyes seemed to connect with my pain. "Don," she said calmly, with her hands on my forearm, still looking at me, "bring the purse back into the house."

He started to protest.

"Don." Her voice became firmer, and she squeezed my arm to reassure me. "I said bring that purse in, right this minute."

Weeping and shaking, with my head down, I said in a barely audible voice, "Thank you, Audine."

She pursed her lips and nodded, a gesture I took as understanding.

I walked into the bedroom and sat down. I had absolutely no energy in my system. I felt bereft and alone. I started weeping and protesting to my sister, using language I generally tried not to use in her presence because she doesn't swear.

"You have to be smart here, Terry," Donna counseled quietly. "Wait and talk to Patty, and approach this together kindly. You can both go to Don."

Donna was leaving to return to Indiana, about five hours away, and was planning to return the next day with her family for the funeral. I didn't want her to go but knew she had to if for no other reason than to get clothes for the funeral.

Cindy Davidsmeyer; Carmel Settles; and two other very close staffers, David Gross and Tim Drea, arrived, and we moved to the den to plan Penny's funeral—everything from seating for dignitaries and politicians to flower arrangements. I was still handling the flood of media questions, requests for interviews, and calls of condolences. In some ways, it was like the old days; we centered around a common focus: Penny, and getting Penny elected. In this case, though, we were preparing her final farewell. After I handled the media calls, I turned my attention to writing a eulogy. Because Penny was a statewide candidate for office, her spokesperson would naturally give a eulogy, but I wondered, given the press conference earlier in the week, if I could get through a eulogy or if I should even give one. I spent the rest of the morning sitting on the deck and thinking of how to capture the essence of Penny in her public and private life.

Later, Don's brother, Willard, and his wife, Maureen, arrived. I wasn't thrilled about their arrival. At Christmas the year before, Maureen had behaved so rudely to me that Penny and Patty said they were going to address it with her. At the time, I begged them not to, asked them just to leave it be. When they arrived at the house now, they barely said hello. They sat at the small table in the kitchen with Don and Audine. Refusing to participate in their rudeness, I decided that for Penny's sake, I would be gracious.

"Can I get you something to drink?" I said.

Audine immediately stood and helped me get them some drinks.

I made a grave mistake at that moment: I disclosed to them that I was writing the eulogy. "I am just putting a few memories together," I said. "If you need something, let me know."

I sat in the living room with a notepad and tired to write. At one point, I heard the group discussing Penny's estate. I felt it was crude, but given how things were going, it scared me. I heard Willard say, "You know, in some places, it's customary to divide an estate before the funeral." I felt isolated and alone. I felt as though I was outnumbered in my own home. I panicked, and I thought about Rod saying, "If you need me, call me."

I went to the bedroom and dialed them, and I asked them to come over. Within fifteen minutes, they arrived. They came in, said hello to the group at the kitchen table, and walked to the living room. I hugged them but felt strange to have called them in such a vague panic. "Everything's going to be all right," Jane said, sitting down next to me. And in the safety of their presence, we started laughing a little about how fast they got there. They were in the middle of a cleaning, and they dropped everything to rush over. I felt embarrassed that I had reached out to them.

"That's what we're here for," Rod said. "Don't worry about that." To this day, we affectionately refer to this as "the mercy run," and it became the shorthand in the years to follow. "If you need a mercy run, let us know," they'd say. I calmed down, and they left.

A little while later, Christi Parsons, a friend and a reporter for the

Chicago Tribune who now covers the Obama White House, called me. She wanted to know where I was and how I was. She wanted to see me. Christi didn't know that Penny and I were partners, and as a reporter, I always feared that she would have to report that information if she knew. But I was too tired to think this through. "I'm in Decatur at the house," I said, purposely not saying "my house" or "Penny's house." Just "the house." I gave her directions. She asked if another friend, Michelle Ishmael, who had once worked for Penny, could come. I said yes. When they arrived, I introduced them to Don, Audine, Willard, and Maureen. I gave them an intimate tour of the house, talking about the art and telling them stories of how we acquired it.

"Terry," Christi said, crying, "I am so sorry for you." I was grateful she just met me where I was, without probing or asking about Penny's and my relationship or asking why I didn't trust her enough to tell her. She simply met my grief in the moment. I asked Christi's advice on whether to give the eulogy. "Of course you should give it," she said. "You were her press secretary. You almost have to, Terry." Kicking into campaign-for-Penny mode made me feel better. I knew instinctively she was right. If I needed to do this for Penny, I could do it.

"It would look odd, Terry, if you didn't," she added. She offered her help, and I said I would call if I needed it.

I was grateful on Sunday evening when Patty arrived; I felt safer with her near. When she came in, she seemed somewhat calmer and told me that she had decided to keep her schedule of teaching Sunday school that morning, as difficult as it was. She said that when she went to the class, two young twin girls had come for their first day. She felt comforted by that, being reminded of her and Penny. I was happy for her, and I decided to refrain from telling her the ugly reality of her father's behavior. The purse had been returned, so why not let her have this pocket of relief a while longer?

Her father, however, whisked her into the back office in the house. I could hear his voice rising. I thought it was about the purse. Patty came out of the room, looking shaken. I felt terrible for her. She came into the living room, and her father strode by. "You okay?" I said.

"Yes."

Don picked up Penny's purse and handed it to Patty.

I decided to tell her what happened. "I'll take the purse," she said. I genuinely felt relief. If Patty had it, it was as good as me having it, I felt. And more to the point, I simply didn't want Don to touch or move it. I knew that Penny would have hated that. While I never understood the wellspring of their friction, Penny was plainspoken about their troubled relationship. Once, when we had moved into the house on Sims, Helen and Don come to visit without calling first. They rang the doorbell. Penny's father was standing behind Helen.

"Mom," Penny said, exasperated when she saw him. "You know you are welcome, but Dad is not welcome," she said. At the time, I cringed for her father, unable to comprehend the audacity (though later, I realized it as her courage) of being able to reject her father as he stood on the porch. Her mother came in to the house, and Don left, returning a few hours later to pick Helen up.

"Terry," Patty said after she took control of the purse. "I need to talk to you." I thought Patty needed my advice or was going to tell me how difficult the conversation with her father was, as Penny had dissected these family dynamics with me.

"Let's go into the bedroom." We walked into the bedroom, closed the door, and sat on the edge of the bed.

"Dad said that you are working on a eulogy?" she said.

"Yes," I said, hoping to get her input. "I am hoping that you can edit it and tell me what you think."

She looked pained and folded her hands in her lap. "Terry," she said. "The family doesn't want you to speak at the funeral."

I was taken aback, and I couldn't speak. My head lifted in surprise.

"The family?" I said. "Donnie? Rod? Who, Patty?" Momentary anger overrode my compassion for her, and I pushed her to say that it was her father.

"Well, Terry," she said. "Let's just leave it at 'the family,'" she said, intimating that it was her father's decision. My ire started to rise.

"She was a statewide candidate, Patty. It is expected that her press secretary would speak for her. It would be odd if I didn't, and I'm going to do it whether your dad wants me to or not."

She paused. "You're really putting me in a bad spot," she said.

I still believed that her father was bullying her. "Patty," I said, "even reporters think it would be odd if I didn't speak."

She paused again. "This is so stressful for me, Terry," Patty said. "You know Penny used to say how stress can affect cancer." I couldn't believe she had just said that, but I immediately switched into caretaking mode. My mind flooded. I surely didn't want to stress Patty, who was in remission. I didn't want to lose her too. At least I could save her, right? My mind went completely blank. Then, with that foothold, she said, "You spoke for Penny so long, we want you to just be family at the funeral." I didn't see it until nearly a decade later, but Patty was using the same language that the broadcaster had used about me speaking for Penny, and I think upon reflection all these years later, she may have resented that focus on me as Penny's spokeswoman.

"Patty," I said, anguished. "I don't want to stress you."

"We want you to be family, Terry, and just sit and listen," she said. Then she said, "Thank you, Terry," patted my arm, and walked back into the kitchen.

I kept working on the eulogy. I wanted it to be ready. I was going to do this, regardless of who said what.

Don Jr. had arrived again, and I was so happy to see him. He was kind and gentle, and together we cleaned up and talked after everybody left. He did the bulk of the cleaning, but I managed to pick up a few soda cans and paper plates. He swept and mopped the kitchen floor, vacuumed, and did the dishes. I sat on the floor in front of the glass coffee table and cleaned it with Windex, but even that limited effort was nearly too much for me.

Once the house was clean, we sat on the couch. He said to me, "You know, Terry, yesterday, before you called me to come, Penny came to me, I don't want to say in a vision, but it was a vision." He paused to see how I would react to this statement.

"I believe in those things, Donnie," I said.

"I know it sounds weird," he continued, "but I have visions sometimes. I was on my back porch, and Penny appeared and said to me, 'Donnie, I'm going now.'"

I don't remember everything he and I talked about that night, but I remember being comforted. He seemed centered, quiet, and deep. Late into the night, I went to bed and lay down, although I didn't sleep. The hours felt like a battering ram to my heart. I got up and got one of Penny's suits out of the closet and chose a tam from the rocking chair. I laid them on Penny's side of the bed. I ran the phone cord to the bed and set the phone next to me. Around 5:00 AM, exhausted and still unable to sleep, I became as scared and jumpy as a child in a thunderstorm. Panicked, and almost without thinking, I picked up the telephone and called Linda Hawker. She answered the phone. "Linda, it's Terry," I said breathlessly.

"Terry, what's wrong?" she said. I began weeping. I needed to talk to someone intimately connected with Penny. I realized that what was wrong was that Penny was dead, and that there was really no reason to be scared anymore.

"Linda, I . . ." I started stuttering.

"Terry, is everything okay? Are you okay?" she asked.

"Yeah, Linda," I said, still crying, but hearing her voice was calming me down. "I just . . . I just needed to hear your voice."

"Call anytime, Terry," she said kindly. Although I was unsure why, I regretted making the call. Everything in my life at the moment seemed a paradox, including my relationship with Linda. I felt I had been hunted by her early on; she made me feel trapped sometimes. Linda could be relentless and unkind, and yet I knew that she loved Penny deeply and that she also had a great capacity for kindness.

I got up and got in the shower. I felt empty and hollow. I couldn't think. I couldn't pray. All my energy was gone. I decided that tea would be soothing and that I would sit in front of the fire for a while—perhaps I'd be able to sleep there for a bit. Don Jr. had told me he would be up early to go for a morning run and would be back around ten. Wearing a short green silk nightshirt that Penny had bought for me, I opened my bedroom door to walk to the kitchen for tea. I nearly screamed out in fear as I looked down the hallway, startled to see someone: Penny's father was sitting at our kitchen table, going through our mail. It was not yet 8:00 AM. I returned to the bedroom to get dressed. I walked to the kitchen and said, "Don, would you mind calling before you come over in the morning, and when you get here, would you please knock? I don't want any embarrassing situations."

"I have a key," he said.

"Yeah, I know, Don, that was Helen's key," I said, correcting him as Penny always did about the key. "But it would mean a lot if you would just give me a call or knock before you come in."

Is this was Rod meant? That Don was intrusive and rude? I saw that he was not opening the mail, just organizing it in piles. I decided to be charitable and asked him if he wanted something to drink. He declined. I made tea and felt very frustrated with his presence in the house, particularly because it was so early. I went into the living room and sat down, looking at the fireplace. The phone rang—it was Penny's secretary. She wanted to know what would be a good time to come over to help plan the funeral "Well, Penny's father's already here," I said in an irritated voice, as Carmel knew the tenor of her boss's relationship with her father.

"How about late morning?" she said.

I didn't want to even hear Don, let alone see him. I retreated to my bedroom. The one place that had not been infiltrated by anyone else. Every one respected the privacy of our bedroom. I kept the door closed and was grateful that part of our home had still remained private, used by only Penny and me.

Senator Vince Demuzio, a close friend of both Penny's and mine, called and asked if he could come by. When he arrived, I realized it was his first time to our home. I opened the door, we both started crying. We hugged for a long time, and then he made a joke: "Hey, I haven't hugged somebody this long other than my wife.

"How you doing, kid?" he said to me. He used this familiar salutation whether talking to Penny or me.

"I'm okay, Vince."

"Don't lie to me. How ya doin'?" he asked again.

I started fighting tears. I told him about Don moving Penny's purse, about Don's early-morning arrival, about the eulogy. I told him that I was so confused.

"Yeah, that it is going to look odd if you don't speak. You're her press secretary. Let me work on it."

I felt better. I knew that Vince would pull this off. He left the room and called Patty, and then he came back. "Terry," he said. "Patty's carrying water for Don. He's the one that doesn't want you to speak."

Letting Patty off the hook, I focused my anger at Don for bullying Patty. Not wanting to make it worse for her, I decided to simply let it go and not protest, and I let my eulogy, as with the rest of our life together, be silent.

In the late afternoon, Penny's staff went to the church to overlook the details—choosing a picture of Penny, deciding where the media would be located, and discerning security details for the governor and other high-level dignitaries. It was clear that Patty and Don were the sign-offs on the major decisions, including ones about the media, and as I stood there, the reality hit me: I was burying my partner and had no say in her final arrangements. Deeply sad, I walked away from the group and slid into a pew and sat down, fighting tears. A pastoral assistant who was also in the group making the arrangements excused herself and came to sit with me.

"I'm Therese Allen," she said. "I am really sorry for your loss, Terry." I thanked her. How was it that those who knew nothing about my life with Penny seemed to instinctively see everything, or at least be particularly kind? I wanted to talk to this woman; I needed to confide in someone. Why not a person whose profession barred her from sharing it? She asked me if I was taking care of myself, talking about grief and how difficult times like these are. I was grateful, oddly, that she didn't talk to me about God or Catholic liturgy. I felt a connection to this woman, as though she understood—whether she did or not—that Penny and I were lovers, that I was bound not to talk about it, and that I was in a terribly difficult place with Penny's family. Unlike I had with others, I didn't shirk or reject her kindness. She had purposely stepped away from the decision-making crowd to console me, and I felt that.

"Everything will be very dignified, Terry," she said. Then she said something that really helped my grieving. "I know that Penny," she said, pausing for effect, "and you," she added, "will be pleased with how things unfold tomorrow." When she combined Penny and me in the same sentence, I felt differently about yearning to make decisions. Penny couldn't make them either, I reasoned. And so, Penny and I, in some ways, were in the same boat. I liked thinking of it that way, and it enabled me to stop fighting for recognition or fighting to have a say in how my partner would be remembered. Therese put her hand on my back. I did not try and hide my falling tears. She handed me her card and said, "Please call me anytime."

When we returned to the house, another wave of well-wishers came through to express their condolences. Later, everyone left but Don Jr. (Donnie) and Luanne. As Luanne was leaving, she said to Donnie, "Why don't you make Terry some of your special tea? Or give her something to calm her down?" He said he would. Then, he and I started what became our nightly ritual: cleaning and talking. Again, he really did most of it, sweeping, vacuuming, and wiping down the counters. I couldn't stop crying—I knew, in the eyes of most people, I was simply Penny's press secretary. I felt out of place in my own home. Donnie came to sit with me and said, "I'll mop the kitchen floor in the morning." Then he made me some herbal tea and gave me some homeopathic pills to help me sleep. We sat on the couch in front of the fireplace. "Rest and drink your tea, Terry," Donnie said. While I drank my tea, I pulled Therese Allen's card from my pocket and studied it, contemplating whether to call her.

We sat on the couch, and I sipped the warm liquid. I hadn't eaten and was exhausted, and perhaps because of the medicinal tea, I felt very relaxed and started to cry harder. Donnie held my hand and said, "It's okay."

Later, as the night wore on and Donnie and I sat talking about Penny, I told him how much I loved her. "You were more than her press secretary, weren't you, Terry?" he said invitingly. I could not hold our secret truth one more moment. "Yes," I said, and I wept openly into his shoulder. He was rapt by our story, and he listened and asked questions about our love. He wanted to know how we met and if Penny had ever been in love with a woman before. I told him the great lengths we went to hide our relationship.

"Terry, I knew it a long time ago when I met you at the house," he said. "The love between you was so obvious."

"Really, Donnie?" I asked, genuinely shocked that anyone could have seen through our ruse. "Are you okay with that?" I asked tentatively, still feeling shame.

"I am just so happy that that my sister was loved so well." He let me weep. He told me he understood grief because his first wife had died many years ago. I wept some more. Then I started to tell him the great pain that his father was causing me. I told him about how he behaved with the purse. I told him how he had complained it would cost money to rent the adjacent building to accommodate the overflow crowd at the funeral. I told him that earlier that day, Don had actually looked down at my shoes, and said "Uh, whose shoes are those?" I told him that I almost vomited when his father asked me that. Donnie looked pained and sat for a long time, listening. Then he said to me something that seemed odd to me at the time. "Terry, I have to ask you something," he said. "I don't want to ask, but I have to ask."

I had no idea what he was going to say. For some reason, I wondered if he was going to ask me something religious or spiritual.

"Please tell me you guys had a will," he said, echoing his brother.

Again, I lied. "Yes, we have a will."

"Oh my God, I am *so* relieved," he said, putting his hand over his chest and exhaling, the exact same gesture that Jane had made. "We've been through this before." Penny had told me of the difficulties of Marsha's estate and I witnessed firsthand some of the troubles that enveloped the family after Helen died. Rod, Jane, and Donnie were now apparently worried that problems would ensue with Penny's estate.

I felt a mixture of sickness and relief after coming out to Donnie. We stayed up talking well into the night. The freedom to talk about Penny and our love and to share stories was one of the most relieving rituals in my grief. I later understood why Jews sit shivah in the aftermath of a loved one's death.

We turned out the fireplace around 2:00 AM. "Everything is going to be okay, Terry," he said. "Don't worry."

I didn't believe him. I knew my life would never be the same without Penny.

CHAPTER TWENTY-TWO

FIFTEEN ROWS BACK

I must have finally dozed off because a few hours later, I awoke and saw a Decatur police officer standing at the foot of our bed, saying, "Ma'am? Ma'am?"

I looked at him, clearly frightened but finally awake.

"Are you Terry Mutchler?" he asked.

"Yes," I said, very confused at the presence of this uniformed, armed man in my bedroom and the sounds of police traffic on his walkie-talkie. Was I dreaming?

He turned down his radio as I lay there under the white down comforter. "Your family was concerned. They had tried to call you several times but nobody answered the phone. They called us to do a welfare check. Do you want me to get that?" he said, motioning to the green phone next to me that was ringing. I hadn't even heard it

"No. Could you step into the hallway so I can get up, please?"

He walked from the bedroom, and I noticed that he had his thumb hooked in his shiny black leather belt. I threw on a white shirt and some khaki pants and walked into the living room where he stood, looking around.

"Officer, how did you get in?" I asked, still somewhat groggy.

"No one answered the door bell, and I tried the handle. It was unlocked," he explained.

I didn't hear the doorbell that morning. Don Jr. had stayed in the guest room but was gone, and I assumed that he had gone out for a morning run again.

"Terry, Are you okay?" the officer asked.

"Yes, thank you," I said, my voice cracking and shaky. "I haven't had much sleep since Senator Severns died, and I guess I didn't hear the phone," I said.

"Yes, we were all sorry about that," he said. "Um, you really shouldn't leave your front door unlocked."

"Yes, Officer, thanks. I'm sorry to bother you."

He said something into his walkie-talkie and left.

I couldn't quite focus on what was happening. I looked at the scuff marks on the floor and thought I should have cleaned it before the funeral, but I didn't care, and I didn't have the energy. I walked to the den and sat down in the chair that we had picked out from Levenger. The chair where so many times I had sat to write a speech or a press release. The chair that Penny would sit in as I sat across the desk, talking strategy or writing letters to the editor. I fingered through the stack of paper on the desk and came across the statement I had written just a few days before. I called my sister Donna and asked if her daughter, Rachel, could do me a favor. I needed to go to the funeral home to drop Penny's shoes off, but I just couldn't bear it. I asked if Rachel could do that for me. She said she would come by.

I heard someone at the front door.

"Terry, it's Donnie," Don Jr. said. He walked into the den, and I told him about my police department alarm clock. "I need to talk to you," he said, somewhat hyped. "Would you come into the living room?" I thought something serious had happened but then dismissed the worry. What else could happen that would matter?

We sat down on the couch, and he scooted to the edge of it and took my hand.

"I don't want you to be upset with me," he said. My stomach started to tighten.

"I got up early this morning and went to Bement," he said. I started to panic and shift in my seat. "No, no," he said soothingly, putting his hand on my shoulder. "It's okay."

Fear encompassed me. "Donnie, you shouldn't have done that," I said, my voice an octave higher.

"No, Terry, he needed to know. I told him that you were lovers. That you and Penny were like a married couple, and that he should respect that. I told him that he needed to remember that this was your house. My dad needed to know that you and Penny were partners," he repeated. "I told him that he needed to stop behaving the way he has been and respect you and your relationship with Penny."

I couldn't believe that he had done this. I didn't know what to do. Penny and I had kept our relationship secret, and although we talked about revealing it to a limited number of people, I was certain her father was not on the list.

I felt sick to my stomach, but I also felt relief, like something had shifted into place, like my soul had weight. Then, just as quickly as the relief set in, I became immediately critical of myself. I felt that I had betrayed Penny by sharing our relationship with Donnie. I should have been able to handle my grief in silence and not share our long-kept secret so easily with him.

"What did he say?" I asked timidly.

"Don't worry about that, Terry," Donnie said. "He understands."

I will never know what he understood or didn't, but things became worse.

A few hours later, family and friends starting gathering at our home. Kristin arrived, making a beeline for me, hugging me hard around my waist and crying.

"It's okay, sweetheart," I said, hugging her tightly. She handed me some letters that she and her brothers had written to their aunt Penny and asked me if I could make sure they were put in Penny's coffin. A friend of Donnie's asked my family to step outside for a picture in front of the house, although I did not want to.

When we walked back through the front door, there seemed to be some commotion in the kitchen. Rod and Jane were sitting in the living room, but Patty, Don Sr., and Willard were in the kitchen. I heard them discussing the funeral procession. Luanne walked into the living room, shaking her head in disgust. She said Willard was upset that I—not a family member—was going to be in a car in the processional ahead of his, when he was Penny's uncle and I a staffer.

Still in press secretary mode, the discussion of processional made me realize that no one had arranged for a police escort, and I knew that without one, there would be chaos, and the timing would be off for our arrival to the church. I called the Decatur police department and identified myself. The desk sergeant transferred me to a police captain. He indicated that the intersections would be blocked so that the funeral procession could proceed uninterrupted. Before he hung up, he said to me, "Terry, I saw you announce Penny's death the other day on TV, and my wife and I can't stop thinking about you, and how you are. We want you to know that you're like family to this community."

I couldn't bear his kindness. I thanked him, scared to death that he was telling me that he knew Penny and I were lovers. He said a police car would be sent over to the house to lead the processional and that one would be provided to follow so that we could all stay together.

I headed toward the kitchen from the den, and Rod and Donnie approached me in the hallway. Each of them put an arm on my shoulders, and they were tearing up. Rod said, "We want you to sit with us." The church was working with Patty and Don on the seating arrangements, and yesterday, I had only seen the section that was reserved for the family. I wasn't sure what that meant, but I assumed I would be sitting with Patty. I told Rod and Donnie that that was already arranged and I was sitting with Patty. They seemed somewhat confused, but Rod said, "Good, I'm glad."

Then one of Penny's staffers asked for everybody's attention and explained how the processional would work. When the family arrived at the church, they would drive into the cul-de-sac, and their cars would be taken to a parking lot. Everyone else, including staff, would drive directly to the parking lot and then walk back to the church. They would enter the side entrance of the church, not the main front entrance, but the door would be very close to the front of the church, where they would be seated.

My brother Dave was standing with his hand on the mantle, listening. He seemed to flinch, but I didn't know why. He leaned in and whispered something to his wife, Cecilia. After the instructions were given, Dave motioned me to him. "I want you to ride with me," he said.

I said, "I'm gonna ride with Donna."

He said, "No, I really want you to ride with me."

He seemed insistent, so I said, "Okay."

As we gathered in the kitchen to leave for the event, the doorbell rang. I went to answer it. A neighbor came to the front door. He and his wife had brought me a single red rose and a sympathy card with "Terry" written on the front. I inhaled, trying to stop the tears. I couldn't say anything. Nothing would come out. I wanted to spill it all right there, to thank him, to scream, to weep, something. But nothing would come out of my mouth, and I kept my head down. He said, "We'll talk later. It's okay, Terry."

We got in our cars and pulled out in order: Patty and her family in the front; Don and Audine; Rod, Jane, and Donnie; me, my brother, and my sister-in-law; Willard and Maureen; Donna and Gary; and then Penny's staff. I was stunned at the crowds lining the sidewalks as we drove through the city. Some saluted. Some cars that were ahead of us realized Penny's funeral procession was behind them, and they pulled over to the side of the road, letting us pass. Unbelievably, some people got out of their cars on the side of the road and stood to watch as the family of Senator Severns drove to the church. I saw one man take off his hat. I started weeping. Dave kept clearing his throat, and Cecelia kept saying, "Oh, Terry Lee." Police officers were positioned at each intersection of the route, and as we drove by them, they would salute the processional. My tears were now streaming, but I suppressed my weeping by holding my breath. As we approached the church, I could hear the tolling of the massive bells. Single repeated gongs. My weeping intensified. I did not want to face this.

When the first cars of the processional turned into the church lot where we were to enter the church's side door, the funeral director, believing that all the family had arrived, waved our car to the parking lot at the end of the street. My brother simply followed the car in front of him into the cul-de-sac. The funeral attendant tried to wave him forward to the parking lot. Dave paused for a second. Then he said, half to himself and half to me in his distinct police sergeant voice, "You are not walking from a parking lot." He rolled down his window as he was driving past a clearly upset attendant. "We have another family member here," he said. The attendant opened the door, and I got out and walked into the side door of the church with Cecelia.

The dignitaries and guests were mostly seated, and all of us that were at the house were the last to arrive at the church. We were greeted by the church staff, who had the seating arrangements pre-planned. It had to be precise because there were so many dignitaries coming to the funeral:

Governor Jim Edgar; Secretary of State George Ryan; the gubernatorial candidates; Speaker of the House Michael Madigan; Senate President James "Pate" Philip; members of the legislature. John Carpenter, a vice president at American Airlines, had arranged for a charter from Chicago for business and political types to be flown in.

I stepped into the church, and the sight of the more than 1,000 attendees, many crying, took my breath. I started to cry anew. I stood with the cluster of family for a moment, and it seemed all eyes were focused in my direction. For some reason, my eyes caught Senator Judy Baar Topinka, whose reddish hair stood out in the crowd. She grimaced and put her hand over her heart and nodded. I nodded back, an unspoken greeting traded between us. I saw Julie Curry in my peripheral vision but knew better than to make eye contact with her, for I would certainly collapse weeping if I did. I spotted Patty in the front row and I made my way toward her. Therese Allen, the pastoral assistant who was so kind to me the day before, walked over to greet me with a handshake and a hug. "I'll escort you to your seat," she said. I was grateful. We walked to the main aisle and started toward the front. But Therese stopped well short of the front row where Patty and her family were sitting.

My seat at my partner's funeral was about fifteen rows back from the front of the church and a little off to the right. Patty was in the front row. I looked at Therese confused and remained standing in the aisle.

"I'm sorry, Terry," she said as she moved her hand toward the seats. It was clear to me that this had been discussed and that this seating arrangement was purposeful. Don Sr. and Audine were in the row behind Patty, and other family members were in the pews behind them. Now I understood why Rod and Don Jr. had approached me about sitting with them. They knew I was not going to be seated in the front. I also realized that this is why they looked confused when I said I was sitting with Patty. What I didn't know until more than a decade later was that Rod, Don, and Patty had discussed where I would sit. They wanted me to sit with the family. "She is not sitting with the family," Patty had said, despite their protestations.

Rod was clearly distraught about this seating arrangement. He kept turning around and motioning for me to come sit by him and Jane. I felt a crush of feeling: If I moved, I would be in the way; it was too crammed as it was. Moving up would draw attention to me, which I did not want to do. I wanted to be near my sister, Donna, and yet I wanted to be closer to Penny. There was nothing but heavy confusion and blinding pain within me.

"I'm okay," I whispered, nervously nodding my head.

As we sat down, Therese, still standing at the pew, said to me, "Let me explain how this will work at the end of the Mass." She said the family would be leaving the church first to begin a receiving line while everyone else stayed seated. Then attendants would dismiss each pew. "So, I will just follow the family when they get up?" I said, wanting to be sure I understood on a day when I was not thinking at all. She bent to the side of the pew.

"No," she said, calmly. "When the family goes to the back of the church for the receiving line, you and your family move to the right aisle, not the center aisle, and go into that vestibule," she said, pointing. "The family will greet the dignitaries and guests. After that, just go to the convention center with the rest of the public. There will be a presentation of flags."

I nodded mutely, honestly not understanding one thing that had just happened. At that moment, I remember hearing Pachelbel's Canon for the first time. Penny had said to me recently that Marsha had wanted this song to be played at her funeral, and she had told me she wanted the same thing "when the time came." To this day, when I hear Pachelbel's Canon, I either turn it off or walk out of hearing range. I cannot bear to listen to that music, although I once loved it.

U.S. Senator Paul Simon, clad in his trademark bow tie, rose to eulogize Penny in his somber and gravelly voice, and he talked of his first meeting with her when she was young and how her fire for politics never diminished over her entire life. Senator Demuzio came next and captured Penny to a tee, with humor and grace. When Vince said his final farewell and referred to his private nickname for Penny—"Princess Spring, Summer, Winter, Fall"—I bent over my knees and wept. When he stepped down, he looked at me. I looked to my left at the crowd of dignitaries and noticed that many were watching me, assuming I would speak next. For a moment, I thought, *Terry, just get up and speak.* Instead, I sat still.

At the end of the service, the attendants started with Penny's family, and they were dismissed and ushered to the back of the church to form a receiving line. The ushers skipped my row and went to the row behind me.

My family, not briefed on the arrangements, looked to me to move into the center aisle. I simply motioned for them to slide out to the right. The people seated behind me seemed confused also, as though they were waiting for my family and me to exit. Then the ushers returned and again motioned them to go out the back of the church and greet Penny's family with everyone else. Everything felt so very far away. As we stepped into the off-to-the-side aisle and the rest of the church went out the back, my family followed me toward the small vestibule, which was tiny and cramped with coats. I held Gary's hand with a death grip as we squeezed into the dark wooden room. We just stood there, all of us looking at each other somewhat stunned.

Cecelia started weeping. She hugged me. "Oh, Terry, I am so sorry," she said, and she wept openly. I was buckling in a way I had never experienced, and I knew I was either going to pass out or run. My flight mechanism took over, and I raced out of the room, leaving my family alone there. I ran out the side door of the church, pushing hard through the doors, ignoring the congregation that was waiting to receive Penny's family. I stood in the parking lot bent over, trying to catch my breath and dispel the dizzy feeling that was overtaking me. Eventually, my family found me. I had regained some composure and stood talking to them. My sister asked, "Why aren't you in the receiving line? Or at least why aren't we greeting the family like everybody else?" I didn't know what to say. We just stood there.

In front of the church, Penny's family received dignitaries. A very young Sen. Barack Obama shook Rod and Jane's hand, and unlike the other lawmakers, lingered. "Penny and I were friends," the now President of the United States said. "I'm really going to miss her." He echoed this to ABC news. "She had integrity and she had vision. She took me under her wing immediately when I came down [to Springfield] and gave me all kinds of terrific advice and tips. She will be sorely missed."

A few minutes later, to my amazement, several dignitaries came walking around to the side of the church. At first I thought they were going to their cars, but that didn't make sense because their drivers were parked in a lot in front of the church a half a block away.

"I wondered where you were. I was trying to find you, Terry," said Cook County Recorder of Deeds and Penny's opponent, Jesse White. He hugged me, and for a moment, I couldn't let go. It felt like another unspoken truth as he held me and then stepped back and took both my hands in his. "I am so sorry," he said to me, two tears dripping down his cheek. "I know you were family to Penny, and I know she is grateful for all you did."

"Thank you, Jesse," I said, while crying with my head down. "I know we will be speaking in a few days regarding Penny's endorsement of your campaign." Senator Demuzio walked over while wiping tears from his eyes, something I had never seen the Majority Whip do.

"Vince," I said. "Penny would have loved that eulogy. She really loved you."

"Terry, she really loved you, kid. I am sorry you didn't get to speak. I hope that I covered everything you would have." As I stood talking to him, many other people made their way over to see me, and a makeshift receiving line began. Senate Minority Leader Emil Jones; Representative Julie Curry; American Airlines Vice President John Carpenter and his wife, Leslie; staff members; members of the community that I had met over the years; and many people that I hadn't met offered me their condolences. I saw the man who always delivered our pizza, although he didn't know I was always hiding nearby, and he introduced himself to me as "Penny's pizza delivery guy." Another friend of Penny's, Skip Dempsey, who was president of the Pipefitters and Steamfitters Union, walked up. His eyes were red, his head was down, and he was having a tough time speaking. Skip adored Penny, and they had been friends for decades.

"Terry, I am so sorry," he said, openly crying. I patted his back. "She really loved you, Skip, and appreciated all you did for her." He cleared his throat.

I stood there with Donna, greeting those who came to greet me and introducing them to her. There was strange relief in the moment. Was it because I felt like I was campaigning again? Shaking hands? Was it that they made a point to find me and console me? Was it just suspended reality? In retrospect, that moment on the side of the church seemed like a second-class citizen line—perhaps what it felt like before the civil rights movement for those that were forced to use segregated water fountains. Nonetheless, I later realized the power of ritual in healing, and in that moment, on the side of that church, the expressions of comfort and kindness offered to me as a grieving young widow, even though that was not explicitly stated, released a measure of my pain.

CHAPTER TWENTY-THREE

AND JUSTICE FOR ALL?

As I finished greeting people who came to see me at the side of the church, mourners and family alike walked across the street to the civic center, where there was to be a presentation of four flags to members of Penny's family. A flag presentation is a posthumous honor usually reserved for members of the military, law enforcement officers, or fire fighters who have died in the line of duty. The city had decided to present this honor to Penny's family for her service. On the way to the civic center, Luanne came up behind me, leaned in, and whispered, "I was trying to find you. I want you to come with me. Don't stand in the crowd for this flag presentation."

I didn't understand, but I didn't protest either. I thought she wanted my help organizing the presentation or maybe she had a spot for a better view. She walked me to the area where Penny's siblings and father were standing, waiting to be escorted outside. Don said to me, "This is for family."

I simply said, "Thanks," and ignored him otherwise, deciding not to explain that Luanne wanted my help. I wished she hadn't stepped away. I saw her speaking to a member of the honor guard, and I watched her hand him a flag.

Luanne came back and said to Patty, Don, Don Jr., and Rod, "Okay, the family should walk outside and stand on the areas marked on the red carpet." Then she whispered to me, "Don't say anything, but when the family walks outside, just walk out with them. You're going to receive a flag." They started walking out, and she had my arm and guided me toward the door.

"Luanne, listen," I turned around and started to protest.

"Terry, it's okay, really." She turned me back toward the door and gently pushed me outside. I followed Rod and stood next to him. The honor guard marched toward us. I was unable to lift my head to face the man who saluted me in slow motion with crisp white gloves. Head down, I clenched my teeth to cage the wail that fought its way from my heart to my throat. My locked jaw kept the yelp inside my mouth.

Lt. Jerry Sullivan of the Decatur, Illinois, Fire Department Color Guard stood squarely in front of me. I could not look at his face. Instead, I looked at the face of his silver buttons. He raised his right hand in slow motion to his brow. He turned his entire body to the left to face another member of his honor guard, who handed him a folded flag. He then turned again to me. He handed me the triangular cloth, white stars showing, and said, "I present this flag in honor of Senator Severns's service." I received it with both arms and pulled it to my chest.

With his left hand, he gently tugged each of the cloth-covered fingers of his right hand, removed his glove, and shook my hand. In the near distance, I heard a deep-voiced command:

"Present arms."

"Ready. Aim. Fire."

Crack.

"Ready. Aim. Fire."

Crack.

"Ready. Aim. Fire."

Crack.

I lifted my eyes, not my head, to a nearby mound of dirt, where a young black-haired man stood in a black suit and raised a silver bugle. I hugged the flag to my chest tightly and wept as I listened to death's ageless heralding, "Taps." In the crowd, I saw a woman that Penny and I knew— she was married to a man but was a closeted lesbian. Her shoulders were heaving as she wept.

I wasn't supposed to receive a flag that day. I didn't know I was going to receive it until just moments before, and neither did Patty or Don. In fact, I later learned, it had been planned as a secret to ensure that I would receive a flag in this ceremony without protest or problems after Patty and Don had insisted that I not give a eulogy. It was bootlegged benevolence for which I am forever grateful. Everything about our relationship was a secret. And on this day, even the American flag was a secret.

CHAPTER TWENTY-FOUR

MORE AFTERMATH

Back at the house, I started to faint. Audine helped me into a chair and got me some food. "You've been taking care of everybody else," she said. She handed me a plate, and remarked how she always liked this plate "of Penny's." Then she awkwardly corrected herself. "I mean, it's your plate too," she said. "Of course it's your plate. It's your kitchen." I realized that Don Jr.'s revelation to them, as uncomfortable as it had made me, may in fact have had an effect. *Maybe everything will be okay after all*, I thought.

Later that day, I said goodbye to my family. Dave said something I hated. "When you go back to Chicago for a few days, if anything really means something to you—Penny's license, her passport, anything you can carry with you—I'd pack it and take it with you."

My face was red with anger, I was nearly shaking. "You can be such an asshole. Not everybody operates like cops and robbers."

With calm, understated ease, he said. "You can call me an asshole, but I have a bad feeling, and if I were you, I'd take some things with me if they were important to me."

I shook my head and walked away.

I desperately wanted to be alone in my house in silence, communing with Penny. But when I was finally alone, it felt like a painful flame burned within me, and I could not be still. Basic tasks brought on a sometimes hour-long internal debate about the most mundane things. Weeks before, I was operating at the highest level of political campaigning, and now I was struggling with questions like, "Should I brush my teeth now or wait until after I get undressed?" Making coffee became an IQ test. I felt like I was relearning everything. And I kept losing things. I would misplace my wallet, my coat, or a brush. I would get very angry with myself, as the time it took to find the lost things cost energy I did not have. In short, I was exhausted.

I didn't sleep much the night after Penny's funeral, and I was awake but tired when the phone rang at 6:00 AM. "Hello?" I answered groggily, the tears already flowing. It dawned on me that when Penny was alive, I never answered the phone in our house. And now that she was dead, I was answering it. It didn't seem quite right.

"Uh, Terry, I drove past Penny's house this morning, and you left all the lights on. That's very expensive," Don reprimanded.

I felt a surge of sickness and anger at once. My mind raged at this thoughtless man who thought it was appropriate to call me with this comment at all, not to mention at this time of day. I wanted to once and for all tell him that I felt he was callous person. But my anger was tempered because of Patty. I didn't want to make things more difficult for her.

"Thanks for the tip," I said and hung up. I couldn't shake the rage. But the grief was more powerful. I started trembling. I realized anew that Penny was dead. Those were the hardest moments of grief, when I would forget and then remember suddenly that she was gone.

I began to weep uncontrollably, exhausted but still unable to sleep. I needed Penny to help me through this, and Penny was dead.

Later that day, I craved to have a real conversation with Patty about Penny's death. I asked how she was, and she said fine, shortcutting my attempts to talk substantively. Before we hung up, she asked me if I had made any progress with the will. I said, "No, I haven't gotten to that yet."

On Wednesday, I felt even more lost, and unsuccessfully tried again to write the will. Patty had called, and we spoke about the Senate memorial service, which would be held the next day. "How's the will?" she asked.

"I am having a hard time doing it," I said, wanting to talk.

"We really need to get that done, Terry," was all that she said.

I ignored the low-grade anger I felt. I resented both having to write it and the pressure I was feeling. I felt as though Patty were pushing me.

I turned my attention to the task of returning calls to the media. Reporters had questions about Penny's Senate seat: Who would take over?

Would the campaign endorse Jesse White in the secretary of state's race? My old feelings of hating politics resurfaced; the woman was not even dead a week, and politics took precedent over any semblance of personal grief. Without Penny, this was no longer fun on any level. I finished the calls, gave up on the will, and decided to go to town and do some errands. I went to pick up Penny's dry cleaning and to pay my cell phone bill.

As press secretary, Penny's campaign had paid my cell phone bills and any expenses I incurred in relation to her election. Penny had given me one of her campaign checkbooks, and she signed the checks in advance. I did what I always did—paid the bill with a campaign check. I also went to the newsstand and ordered about fifty Sunday papers from the day her death was announced. I have no idea why I ordered so many. I stopped at the bank to cash my work checks. Though she would tell me to just use the checkbook I had, I insisted that for my work, the whole check should be written in her own hand. I had several checks that I had not had time to cash while she was sick. I went to the bank, and they refused the checks. I explained the situation—that these were written before Penny had died, and I hadn't had a chance to cash them. They refused to honor them. I had no energy to fight with the bank. I decided to consider the lost wages a gift to Penny.

The next morning, a second memorial service for Penny was held in the Illinois Senate. I walked past the brass rail where I first met Penny. My chest hurt badly, but I knew that no matter how beloved Penny was and despite that she had just died, politics was politics in Illinois, and Penny's endorsement of a candidate in the secretary of state's race and Penny's replacement in the Senate would soon override any normal patterns of grieving. And facts were facts: I was still her press secretary and had work to do, no matter how much I didn't want to do it. Patty pulled me aside to ask me again if I had made any progress on the will. She later called two or three times to ask if I had finished it. I couldn't write it when Penny was alive, and I surely could not write it now that she was dead. And yet to not finish it meant that what Penny didn't want to happen—her father taking a portion of the estate—would happen.

Unanchored, unmoored, and unsure of what do to, I went home. I wanted to lie down and rest, but I had to do the will, no matter how painful to write; Patty wanted to file it on Monday. I was not a lawyer yet, and only had a textbook version of how to write a will. And, although Penny had suggested that we auto-pen her signature, I knew that legally that wasn't a good idea. I pondered consulting John Keith, but I knew that if I told him Penny died without a will, he would not be able to help me. And without a will, Penny's father would take fifty percent of the estate, and Rod, Patty, and Don Jr. would split the remaining fifty percent.

I typed the basics. Then, I typed: "Marital status: Married," and then hit delete. I did this a few times, and then I finally typed: "Single." I shook when I wrote that word. I felt sick. I felt as though those twenty characters cauterized a lie into my soul.

I continued to outline the will, bequeathing $1,000 to Penny's brothers and $250 to Don. I finished a draft of the outline, but I could not get over the untruth of Penny's marital status. And to make matters worse, I regretted that I wrote this will at the desk where we had written so many other enjoyable speeches and letters. I should have preserved that space for our happiness. I printed out the two pages, set them on the desk. My mind kept repeating the words "Marital status: Single" as though I were suffering from a mental ailment. I went to our bedroom and lay down. I decided to forget it for a while. Except the $250 to Don looked harsh. And I thought it looked even harsher to not say anything kind about Penny's father. I remembered hearing Penny talk of the hard feelings created when Marsha explicitly cut Don out of her estate. So explicit were Marsha's wishes that when Helen died years later, there was a terrific argument and legal action to prevent Don from taking any of Marsha's remaining money that had become part of Helen's estate.

I struggled with the right thing to do. Perhaps it was to simply let it be that Penny had died without a will, intestate. But knowing how vehemently Penny didn't want her father to have anything from her estate, I knew that was not an option. I recalled Penny's admonition the night before she died to "be generous. Not too generous, but generous," and I decided to let that be the guiding principle. And I knew how much Penny said she didn't want to stress Patty. So I reasoned that if I injected some kindness about her father, that would make Patty's life easier.

Instead of leaving Penny's father $250, I upped the amount to $1,000. I also added some language that would, I hoped, temper Don's heart toward Patty, still believing that he was pressuring her.

I finished the will on Sunday, and early on Monday, I drove to Springfield for the electronic signature. I thought that nothing could be worse than Penny's death, but now it seemed that each day without her was worse than the day before it. I simply wanted to crawl into our bed and never wake up. I told Patty I had finished the will, and she immediately drove to Decatur to pick it up. When she was at the house, Luanne stopped to take me to dinner.

"Don't mention this to Luanne, okay?" Patty said as she leaving.

"I am not going to mention this to *anybody*," I said, believing I was stating more than the obvious.

I waited for Patty to say more—to acknowledge the will or the effort it had taken, to say, "I'm sorry," to say anything. Instead, she said, "Thanks. I'll take care of this."

"Patty," I said, somewhat indignantly. "I need a copy of this. And I want to be there when you file it." I was trying to be visible.

"Well," she said, somewhat stumbling. "Yeah, I guess that makes sense."

Makes sense? I thought. *What the hell is happening here?*

I was preoccupied with the bizarre nature of her remark and was distracted at dinner. Luanne spoke candidly about the flat-out meanness of Penny's father. She warned me to be careful of this family's politics, and to not let them push me around.

"Remember, Penny wouldn't want that, Terry," Luanne said. I didn't know what to do, who to trust, or what to believe. I just wanted something I could not have: Penny to be alive.

On Tuesday, March 3, 1998, Patty and I walked in to the Macon County Courthouse and filed the will. I felt shaky and scared and sad. Now that we had gotten past this hurdle, I was certain she and I would collapse into our friendship and begin to grieve Penny together. "Let's get lunch," I said, but she declined.

I wanted to lie down on Rod and Jane's couch and sleep—but I didn't feel I knew them well enough to ask. I went home. Thankfully, they came by. For some reason, I didn't immediately run from their kindness or offerings. With them, I was able to be real with my grief, even without coming out to them. They knew that I needed to process her death, and they gently pushed me to talk and grieve with them.

That week, I felt that I needed to get back to law school no matter how terrible I felt. I was both aching and numb. I couldn't understand the duality. Numb, I would try and do things, but when the pain hit, I would be stuck wherever I was in that moment, the task left undone. I yearned for Penny. My home had become a house. I missed our routines, watching television with her, or reading with her.

I slept on Penny's side of the bed and woke up at 2:00 AM and lay there, feeling the weight of the world on my chest. I decided to leave for Chicago. I convinced myself the sooner I got there, the sooner I would be home. When I reached my apartment before dawn, I was scared, lonely, and sad. I later went to class, but the pain of sitting was unbearable and I would take several bathroom breaks, just because I couldn't stop crying.

That Friday, I hurried back to Decatur to be in my own bed. When I opened the garage door, the Volvo was gone. My immediate reaction was that somebody stole the car. But I couldn't figure out how that could have happened in a locked garage, particularly when I couldn't find my key. I picked up my cell phone and immediately called Patty. "Oh my God," I said. "Somebody stole the Volvo." I started talking a mile a minute.

"Slow down, Terry," she said. "I have the Volvo. I thought it would be better here than at the house."

I was angry. Even though I loved Patty, she had overstepped her bounds. Like with the purse, I didn't want to move anything yet, not even the car. Part of me wanted to call Rod and ask him to deal with it for me, but I didn't want to engage him against his sister.

"Patty," I said, frustrated. "I have lots of stuff in the car, including law books in the trunk. I need those." Then, I told her I thought it was probably a smart idea not to have the car at the house. Why I said this, I don't know. I was so unsure of myself I wondered if I was thinking clearly at all. I felt like I was twisting apart inside. I wasn't sure of anything any more. I didn't care about anything anymore.

Inside the house, things were decidedly worse. My countless sympathy cards were gone. I was too angry to call Patty at that moment. I pushed the button on the remote and the television flicked on, but the cable had been cut. This was too much. I picked up the handset in the kitchen to call Patty a second time, and the line was dead. As odd as it sounds, I completely forgot that Don Jr. had told his father that Penny and I were partners, and I was behaving as though the secret was still in play. I called Patty from my cell phone and said with force, "There's no cable or telephone in the house."

"It was a waste of money to have the phone and cable on," she said, a bit nervously.

I wanted so badly to speak up for myself to say more; to complain, to demand, to simply take control. But I could not. I felt like a ship without a wheel, at the mercy of the waves.

"The sympathy cards," was all I could say.

"Dad said he would go through them," she said. I felt in that moment as though my voice were buried in my stomach, as though not a sound of self-defense could come out.

Defeated, I said, "I'll deal with all this later. I'm going to my sister's for the weekend." I am not sure why I told her this. Maybe I felt that by saying I would deal with this later, that somehow I was preserving my right to an appeal at a later time.

"I think that's a good idea, Terry. There won't be anything for you to do there," she said.

It's my own fucking house, I thought. *What does that even mean nothing for me to do here?* I silently yelled to myself, and I started to hang up. Then Patty added one more thing: "Oh, and we are going to need the campaign cell phone and computer returned."

What I failed to understand was that now that I had given her the will, I was only in her way.

Disgust and rage were building within me.

I refused to acknowledge or admit the warning signs that were right in front of me. David's words were coming back to me. He couldn't be right, could he? I decided to put a suitcase of things together, not because Dave was right, I reasoned, but because some things that were usually in Decatur would comfort me in Chicago. I would have a few more of Penny's things with me. I took the hundreds of love letters that Penny had saved in the top drawer of our dresser. I took her wedding ring, her passport, a cloth ribbon she had saved from our first Christmas together. I took some silverware and a cup that she liked to use. I took one of her favorite scarves, although I had many of hers in Chicago. And I took two of our favorite pieces of art from the dining room. I put those things in my car. In a separate suitcase, I put the red and white striped shirt Penny wore on our first Memorial Day date. I put some of her writings in the suitcase, along with a letter that her ex-fiancé had written to her long ago that she had shown me once and we laughed about. While I was packing these things, the doorbell rang. Another Decatur police officer was standing at the door.

"Hello, Officer," I said. "Can I help you?"

"Ma'am, we had a call that someone was in this house that shouldn't be," he said. My anger was molten, but I didn't express it.

"Well, Officer," I said, "you have some misinformation. I live here. This was Senator Severns's house, and I lived here as well," I was shocked at my own bravery and disclosure.

"That's not the information we have. Do you have some ID?"

I asked him to step in out of the cold, while I retrieved my license. "I'm Terry Mutchler. I was also Penny's press secretary." A flash of recognition came over him. "I thought you looked familiar," he said, smiling.

I felt deflated producing my identification in my own home. I wondered if Don or Patty had called the police, but I still didn't want to believe that. I walked down to the basement and closed the blue suitcase. *This is ridiculous,* I thought. *I am not going to behave this way. This is my house.* I was angry at myself for letting fear get the better of me. *So what?* I thought. *They disconnected the cable and the phone, and I'll just reconnect it in my name next week.* They were grieving too and probably thought it was a good idea. But why couldn't I speak to Patty? Why couldn't I simply say, "Patty, Penny and I were partners, and you need to start behaving as such." I was still afraid of my own truth.

Although it was 8:00 PM and decidedly not a good idea given the hour, I drove to my sister's house five hours away in Indiana. On the drive, I was trying to figure out what was happening and why I couldn't speak up for myself. While these feelings were foreign to me, I didn't realize until years later that the muteness I was experiencing was reminiscent of a time in my youth: after I was sexually assaulted, I could not speak or ask for help. I only permitted myself to look at these feelings on the periphery.

I arrived at Donna's house and lay down on the couch. I was facing the back, and around 3:00 AM, I thought I heard Penny's voice. *Can someone go crazy this quickly?* I wondered. I nestled into the couch and ignored the sensation.

"Terry," I thought I heard Penny say.

I was on edge and listening. "Terry, turn around." I shook my head, thinking I was hallucinating or dreaming. I heard it again: "Turn around." Fearful but certain that I had heard her voice—or *a* voice, or something— I rolled back to look over my shoulder. Penny was standing next to the bookcase, her feet about two feet off of the floor. She was smiling, healthy, and looked about twenty. I immediately sat up, jumped off the couch, and reached for her, but she disappeared. I sat back on the couch, calling for her. She had been as visible as my hand in front of me. Now she was gone, but her presence felt very real even though I could not see her. The experience did not scare me. I did not feel sad, but rather deeply soothed. I had been aching in her absence and missing her, and just seeing what I believed to be her, brought me peace. I slept deeply for the first time since Penny's death.

The next day, ignoring Patty's callousness from the night before, I called her and told her what had happened, that I had seen Penny. Patty sounded shaken and very sad. "Did she say anything about me?" she asked. I could tell she too was aching for Penny. Feeling hopeful and wanting to soothe Patty, I told her that I was feeling stronger and suggested that she identify a few things in the house that might comfort her, as I had, and take them back to Bloomington. "I know it sounds silly, but I took two forks, two knives, and two spoons, and it makes me happy because Penny and I have eaten off of them together." I felt a measure of my old self returning. I felt generous, as though I had the strength to help Patty get through her grief.

CHAPTER TWENTY-FIVE

LOCKED OUT

I returned to Chicago and law school feeling a little bit better. Seeing Penny, even if it was a dream, brought me a particular happiness. On Thursday, at C's North, the euphoria of seeing her was not enough to keep my hard grief at bay. That night, Patty called me, and I was happy to hear her voice. She said, "Terry, things are moving a bit fast for me. We were looking for a photo of Penny being sworn into the Senate in 1996, and we can't find it. Dad said he thought he saw it near your stuff in the garage."

I was crushed.

"What photo are you talking about?," I said curtly.

"The one where we are in her office after she is sworn in," she said. "You know, Patty," I said disgusted and with a little sarcasm in my voice. "The Senate probably has a hundred of them. I'm sure you could call Cindy Davidsmeyer and get one."

"Well, Dad was pretty certain that it was near your stuff."

"I don't have the fucking picture, okay?"

"Well, Terry," she said, unflustered. "We just wanted to keep it in the family."

I caught my breath. *Keep it in the family.* Those words punctured my heart more than any other during the long aftermath of Penny's death. The lines were clear. To her, I was not family. I had been family until Penny died, but now, clearly, even after Don Jr. told them Penny and I were partners and after I wrote the will that gave everything to Patty, I was no longer one of them.

"And, Terry," she continued. "I think it would be best if you returned the silverware."

I didn't think that my grief could get worse. But in that moment, low-burning shame and anger collided with my grief, sapping me of every fiber of energy. I stumbled to my bedroom. I took half a sedative that Jane had given me. Maybe when I woke, this nightmare would be over.

I woke the next afternoon. I had two desperate needs: to be home, and to maintain some semblance of attendance at school—forget about absorbing the material, I just needed to be there. I contemplated with-drawing but was afraid I would not have the energy to continue later. I didn't want to lose Penny and law school. Like every Friday, I finished classes, packed, and went to Starbucks before starting the three-hour drive to Decatur. This Friday, three weeks after Penny's death, I could not stop crying as I walked in for coffee. In a glass jar at the register, they had a fresh batch of lemon knot cookies, and I started crying anew. Penny loved lemon knots. Decatur didn't have a Starbucks, so I often would bring her the glazed, sugary treats on my commutes home. She laughed hard when I disclosed that I had to put the cookies in the trunk because despite my good intentions, the cookies sometimes didn't make it to Decatur. The barista was patient as I wiped my eyes and tried to speak. She asked if she could do anything, and once I ordered, she handed me a glass of water while I waited.

I didn't know how to mark the third week anniversary of Penny's death, but I needed to be home. I longed to talk to her, to hear her voice. Our apartment in Chicago didn't feel like a home without her, and I was glad but scared to be on my way back to Decatur. I hadn't even wanted to leave Decatur at all, but I hadn't wanted to stay either. I couldn't calm myself. I kept moving even when I didn't want to simply because I knew that soon, I would be home in our bed. I was obsessed with our bed. I longed for its comfort, even though I knew Penny would not be there. It was the one place that she and I had shared completely alone. I had hardly been able to sleep since her death, and I believed that if I could slip under the covers of our bed tonight, I would sleep, and I would be safe.

As I pulled onto the highway, each mile brought a memory. By the time I reached the Champaign exit on I-57, about forty-five minutes from home, I wasn't sure I should be driving at all. I ached. I was nauseous. I was exhausted, and my mind was not on the wheel. Between the rain and my crying, it was hard to see. Champaign held so many memories for us, and as I drove, I kept reliving the hours we spent at Kanfer's art gallery and Pages For All Ages bookstore; walking the campus of the University of Illinois in the Fall; eating at the Mexican restaurant on First Street. My mind even replayed the long hours we spent at the school's veterinary hospital with Penny's sick cat. I remembered the many times early in our relationship when we opted to drive to Champaign to go grocery shopping so we could shop together, as opposed to shopping ten minutes from the house where we couldn't be seen together. As I drove, I wanted to speed past these memories.

When I hit the last stretch of the ride, each mile and minute felt like a battering ram to my heart. Struggling, I stuck my head out the window hoping to refresh my eyes. When that got too cold, I splashed water from my water bottle on my face. At the very end of the drive, I was alternating between singing to stay awake and praying out loud, *Lord let me arrive home safely.* I envisioned that I would get there and pretend that Penny was away campaigning. I would take a long hot shower, find her red scarf with the scent of Calyx perfume, and lie down and sleep. I couldn't think beyond that. I didn't care beyond that. I just wanted to be at home asleep in our bed.

As I neared the house, I started to feel better. I started to calm down. I could breathe. My stomach was unclenching. I finally pulled into our driveway that rainy Friday night, and I exhaled as though I had victoriously finished a race.

I had made it home.

I reached up to my visor and pushed the button on the gray garage door opener.

Nothing happened.

I pushed again.

Nothing. No noise of the door engaging, and no motion. Nothing.

It must be the battery, I thought. "Fuck," I exhaled in a tired, tight voice. "It figures."

I opened my car door and darted up the two steps to the side door. Cold rain pelted my back. I fumbled with the keys for a second and dropped them on the concrete step, my headlights only providing minimal light. I picked the keys up, fumbled again to find the right one, thrust the key into the lock, and turned it. Nothing.

I turned harder.

We never had trouble with this lock, I thought, as I gently tried to shimmy it and force the door open with my body.

I took the key out of the lock, pushed it back in, and turned it hard. Nothing again.

I pulled the key out and looked at it. Standing in the rain, I held the key up to darkness and strained to see if it was the right one. Then I bent over, eye level with the lock, and put the key in again. Again, the lock wouldn't budge.

I made fists with my hands, tilted my head to the side, and screamed through my clenched jaw, "AHHHH!" as I realized the lock had been changed.

My body seized. I couldn't breathe. I doubled over as though I had been hit in the stomach with a two-by-four, staggered backward, and stumbled off the bottom step. I remember putting my left hand on my left side and squeezing trying to squelch the physical pain. I walked to the mailbox about twenty-five feet away as if trying to walk it off, hands on my waist and gulping for air.

At the end of the driveway, I turned. Through a sheet of rain, I looked at the darkness of the house. I was locked out.

I knew Penny was not in the house. She was dead. But for me, she was in the house. She was in our bed waiting. I panicked. I felt as though I couldn't get to her. I thought about smashing a window. I heard myself scream in my head, but nothing came out. I collapsed on the curb. I put my hands on my head, grabbing the hair at my temples and pulling it, and I started wailing into the rain. I didn't recognize the sound coming from my own mouth. It was more yelp than yell.

I do not know how long I sat there. I remember shivering. I remember gulping for air. I remember my khaki pants and white shirt soaked through to my skin. I remember a neighbor trying to get me to go inside her home. I looked at my white Toyota Corolla and thought how far away it looked. I became very confused. My head hurt as though I were doing a complicated math problem.

Finally, a surge of energy hit me. "Call Patty, Terry," I said. She would flip when she realized that the locks were changed. I stood up and strode to the car, backed up the driveway, and whipped around the corner. I had given back the campaign cell phone and had not replaced it with a personal cell phone yet, so I sped to a payphone at a nearby school parking lot.

I punched her number, and Doug answered.

"Hi, Doug. Is Patty there?"

"No, she's not." He wasn't warm but he wasn't cold, and for a moment, I thought about how all of us were aching with Penny's death.

I had wanted to talk to Patty, not Doug. I didn't want to tell Doug that the locks had been changed because I thought he might call Patty and tell her too abruptly. I thought it better to break the news to her gently.

"You're not going to believe this," I said. " I just tried to get in the house and my key won't work. And the garage door won't work either. I'm not sure what's up."

"I know," he said.

"I can't figure out what's wrong with it," I continued, almost talking over him, not really absorbing what he had just said.

"What do you mean, you know?" I asked warily, coming to my senses.

"Patty's on her way there now," he repeated. "She should be there about ten thirty."

I hung up the phone and leaned against the metal box, confused.

I got in the car, turned up the heat, and drove back to the house. I fell asleep in the car listening to a sermon on CD, waiting for Patty to arrive.

I woke when I heard the garage door open and saw headlights.

Patty pulled her van into the garage, and I started my car and pulled in next to her. The garage door closed. I walked up the two steps from the garage into our small laundry room. Although soaked, I hugged her and then apologized for getting her wet. I was glad to see Patty, and yet it was hard to look at her—as Penny's identical twin, looking at her brought up images of Penny.

I wasn't sure how to broach the fact that the locks were changed, that I was convinced her father had done it, and that we were going to have to confront him.

"Wow, I'm soaked. Let me change," I said, walking away.

I walked across the kitchen and through the living room. I felt as though I were walking through an invisible force field that was slowing me down. I grabbed a pink towel from the linen closet, popped my barrette, and tried to towel dry my hair. I hung my shirt and bra over the shower door. I pulled out clothes from the walk-in closet that was literally shin-deep in neglected, crumpled laundry, and I changed. I figured I would take a shower later, once Patty had left and I was alone.

I walked back to the kitchen. Patty looked stricken. "How are you?" I asked.

"I'm okay," she said, and it was clear that she was not. Of course she was not okay. Her identical twin had just died. How *could* she be okay?

"Hey, I just talked to Doug. He said you were on your way down. Patty, my garage door opener wouldn't work, and neither would my key. Did your dad change the locks?" I asked gingerly.

"I'm glad you raised that, Terry."

Raised that? The phrase didn't even make sense.

"I had the locks changed like we talked about."

I had told her a few days before that I was thinking of changing the locks for two reasons. Penny's mother had always had a key to our home, and when she died, Penny had wanted Don to return the key but didn't know how to ask him. They had finally reached a détente in their troubled relationship, and instead of asking for the key's return, we decided the better option was to simply change the locks. But as with many things at that point in our lives, we didn't find the time to do it. Patty and I had talked about changing the locks after the purse incident. I wasn't asking her permission when I brought it up, I just wanted her to feel connected and part of this entire process because I felt as though we were in this aftermath together. I trusted her. If she had done something, anything, I believed it was in Penny's best interest, and so her changing the locks felt as though she had done something for me that I hadn't yet had a chance to do myself.

"Patty, I'm relieved," I exhaled and felt almost happy. "I thought your Dad changed them without telling us. Man, do I feel better. Wow."

I sat on one of the barstools that Penny and I decided to buy after months of searching stores in the United States and Mexico. Then I got up and walked to the sink for a glass of water.

I noticed that Patty seemed ill at ease, as though she wanted to say something more. She picked up my garage door opener off the counter.

"I'm going to change the code, and you should be able to get in an out of the garage," she said. I didn't even know garage door openers *had* a code.

"Thanks," I said still not comprehending what was happening.

"I think it's best for me to be the one who has the key," she said, looking at me. Her face looked pained, and she couldn't stop blinking.

It still didn't compute. "Your dad will probably be upset not having a key, but we can figure that out," I said, genuinely feeling that we would tackle this together, as the two of us had tackled so many things in the last several months, helping each other as we cared for Penny.

"Terry," she said calmly. She paused and winced. "He does have a key."

Then I realized I had been locked out of my own home. The person Penny and I had trusted most, that I had wanted to include in the aftermath of Penny's death, had changed the locks on my own home. I had been worried about the wrong person.

I couldn't speak. My sides ached, particularly my left side. I felt as though I had no air in my lungs. I stood there frozen. I couldn't protest. I couldn't fight. I couldn't say anything. I gulped my water, hoping to douse the imaginary reddish-yellow flames that were consuming my insides.

I felt as though I had split into two people, two Terrys: the lesbian Terry whose mate had just died and who was grieving deeply and needed help, and the press secretary and good friend Terry, who created a life of lies very carefully to keep her love and partnership a secret.

Both Terrys remembered something Patty had said to me just a few weeks before, on February 20, a few hours before Penny died. "I just want you to know, Terry, that I consider this your house as much as Penny's."

"Thank you, Patty," I had said, hugging her and feeling in my heart that she really understood how much I loved her sister and that we were mates.

But now that Penny was dead, Patty apparently had changed her mind about that sentiment. Patty had a key. Don had a key. I did not.

An invisible prison appeared around me. I instinctively knew, standing at my own kitchen counter, that one of the two Terrys would be imprisoned. The person closest to Penny and me, and to our love, chose to address and acknowledge only good friend Terry. She was going to let her sister's partner and the truth die with her sister. When she changed the locks to the house, Patty led both Terrys to the door of that invisible prison and waited to see which one would speak.

In grief, confusion, loyalty, and perhaps the retriggered trauma of my youth, Penny's partner Terry didn't protest. She walked into the silent vault that she and Penny had laid, brick by brick, and lie by lie.

I relinquished the key of my truth.

While Penny's partner—the imprisoned, lesbian Terry—stayed silent, press secretary and good friend Terry tried to organize and separate the things in the house that were solely mine. Unable to put these things in a moving truck that night, the plan was for me to return the following weekend. As I wandered through my home, dazed and traumatized at having been locked out, I wanted to be alone, away from Patty. I went to the guestroom, where I had kept my law books. I was sitting on the floor going through them, and she came in.

"Terry, I found the suitcase," she said as though I had hidden a bomb. "The one where you had put Penny's writing and a letter from Michael," she said. I immediately felt shame and a terrible piercing pain in my stomach. My instinct was to lie.

"I know you did it, Terry, because the red and white shirt that you told me about from the first time you . . ." she stumbled over her own words. I think she was going to say, "went on a date." She continued, "The first time you and Penny had fun together. So I know you packed it."

"You went through my things?" I said.

"Dad was here, and he didn't know whose it was," she replied.

A flash of anger came through me. "Why was he here, anyway?" I said, hotly. "You know Penny couldn't stand him."

"He was helping me," she said. She went on, "Terry, I have a question. The letter from Michael, talking about Penny's anger, why would you take that?" she asked.

I didn't want to explain to her that history. I didn't want to explain that Penny had shown it to me as we were talking about Michael Venutto, her ex-fiancé. I didn't want to explain that Penny had told me that after they broke up, she wasn't over him. That after they lost touch, she used to fly into airports and would look at phone books hoping to find out where Michael was. I didn't want to explain to Patty that she told me how the relationship started and why it ended. I didn't want to explain that about three weeks into my relationship with Penny, she had a meeting in Chicago but flew home early on the state plane so we could rendezvous at home that night, and that was when Penny told me of her phone book habit. She said to me that she realized that if she ran into Michael now that we were dating, she would simply say to him, "Nice to see you, Michael, but I have to be going, I have to get home." I didn't want to explain to Patty that Penny's revelation started a discussion about Venutto, and I had asked her what he was like, and Penny had dug out the letter and showed me. "This is what he was like. Kind of an ass," Penny said, and we mockingly edited his letter, laughing very hard.

"Terry," Penny had said to me that day. "I don't care about anybody else any more. I finally have found home."

I didn't want to explain any of it. I wanted to cherish that moment between Penny and me alone.

"We had an old joke about it, Patty," I said flatly.

"A joke?" she pressed. "What kind of joke could you have about a letter like this? You know what I thought, Terry?" she said, answering her own question. "I worried that you were going to write a book about Penny. That's what I thought. And this would be terrible."

I was weeping at this point.

"I guess you're not the Terry we thought," Patty said.

I wanted to flee. I didn't care about anything anymore. What happened that night was similar to the aftermath of being sexually abused: You are blamed; the abuser explains how you are in the wrong or deserved whatever action just happened. I took an old love letter of my spouse's, and somehow that was proof that I was a bad person. Years later, Jane told me that Patty had told the family that "Terry's not the person we thought she was" and that she cited the fact that I had bought newspapers and paid my work cell phone with campaign checks. I figured she must have told my fellow staffers as well. In that moment on the floor in the guest bedroom, I knew I was trapped because I knew I would not be able to claim my lesbianism or my relationship with Penny. I couldn't speak, much like I couldn't speak as a child. My loyalty to Penny and my own homophobia, coupled with an avalanche of new grief, simply would not let me do anything else. I got up and walked into my bedroom and lay down on the bed, ignoring her.

Patty left Saturday afternoon, and I made no headway packing. Instead, I walked around weeping. I felt anger and shame that I could not walk in and out of my own front door. Access to my own home was limited to a side door through the garage. A few hours later, Patty called my cell phone. She and Doug had noticed that some of the art in the house had certifications of authentication but some pieces did not. "Do you know where they are?" she asked demandingly. I was sitting at our desk in the den. I was disgusted. I was angry. And still, I was unable to speak my mind. "You're the executor. Why don't you call the galleries and ask them for a printout of what we bought?" I hung up.

Rod and Jane, knowing I was back in town that weekend, suggested that we have dinner. They brought a homemade meal over that Saturday night. I didn't know how I was going to explain what had just happened. When they arrived, I rushed outside to open the garage door, knowing that I could not open the deadbolt doors to the house to let them in. They walked through the garage, and Rod asked, "Why didn't you just open the door?"

I chose not to tell him the truth. I didn't want to cause family strife, and I was still feeling gun-shy about who to trust. In retrospect, all these years later, had I told Rod, I believe he would have intervened and that the crazy tormenting that was to come may have been less tangled. When they left, the trunk of my car was up, and Jane noticed the stack of newspapers I had bought for Penny, and I gave them a few.

After they had gone, I became terribly sad. I wanted to tell them the truth, but I wasn't sure of anything anymore. Patty didn't seem to trust them, and I didn't know them that well. And yet, they seemed genuine and kind in their care of me. They always asked if they could be helpful. I didn't understand how they, not knowing me, could be so generous and how Patty, who knew me well, barely asked me how I was doing. In fact, she never once, even to this day, said she was sorry for my loss of Penny. Rod and Jane couldn't stop telling me. I wanted to tell them the truth, but I was confused and scared.

The next weekend, I rented a U-haul to retrieve my things. When I arrived, Patty and Doug were already there, hovering. I spent forty-eight hours packing items under their watchful eyes, but I got away with a few things that were Penny's—a few of her scarves, some pictures, towels, dishes, and a yard tool that Penny loved that Patty believed belonged to the good friend Terry. Both Terrys walked away from everything else: the hundreds of books; our Chagall's, our Rafaelli's, our Kanfer's; our silverware; our Mikasa china; Penny's jewelry; our towels. I walked away from every item within our home. Grieving. No protest. No voice. Dazed. Lesbian Terry paced the prison floor, looking for Penny, wanting to die and to search the afterlife for her.

Doug and Patty helped me pack and load the truck. Penny and I had built a life together, paid for it together, and the airless prison of lies that we created would now suffocate me; I would die with no witnesses to the truth.

On Sunday morning, having been awake for the better part of seventy-two hours, I stood on the driveway of my home. Patty and Doug stood with their arms around each other's waist. "I don't ever want to be here again," I said more to myself than to Patty.

Patty handed me $250. I felt as though I was going to throw up, but even then, I could feel a low-grade boil of anger within me. That anger could have saved me, but it was too distant to tap into. If I could have said something, anything, Patty's fear of her sister's reputation being ruined would have enabled me to stay in my home. But I could not speak for myself, let alone for Penny.

Good friend, press secretary Terry accepted the mostly $20 bills as Patty said, "We want to give you this to help with the move back to law school. Love you." They waved. I put the U-haul in reverse. Lesbian Terry, Penny's partner Terry, sat down on the prison bed and wept bitterly as she watched good friend Terry drive away.

CHAPTER TWENTY-SIX

"NO HOMELESS HERE"

I was an empty shell of myself. Anytime anyone tried to speak to me kindly about Penny, I pushed them away—sometimes harshly. I was drinking heavily and unable to concentrate. Things I liked to do were so inextricably linked with Penny now, and I couldn't bring myself to engage. It was too painful to read newspapers, let alone a stack of them on Sundays. Discussing politics was out of the question, and even walking down Michigan Avenue brought more pain than peaceful distraction. Several lawmakers, presuming that Penny was only my boss, called and asked if I wanted to come work for their campaigns, as if they were doing a favor for Penny by picking up one of her staffers. *If they only knew the truth, they wouldn't ask me*, I thought.

In late March, I started to write again in the Italian journal Penny got me for Christmas. Looking back, I don't even recognize my handwriting. Grief was present everywhere. Carmel Settles had stayed in touch with me and would pass along notes that came to me at the office. One day, she left me a message saying that somebody from hospice was trying to reach me. There was going to be a service for caregivers of hospice patients who had died the previous month. I decided to attend.

When the speaker said it's important that the primary caregiver be acknowledged, I started to feel soothed, perhaps because I was in need of that recognition. The speaker then said, "When we call the name of your loved one, would the primary caregiver please come forward to be recognized."

"Penny Severns," she said.

Crying, I stood up from the pew. But Penny's father was in front of me, and he strode to the podium. I felt angry and sick, and at the same time, I felt sorry for him. They handed him a plant. I looked over at Patty in anger and motioned my head for at least her to go forward. She quietly shook her head, which I took to mean, "don't do anything."

My feelings were so raw, my anger so high, the secrecy so toxic, that I simply got up and left. I later learned that Rod and Don Jr. were not even aware of the memorial event.

I returned to Chicago, and my anger and sadness collided daily.

Weeks went by. The pain was not subsiding in any way. One day in the spring, one of my first-year professors asked me to stop by his office. He was thinking about throwing his hat into the ring for a Chicago City Council seat. Would I help him? I impolitely told him I didn't work in politics anymore. A law school professor asking me about politics seemed too close to home. I wanted to separate myself from politics. If I would have quieted myself and listened to that small voice, I may have chosen different, healthy ways to handle the pain and confusion of death, even of having a closeted lover. Instead, I chose the familiar elixir that brought so much havoc to my young life, the elixir that brought violence and pain and left no room for comfort: alcohol.

I strode to a nearby bar to drink; my anger was rising to the surface like mercury in a thermometer. I started drinking fast and hard. Finally, I was so drunk the bartender wouldn't serve me another, and I took the train to a bar I discovered on Western Avenue, about twenty minutes away. The bar was called Spynners and was owned by a lesbian named Maureen Sullivan, who on a few occasions let me bartend very late at night, which really meant drinking for free in the early-morning hours before closing.

I had found this bar by accident a few weeks before. I hated the place, really. It represented everything my life with Penny wasn't. It was dingy, with worn-out barstools. Walking into that dark place, I felt a slow burn inside me, the same burn that whiskey produced when it exploded in my chest. I wanted to burn the memories of the fine restaurants, fine wine, first-class travel, and love. Class and comfort hurt too much. I needed grit, and this place surely had it. I needed everything that was opposite of my life as I had known it with Penny. Maureen, who people called Mo, was a sharp businesswoman with a common touch. I enjoyed the darkness and dark wood of the bar. I also enjoyed spying the life of working-class lesbians from a distance. I went there frequently, and Mo and I developed something of a friendship. I found that in bars, where many people lie, I could tell the truth about my life, perhaps because I was sure that people either would think I was lying or would be so drunk they would forget my story. Then again, who would make up a love story with such a terrible ending?

I don't clearly remember leaving Spynners that night. But I awoke with a pounding headache and cold, dirty tile against my right cheek. I didn't move until I was sure where I was and that I wasn't going to throw up again. I lifted my head off of the tile, the imprint of the grout paths grooved in my splotchy reddened face. The hallway swirled. My back hurt. A pool of chunky vomit lay on the floor in front of me. I angled up and put my back against the wall. I vaguely remembered leaving the bar and walking to the apartment of my colleague's. I guessed that's where I was, although I wasn't entirely sure. I knocked, or rather, I let my hand fall against the door. No answer. I reached into my jacket pocket and had no wallet, no keys. I looked around. I remember saying, "I am sorry, Lord."

I managed to stand up. I stepped outside. The air was cold. I realized I didn't have my overcoat. I tried to hurry to Lawrence or Western Avenue to find a phone but couldn't hurry because my muscles ached and moving too fast made me nauseous. It was 6:00 or 6:30 AM. I walked across the frosted grass of Goss Park, the frozen dew reminded me how thirsty I was. I swallowed what felt like paste. I saw a bakery with a pink neon sign that read, "Open," I asked to use the phone. A short Asian woman came around the counter quickly and started to shoo me away with both hands. "No homeless. No homeless here," she said.

I didn't have the energy to protest or explain.

"You leave."

I *was* homeless, in a way. I started to walk toward the El Train. Maybe I could sneak on a train and get home. Or, maybe I could explain my situation to the transit cop. Instead, I spotted a pay phone. I leaned my forehead against the top of the box. I put my hands on the cold metal sides and then put my cold fingers on my eyes and cheeks to sooth the burn. I collect-called my friend Ed Kennedy, who lived nearby, and told him I needed a ride. Then, I stood there waiting. Alcohol hadn't numbed the emotional pain, but maybe the Chicago weather would. When I got in the car, he started laughing. "Wow," he said in disbelief. "All you need, my friend, is a shopping cart."

We drove to Spynners, and Ed and I walked to the back door. Mo was doing the early-morning cleanup. The smell of stale beer made me sicker. I staggered back, and Ed went in and retrieved my coat. Maureen handed him my keys and wallet. "I don't know what happened," she told him. "I turned around, and she was gone without her coat, keys, or wallet. Is she okay?"

I didn't hear his reply.

He drove me home. I didn't say much, and he didn't either.

"You going to class?" he asked as I pulled in front of my building. "I could wait for you and we could go together."

"What do you think?" I said sarcastically, looking down at my disheveled self and shutting the car door.

He rolled down the window. "Hey, Mutch," he called after me. "People usually crack up in the first year of law school, not the third. What's going on?"

I kept walking.

"Okay, see you later," he said.

I walked up the few steps into the well-groomed and beautifully landscaped courtyard. The property and apartments were advertised as Frank Lloyd Wright–inspired living. Prairie-style lights adorned the building. A fountain sat centered in the walkway with four massive ceramic planters filled with prairie grasses at each corner. An oversized blonde wooden archway with windows welcomed visitors, and a gas fireplace warmed the foyer-lobby that was filled with art and prairie-styled furniture.

My head was swimming with memories and pain, mostly shame at how far I had fallen. I didn't know what to do. I didn't know how to move forward. I didn't believe that I had anyone to talk to. Asking for help growing up was never easy; my family saw it as a sign of weakness or failure. And how could I disclose my relationship with Penny? I walked into the house and dropped my coat on the floor. I walked into the bathroom. I looked at the long counter next to the sink, and I started to cry. I used to sit on this long counter and talk with Penny while we were getting ready for bed or getting ready to go out. If I could just dial time back for a moment and have her here, talk to her, I could get my bearings. I ached to have one more word. I looked at my vomit-stained shirt. I kept staring at it, and I realized that I hadn't really looked at myself since Penny died. Finally, I summoned the bravery to look at my whole self in the mirror. I started to cry again. My eyes were bloodshot and swollen. There hadn't been many days that I'd been sober in weeks; most days, I was full-blown drunk. I was gaining weight fast. My long hair was unkempt. I smelled. I really did look homeless. For the first time in my life, I understood how people crack up. I looked long and hard at the person I had become in the two months since Penny's death. I realized I had actually worn this very outfit to give a speech for Penny when she was too sick to address the Independent Voters of Illinois, and had won the endorsement.

The charcoal gray pants had been dragging the ground and there were holes in the hem. The white shirt was wrinkled and stained, the cuffs frayed and gray. The shirt and pants were ruined even before the night began, and yet I insisted on wearing them. Those clothes were a time machine to happiness.

The fog of drunk moved back, and a moment of clarity moved in.

What am I doing? Who am I becoming?

Thoughts of Penny's grace and beauty flooded me, followed by painful thoughts of how disgraceful and sick looking I was at this moment. I was becoming someone else. I wondered how Penny would have handled my death had I died, and I was convinced that she would do it with dignity and grace. I wondered how I could be letting her down so badly. I wondered why I couldn't simply speak to Patty about what was happening—about why she wanted to shut me out. I had spoken for Penny before she died. Why couldn't I do that now? My mind replayed so many things—Penny's words in bed the night we knew the cancer had returned: *I love how you make me feel.*

And that memory made me think of a time when she was in the thick of a troubling campaign issue and was looking for a solution, and we had found one together. She had said to me: "You always know what to do. I love your strength."

Strength? Always know what to do? I had a vomit-stained white shirt, ripped pants, and no idea what was going on in law school; I was trapped in the lie of our life. I was held hostage in a dank basement of secrecy, and I knew that no one was coming to rescue me. Even the people closest to me had no idea why I was falling apart. Then another thought stung me: if Penny saw me now, in this moment, she would never fall in love with me. I started to cry harder. Although I couldn't see it clearly, I knew I had to find the Terry that Penny had fallen in love with. The Terry that I had abandoned when Patty changed the locks. Deeper, I had to find the Terry that had abandoned herself when she agreed to live a secret life. Deeper still, I knew I had to find the Terry that entered a life of silence after being sexually abused as a child. I knew that Terry was the strong one. The real Terry. I knew she lived in the basement of my soul; I could feel her pacing, and I was the only one who could free her. But how? How could I sew these realities together? The instant I thought about speaking the truth to anyone, my soul felt like it was collapsing, like an unshored construction hole. And I never slowed down enough to see my way through to the truth.

I thought of my faith. But how could I ask God for help? All of this was my fault because I disobeyed all that I had been taught, plus, I had gone back on my deal, hadn't I? I thought of the story of the prodigal son who, standing in a pit of mud, realized he didn't have to live this way and could find his way home, even if it was not to be an heir but a servant. I had to find home. I had to find me.

First things first.

I had to sober up. I knew it. Yes. That was it. I would take a shower, clean the house, and eat a homemade meal. I would open the law books. I would find that Terry where Penny had left her: studying to become a lawyer. A beam of hope seemed to pierce my drunken self. With my political instincts, I knew I had the makings of a plan: become sober, and each step beyond that would be clear.

I threw the shirt in the garbage, not even wanting to try and clean it. I threw up again. Clouds of confusion swept back in, blotting the pockets of clarity. I decided, perhaps as all drunks do, that I was never going to drink again. I stripped, took a shower, and stood there washing my hair for a long time. I decided to use the shampoo that Penny liked. I didn't really like it myself. It had a scent of pine needles. But now, because it was hers, I used it as sparingly as holy water. That, and her Borghese creams. I wanted to always have something of hers, something left unused, something more. But this was the start of something new, and I needed to mark it. Using something that she had loved was a good way to begin, I thought.

I was hopeful. The imprisoned Terry finally calmed down, stopped pacing, and waited for me to free her. Now we had a plan. She had a way out. She too could rest. For the first time in weeks, it felt like the inner Terry, the lesbian Terry, was going to lie down on the prison bed and sleep. As I put cream on my face and elbows, I gave the imprisoned Terry false hope that I was finally going to pay attention to her and value her. I felt a small sense of normalcy.

I called Rod and Jane and talked with Jane for a few minutes. I completely ignored the truth of what had happened the night before, what was happening now, and where I was. I was doing fine, I told them. They seemed relieved. I lay in my bed trying to remember how I ended up so drunk. I always had the energy to tease apart whatever horrific thing happened, but I had no energy to focus on the core issues of secrecy, truth, and freeing myself. I wasn't out in any aspect of my life.

Still drunk and now woozy from crying so hard, I pulled out the Ziploc bag that held strands of Penny's black hair, worried that I was "mentally ill." I held them to me, hoping for a scent of her, though only the plastic aroma was present. I didn't care. I had her hair. It was part of her, and part of her was enough. I closed my eyes and held her hair in my hand. I laid the black locks on the pillow and went to sleep.

I dreamed that I was standing on the top of a sand-colored train trestle several hundred feet in the air. The bridge had elaborate carvings and arches. I could see the expanse of train tracks for miles in each direction, with golden and rust-colored wheat blowing gently east and west, inviting ease. But I was not facing either direction; instead, I was standing on the edge of the trestle, looking down. Below was a river. The whitewater was churning. I looked east, and I saw a train coming toward me. I looked west and saw a second a train. The locomotives were headed toward each other at great speed. I saw Penny in the window of the train heading west, pounding on the glass with the flat of her palm. She was wearing the red-striped shirt. She was screaming for me to help her. She was screaming my name. Her voice was muffled behind the glass, but I could see her lips move in slow motion: TEERRYYYYY. I saw the trains were on the same track. I started to shake. My knees were buckling. I knew I could not save her, but I jumped from the trestle to try. I screamed her name as I fell. I remember feeling the sensation of my shirt lifting up, exposing my belly and covering my face so I could not see her. Before I hit the river, I awoke. I was in my bed, shaking and screaming her name. I got up and sat on the edge of the bed. It was 11:00 AM. I could no longer stand to be with myself. The inner Terry was telling me she was with me and that it was okay. It was just a dream. I needed to be as far away from the inner Terry as possible. I hated that Terry. If I could have killed her and lived, I would have.

I was sobering up. I had to run. I had to get out. I couldn't stay here in this apartment. I didn't have the energy to clean, the clarity to study, or the desire to cook a meal.

I decided, though, that a little food would be good. I drove to Poor Phil's in Oak Park, a few blocks from my house. The Terry who thought I was coming to help her escape the prison basement started talking to me: *Why don't you just order something and have it delivered? Why don't you sit down on the couch where you and Penny have lain? Why don't you try and sleep a little more? Put on a tape-recorded sermon. Remember, He is a very present help in times of danger.* I remembered as a child being ridiculed for crying and being told to "get over it." To accept inner Terry's kindness was equivalent to being a wimp. I was having none of her nonsense. She tried one more time: *Why go to a bar? You can get food where there is no alcohol.*

I stepped outside, and the sunshine felt good. But the emotional pain was bearing down again, perhaps somewhat like birth pangs. My body felt a little better, but the pain of Penny's death was chasing me hard, convulsing me. *Just get some food in you, Terry. Anything but alcohol.* I parked further away from the bar so I wouldn't have to worry about feeding the parking meters. Despite my own protestations, I knew I was going to be there a while. I walked in and slid onto a barstool. The bartender gave me a menu and a beer list. I thought, *I'm not going to drink. I'm just going look at the names of the beer.*

My mind flashed with memories of Penny and me and a group of friends being in the back of this bar. My eyes landed on a beer called John Courage. I ordered one solely for the name, and I ordered a Scotch. "You want both?" the bartender asked, his eyebrows up.

"Yes."

Food would slow down the speed at which I could get drunk, which would bring momentary relief with no pain for a second. I started drinking and kept drinking. I knew I would be standing in front of the mirror again at some point, but for now, I didn't care.

Tomorrow, I would never drink again. *Tomorrow,* I would study again. *Tomorrow,* I would clean my house. *Tomorrow,* I would cook again. *Tomorrow,* Penny would be alive again.

But every tomorrow looked much like the day that preceded it: steady pain. I couldn't sleep; memories tortured me. I couldn't focus on work or anything else. I longed to be back in my home, at least to be around things that were familiar to me.

I was aching for Penny and any semblance of the life we had. Kristin's birthday was coming up. I had sent her one of the most expensive hand-blown glass paperweights that Penny and I had bought. Granted, a $500 glass paperweight was perhaps not an appropriate gift for a young teen, but I had done it because it was something that Penny and I had enjoyed together, and I wanted Kristin to have it. Patty called me to thank me, but her voice was tentative and I knew there was more to come. She said, "You know, if you want to send a card, that's fine, but you shouldn't send gifts." I didn't give the remark much thought until a few months later—I was just happy to have shared something of ours with Kristin. The call depressed me. I both longed and hated to interact with Patty.

Again, depressed and grieving, I was falling behind at school. Mail was piling up, and I had not responded to an invitation to attend a moot court banquet, an end-of-the-year celebration for moot court staffers or, in my case, students lucky enough to have participated on the national teams. The last thing I wanted to do was go to a social event with my colleagues, as I knew that I would inevitably end up drunk, crying, and not able to tell them what I was crying about. But a law school pal, Klint Bruno, really wanted me to go to the banquet with him.

When I arrived at the banquet, my heart was pounding fast and it hurt; my hands were sweating and I didn't know why. I couldn't catch my breath. So many times since Penny's death, I felt like a foreign creature to myself. This "creature" was really just the lesbian Terry that good friend Terry self-banished to an inner secret prison. Scared and panicked, I would often ask myself, *What is* happening *to me?* The thought of walking into a crowd of people—mingling, shaking hands—petrified me. That fear was so out of character for me. I love crowds and talking—the energy and excitement in meeting new people and shaking their hands, saying hello, is a rush. I relished the scores of times I campaigned with Penny, or for Penny, and, when she was sick, standing in for her at critical debates between the other candidates for secretary of state.

But this day, I felt clumsy, sick, and tired. The inner Terry, the lesbian Terry, was awake; she was panicked and shaking the bars of the prison cell I put her in, begging for me to let her out, at least to hear her. The inner Terry was aware of the fact that I would be "campaigning"— meeting, talking, and laughing—without Penny. The outer Terry didn't understand what was happening and was confused, tired, and lonely. I stood outside of the restaurant for quite a while, bent over and trying to catch my breath. When the first swarm of law school chums emerged from a cab, I rode the wave of their energy through the doors and made my way to the open bar.

That night, I happened to be seated with one of my first-year professors, George Trubow, and his wife. We laughed hard and drank hard. He was taken aback at my blunt, sailor-like language when we discussed politics.

Trubow's wife had heard of Penny, and so talk inevitably turned to her and her recent death and who would win the secretary of state's race. We talked of Penny "my boss," politics, and my work as a reporter. And each word that came out of my mouth—chosen carefully by good friend, press secretary Terry—was matched by the inner Terry's silent screaming: *We were lovers; I was locked out of our home; I am locked into this secret: LET ME OUT.*

"She was really a beautiful woman," Mrs. Trubow said. "How tragic that she died at forty-six, with so much more to give."

"Yes, and she would have been the first female governor of the state," I heard myself say as though I were working a room.

At that moment, the inner Terry started crying; she sat back down in her prison cell and said to herself: *You can't imagine how lovely she really was, how much we loved each other, how much I ache for her, and how lost I am without her.* I felt as though my spoken words were time-delayed before they came out my mouth. I felt as though I was translating the foreign language of grief in my head: I was thinking grief, speaking lies, and voicing campaign pitches. Drinking, I refused to watch my true life on the screen that no one but inner Terry saw.

Trubow said he had been in national politics previously, and mercifully, the conversation shifted. He had worked at the White House for the Ford and Carter Administrations on privacy issues. He reminded me that he had the opportunity to pick one student each year to serve as a law clerk in the White House.

I thought he was kidding, and the more I sipped the Scotch, the more my heart churned. How odd to be thinking of politics—and the pinnacle of the White House—without Penny. She would have loved the thought of me working there and being in D.C. But even thinking about it felt like a betrayal to me.

"The job starts next month, and the school pays a living stipend. Two thousand at the beginning of the summer. Two thousand at the end. One thing though," he said of my neon language. "You might not want to sound like a Teamster at the White House."

"Fuck yeah, I can do that, George," I said purposely trying to irritate him. Inside, the inner Terry lowered her head embarrassed. She knew that parole was not in sight.

I drank heavily that night, as I did any time I could get my hands on something to drown the ache. I put the White House out of my head. Many people wanted to talk to me about Penny, and when I got home, I felt like I was dying. I didn't get out of bed on Sunday. On Monday, I stayed in bed again. Trubow's secretary, Gwen, asked if I had sent my résumé. I truly had thought Trubow's invitation was a product of happy hour. I dragged myself out of bed, printed my résumé, and stepped across the hall to ask the Apartment Rental Office if I could use their fax.

Within two hours, I had myself a shiny clerkship in the Executive Office of the Clinton White House in the Office of Management and Budget, working on privacy issues for Y2K Chief John Koskinen.

CHAPTER TWENTY-SEVEN

"I COULD DIG A DITCH"

That summer, the summer of Monica Lewinsky, I served as a law clerk at the White House, working on privacy issues. Just months after Penny's death, I was still a mess in every way. Though I was making my way through law school and doing fairly well in the clerkship, I was physically and emotionally spent from grief.

It would take me hours to get up in the morning and often I was late to work, which was not acceptable when you are a clerk at the White House. I didn't want to lose the benefits of this career opportunity on top of everything else, but I struggled at every turn, often hiding in the library of the Old Executive Office Building, writing love letters and laments to Penny in my journal. I missed her so much. I had no idea whether I would finish law school. And except for the law school stipend, I was flat broke.

When I returned to Chicago that August, I was more exhausted than when I had left for Washington, D.C. Law school had started again, and I could not concentrate no matter how hard I tried to keep up with my heavy reading assignments. Penny's loss filled me. I was a shell of myself, and at about $30,000 a year for tuition and living, I felt as though I was wasting my life and my money. I decided to quit. I hadn't thought out a clear plan. Perhaps I would get enough money together to fly overseas and pick up stringing work for the AP, or maybe I'd just go home to Pennsylvania and live with my parents until I could heal. I had drafted a short three-sentence letter to the dean, saying I was withdrawing from school, no explanation. I laid the letter on the table and then lay down on my couch to take a nap. I would deliver it tomorrow and see if I could get a refund on my tuition. I would stay in my apartment for another month and decide what to do. As I lay on the couch pondering these options, the phone rang. Klint, my law school pal who subletted my apartment the summer I was at the White House, asked me if I wanted to go to dinner.

Outwardly, Klint and I were hardly the type to be pals. He was straight, twenty-three years old, the quarterback and captain of his high school football team, and had women falling over him at every turn. I'm not even sure how we became friends other than the fact that he and I disdained the professorial bullying that often accompanies the Socratic method and we were fearless in saying so. I don't remember the moment we met, but I also don't remember law school without him. It seemed he was always there with me, plowing through, laughing, talking, and plotting—politics, law, and women.

He lived a few blocks from me in Oak Park, and we would have dinner together or drinks on occasion. Our friendship deepened several months before Penny had died at a moot court competition in Indianapolis. We laughed and learned about each other; we shared soul-blushing moments of our inner lives. We connected in a way that can only happen outside of a daily routine. At a bar, we devised and refined card games and magic tricks shamelessly created for the sole purpose of him picking up women. My friendship with him felt like we were trapeze artists, on the inside of a secret together with seamless trust.

Yet, in all those moments, I never disclosed that I was a lesbian, or that Penny and I were lovers. Klint knew I was Penny's spokeswoman but nothing personal. When Penny died in February, I remember him telling me he was sorry, and I remember him being with me at school.

When he called that August evening, I told him I wasn't really hungry but that I would be happy to have a drink. We went to a bar and I didn't waste any time ordering a Scotch and soda. He ordered a Coke. He sipped quietly. Unable to contain my truth any more, I finally told him how Penny and I were lovers, and I shared the story of what happened—and what was still happening—in the aftermath of her death.

The drunker I got, the steadier Klint became. Yet no matter how much

I drank, I couldn't drive this pain from my head and heart. Tipping my fourth Scotch, I told him I was quitting law school the next day. He asked me what I planned to do.

"I don't know. I just can't make it through another day," I said.

Pain eclipsed clear thought. I wasn't absorbing the law school material; I really didn't care about anything but that my sweetheart had died. Usually in the last semester of third year, you are cruising along. But I was drowning, and quitting seemed the only escape. The evening had become very, very serious. Finally, I was speaking truth, which brought its own measure of relief. And Klint listened as though life and death were in the balance. While Klint and I were always "real" with each other, neither of us had ever dealt with issues this deep or devastating.

When the rush of truth had slowed, Klint and I just sat there on the ripped burgundy barstools alongside the mostly bearded, leather-clad patrons who were drinking harder than I was. There was nothing more to say. I had just spoken the truth that my life was shattered and that I couldn't make it another day. Both Terrys faced each other, and for the first time, the good friend Terry acknowledged the true Terry inside.

"Terry," Klint said, as if a plan had just dawned on him. "We only have about ten weeks left." I couldn't fathom living through that night, let alone the next seventy days.

"I could dig a ditch with my dick to Springfield in ten weeks. You can do this. You can't just throw this all away."

A stunned pause. That was quite an image. We both started laughing. Hysterically. Sustained laughter that slid down the bar like a spilled drink, with the other hard-drinking patrons smiling in confusion as if to say, *What? What's so funny?*

In that moment, the night's tale seemed to retract in the wind, safe in the telling. I felt better in my heart, even though I was beyond drunk. Somehow, Klint Bruno had created the space for one more day. He dropped me off that night, and inside my apartment, I opened the bottle of Scotch that Penny had given me six years before, and I gingerly poured 1/8 an inch. I wanted to be near a gift that she had given me. I wanted her whiskey tonight. I lay on the couch in my clothes watching the antique regulator clock on the wall that Penny and I bought at an Oak Park store. My body was still, but my mind walked the streets of our life, leaning against the burned-out streetlights of our romance, looking for her. The last time I looked at the numbers, the clock read 5:00 AM.

I tossed and turned on the couch and woke four hours later. I stumbled into the kitchen. I was shaking. I opened the refrigerator and saw a white Styrofoam box of leftover spaghetti from a few days ago. I reached in and grabbed one of the three Rolling Rock beers on the shelf and tried to twist off the lid. I felt scared—not because I was drinking at 9:00 AM, but because I didn't have the energy to turn the twist-off lid. I rooted around the drawer and found a can opener and opened the green bottle, then set it next to the stove. I opened the three-day old spaghetti, put it in a pan, and turned on the burner. I figured it would either warm or burn, and I didn't care which. I stood there watching it, sipping the beer.

The phone rang. It was Klint, reluctantly I let him in.

I was standing at the stove stirring the red mess in the pan. "Ter, what are you doing?" he asked gently.

With tears in my eyes, and still shaking, I said, "Making breakfast."

He walked to the stove and turned off the burner and set the beer bottle in the sink full of dishes.

"Get changed," he said firmly, more stern than I was used to from him. "We're going to breakfast."

I said no. He strode into my bedroom and past the stacks of boxes—all that was left of my life with Penny—and the clothes and papers strewn atop. He grabbed a clean white shirt and a pair of jeans.

"Here," he said, with an unspoken, *If you don't, I will.*

I laughed at the thought of Klint trying to dress me, and I got ready. We drove to the Cozy Corner at the corner of Lake Street and Miriam.

"I don't have any money," I said meekly, feeling as though my stomach were caving in at the admission that I was truly broke. When I had received my stipend at the end of the summer, I paid my bills and, of course, drank.

"Don't worry about it," he said.

He parked and pushed quarters into the meter. We picked a corner booth, and I was sick to my stomach. A combination of grief, alcohol, fear, and embarrassment. He ordered a cheese omelet, toast, and potatoes. I followed suit, gulping the black coffee. We talked, or rather he did. He sat there, knowing the truth, but not saying anything about it—just offering the simple comfort of being near. I felt my stomach constrict when he picked up the check. We walked to his car, hopped on I-290, and headed downtown.

For the next ten weeks, Klint was faithful to that same morning routine: phone call, pickup, breakfast, and I-290 to school. Often in the afternoons, he would come by my house. I would make him tea, and he would study and try to get me to study. Usually, I would lay on the couch and fall asleep.

As the semester wore on, with tired nights and the craziness that accompanies even the most normal law school year, whenever I would want to quit, or whenever some memory hit me, Klint would say, "Ya know, I could dig a ditch . . ." Never any more than just, "I could dig a ditch . . ."

When I was submerged in grief alone, I began to say to myself, *Yeah, yeah, I know, you could dig a ditch.* The memory and the laughter would ease that moment's pain, and I could get through to face the next moment. But the next moments of pain were never too far away.

Sharing my truth with Klint gave me the energy to stay in law school and the courage to come out to people more regularly. It was certainly not a widespread disclosure, but I did come out to professors, fellow students, and more and more friends. In retrospect, it wasn't so much that I was coming out in celebration of my sexuality. I came out more and more because I could no longer handle the grief of my partner's death. In order to share the pain of Penny's death with people, I had to disclose that I was a lesbian. It seemed grief was a primary catalyst to my coming out, and being a lesbian was secondary to that grief.

I began to worry about what would come next in my life. I knew I would have to find work when I graduated. I had decided that I would apply to ten places, and that if I didn't get a job in the first round, I would try and find a way to stay one more month in my apartment and sleep. I felt tired even tying my shoes, and my terrible eating and drinking habits didn't help.

When the Christmas season began, I was terribly sad. Just a year before, Penny and I had traipsed around the city and had dinner at Gibsons. Yes, she had been sick, but we were together. Wanting to flee Illinois, I applied to firms in Louisville, Kentucky to be near my family. All said no. On the advice of a professor who said I had a gift, I applied to the Cook County

State's Attorneys Office. On a whim, I applied for a clerkship at the Illinois Supreme Court touting my writing and my work for Penny. I had an interview that went well, but months later I had no answer.

I was walking down Dearborn Avenue and became desperate that I did not have a job, and I began to pray. *Lord, I have no options. I am desperate. I feel like I am going to die. Please Lord, help me.* Klint called me later that night, and said he would pick me up in the morning to study for our last final. "We can go to Caribou and get some coffee and flirt with the med students."

We went to Caribou Coffee and sat near the fireplace. Two young women walked in and opened their medical books at a table next to us. Klint lifted his eyebrows at me and smiled.

We studied together for the rest of the week, which ended with an exciting call two hours before my last Sales final, on which unbelievably I scored an A.

"Terry, this is Ben Miller," the chief justice of the Illinois Supreme Court said. "I'd like for you to come on board for a clerkship."

I told Klint the news, we went to a dive burrito shop in Oak Park to celebrate, and then we drove downtown for the final.

Of all the people who helped me during the darkest hours of grief, Klint kept me on track to finish law school. Had he not called that night that I came out to him, I more than likely would have quit. His love and support continued for many years to come. He's still in Chicago practicing law and chasing women, and although we talk less, Klint is one of the best friends I have.

CHAPTER TWENTY-EIGHT

BACK TO SPRINGFIELD

I wanted to leave Illinois, but a Supreme Court clerkship was too premier an offer to ignore, even if it meant moving back to Springfield, alone, without Penny. During this time, I had hoped that by Christmas Patty would approach me to return my belongings and to resolve the financial portion of the estate. I fantasized that Patty would come to me to explain that whatever she had done may have looked dubious but that she had had a plan in mind the whole time, and she would return my belongings and estate proceedings.

When a package came from Patty, I knew I was right! I opened it to find a can of beer nuts and a pocket-size photo album with a card that read: "Merry Christmas. We love you. You're always welcome." Despite every disappointment, I rewrote my denial and believed that Patty would present my things to me during the next special event.

I knew Linda Hawker was well connected in Springfield, and I asked her to help me find an apartment. She agreed and offered to let me stay with her and her husband while I searched. Contacting Linda was an odd choice in one way, but I craved to be near people who knew Penny, who had a history with her. When I walked into their dining room, I saw the papier-mâché grapes that Penny and I had bought together on vacation on their table and I froze, staring at them as though I were trying to place them in my own life. It confused me. Linda saw my odd reaction and said that they were Penny's.

"Yeah, I know," I said, feeling as though I had no air in my body. I made the remark that Penny had told me she had bought those in Ixtapa, and I shared the story of how Penny bargained, recasting it as though I wasn't there and Penny had only told me about it.

Linda told me that when Penny died, she was so sad that she felt the need to go to the twin towns of Ixtapa and Zihautenejo to "be near Penny" because Penny had spoken so often about how she loved that part of Mexico. What Linda didn't know was that Penny and I had fallen in love with that vacation spot together.

This episode brought me into a deep depression, and I became so ill that I called in sick during the first few days of my clerkship, absolutely unable to get out of bed. I said I had the flu. My reaction didn't make sense to me. It was one thing to lose my possessions with Penny but quite another to have someone invade my memories. It sounded crazy to say that. It was not rational, but I had always felt like Ixtapa was "our place."

I struggled through work every day the next week. I also looked for an apartment, which was a very sad task. I didn't want to live in a home that Penny had never entered. But I tried to find one that she would like. I found an old Chicago-style walk-up on tree-lined State Street. It had a fireplace, hardwood floors, built-in bookshelves, and an all-glass sunroom. If Penny couldn't be with me, at least I could pick a place that reflected the type of class and charm we loved.

As the first anniversary of Penny's death approached, I was searching for ways other than drinking to relieve my grief. One of the things that was preventing my healing process was that I had been silenced at Penny's funeral. I took the eulogy I had written for Penny and submitted it to her local newspaper. I told no one for fear that Patty or Don would somehow be able to block it. I toyed with the idea of coming out in this piece and writing what really happened in the aftermath of Penny's death, but I could not. I felt tremendous relief when I received phone calls and letters from people who had been moved by the article honoring Penny.

A group of state leaders decided to create a scholarship in Penny's honor. The bipartisan event was chaired by Secretary of State Jesse White. The goal was to raise $150,000 to pay for both a scholarship at Southern Illinois University and a paid internship in state government. To kick off the fundraising drive, there would be a fly-around from Springfield to Chicago and then to Decatur on February 21, the first anniversary of Penny's death.

I had called Patty about this in mid-February, hoping it would jump-start our relationship again. The night before the event, she called and told me that the fly-around was for "family only" and that I would have to make my own travel arrangements, as there would not be room on the plane.

"Patty," I implored. "There is no way I can make it to Chicago and Decatur if I'm driving."

"You'll just have to decide which one you want to be at, Terry," she said.

The morning of the event, I lay in bed weeping. I decided not to go at all, and I felt both relieved and selfish. Thoughts tormented me: *It's about Penny. You should go, at least to one event.* But the struggle overcame me, and I lay in bed crying and in deep pain for the whole day.

The next day, Secretary of State Jesse White called me. "I had been hoping to talk to you at yesterday's event, but it's like you vanished after Penny died. I asked the family about you several times, and they said they didn't know. Today, I heard you were back in Springfield, and I got your number. I just wanted to see how you were."

I was angry that "the family," which I knew meant Patty and Don, didn't pass this along.

I started to accept that Patty was never going to come around. I also knew that I had to get some things off my chest. I decided to write her a letter. After much struggle, I wrote her a fourteen-page letter, begging to help me understand what I had done to deserve to be shut out and asking her to give my things back. The March 18, 1999, letter did contain a lie. Out of desperation, and because I thought it might be a good negotiation tactic, I told her I didn't care about the money or the house, giving them up in the hope of getting my personal items back. I recited all the terrible things that they had done, and said I was specifically haunted by a picture that Penny and I had over our bed. I reminded Patty that she asked me if I wanted it and I had said yes. When I returned to my home, the painting was gone. "I know you said you wanted it," Patty had said to me. "But I had other plans for it too."

I compared my marriage to hers. "Imagine, Patty, that, God forbid, Doug died, and Orville [Doug's father] came in and rummaged through the mail—or went through Doug's wallet—and then Janet [Doug's sister] came in and changed the locks, giving you access to the garage only. It would shock your consciousness, and you would be devastated. It's the same thing—Penny and I loved each other as much as you love Doug, or Rod loves Jane. When Penny was alive and we were together, I was family. When she was sick and dying, I was family. When she drew her last breath, I suddenly ceased to be family. I'm still bleeding from that."

A few weeks later, having heard nothing, I mounted the courage to drive to Bloomington and see Patty face-to-face. Facing Patty was confusing for me—it was hard to see the embodied similarities—and our encounters often ended with me not being able to speak my mind about anything real. I knocked. She invited me in. I told her that I wanted to talk to her about my letter. She denied having received the letter, which she interpreted as "divine intervention."

It was an odd and tense visit. As I left, Patty said to me, "I have something for you, Terry. I've been wanting to give it to you for a while." It was the picture that hung above our bed.

As I was leaving and she was helping me put the art in my car, she said, "Terry, if you ever decide to become a monk, I hope you will return this to me."

I didn't know what to say; it was a very odd statement.

I left feeling as though I had made progress. At least I had the picture. I started to wonder whether it was plausible that she hadn't gotten the letter and this was merely coincidence. Fantasy started again: maybe if I sent her another letter, she would read it, and we would finally be able to work through things to a just result.

I resent a copy of the letter on April 8, 1999, and asked Patty to please let me know that she got it. In early May, Patty acknowledged receiving the letter but said she would not read it, that she would just put it in the bottom drawer of her desk.

I decided to try and forget it and focus on taking the July 1999 bar exam. That spring, I couldn't sleep well and had very little energy. I struggled to stay awake in the bar review classes, and when I would sit to study, my mind would drift to Penny or being locked out of our house.

That June, I called Rod and Jane and asked them to push Patty about spreading the ashes. Many fights ensued, as Patty originally picked a date that conflicted with Rod's intense work schedule. While I had no say in the matter, the finalized date coincided with the worst possible time for me as a law clerk. June was one of the busiest months of the term, and the Judge was reluctant to give me a full day off. Still unable to speak my own truth, he didn't know Penny and I were partners.

I had no experience with ceremonies to spread the cremated ashes of a loved one. In the movies, though, mourners took turns saying a few words, and then each would take a handful of ashes, gently releasing them into the wind or into the ocean. Here, I thought that each of us would say something, take a handful of ashes, as we all were part of Penny's life, and place them in the slight hole dug under the white oak sapling.

Don brought out Penny's ashes. There was no urn. No special box. Just a plastic bag with a twist-tie, not unlike the ones used for garbage bags. He handled her ashes roughly, almost angrily. I felt he failed to realize that this should have been as solemn as his daughter's memorial service was. Here, though, there was no presentation. Don tersely untwisted the tie, took the lip of the bag in one hand and the bottom of the bag in the other, and dumped the ashes into the ground, as though he were empting a cereal box. He then wadded up the bag and put it in his pocket.

I stepped forward. I had decided I was going to speak up in this group of intimates and make plain that Penny and I were partners and that Penny would be devastated at what was happening. Instead, I swallowed my words and the bile that had come up into my throat and gently ran my hands over the bark of the tree as though it were Penny.

Rod, Jane, and I lingered in the rain, crying. They were equally drained and stunned at this callous quickness of a final good-bye to a spouse, daughter, sister, aunt, and friend. To me, it was nothing short of sacrilege. Rod said, mutedly, "Let's sit in the truck a minute." We just didn't know what to do.

Rod and Jane begged me to come back to their house with them for dinner. I refused. Instead we went and got a drink and talked about how badly the ceremony had been handled.

"Did this just happen?" Rod said incredulously. "He handled that bag like he was handling a bag of dog crap," he said angrily. Panic and pain had overtaken me, and the ony thing I wanted to do was to get blindingly drunk. I said good-bye. I went back to the tree. On my hands and knees, in a driving rain in the dark, I dug most of Penny's ashes out of the wet ground and dried them in a box. They now rest in an urn. I drove to Chicago at midnight, went to a bar, and pounded whisky as fast the bartender would serve it. I hoped I would die.

Just weeks before the bar exam, I spiraled into despair. I couldn't study. The week of the test, everything seemed to go wrong. The hotel I was staying at in Chicago had a leaking ceiling, and they had no other rooms available. I spent hours trying to find another hotel but stayed with a friend instead. I struggled through the exam and had to try very hard to keep from crying.

When the exam was over, I felt great relief, but it was quickly replaced by the next wave of grief. Every August Penny and I had taken a two-week vacation. Each day in the Midwestern heat was a keen reminder that my partner was dead and that my life was completely upended. My sadness seeped into anger, with both Patty and with myself. I decided I would seek legal help.

In retrospect, I wish I would have called LAMDA Legal Fund or sought out a full-time legal expert, which I didn't do until many years later. I decided to trust a law school professor, Michael Closen, who I knew was gay and an expert in contracts. We discussed the fact that in the eyes of the law, I had no standing. He suggested that I write Patty another letter, telling her that I spoke to him and that if she refused to meet with me by a certain deadline, I would go forward legally. What I really needed and wanted was to have someone spearhead this effort on my behalf. He suggested language for the letter, but I couldn't quite bring myself to be that harsh with Patty. I drove back to Springfield and put the idea on the shelf until the next month, September 1999.

CHAPTER TWENTY-NINE

THE $1,000 OFFER

The fall of 1999 was the first time since the night Penny died that I had seriously questioned whether I had the wherewithal to go on living.

A former staffer of Penny's asked me to help organize a fundraiser for the Penny Severns Scholarship. I was so grateful for the invitation, but I could no longer bear being identified as a staffer, or not mentioned at all, and I knew that participating would mean that I would have to see Patty and her father. I was anxious about that.

After Patty refused to read the second letter I sent, I tried to ignore her. But my pain would become too much to bear, and in desperation, I would call and ask her to have lunch. Those calls were tiring because she talked frantically about how busy she was. We met a few times, but like the calls, she left no room for real conversation as she was always in a hurry. When I could make a foothold, Patty worked her own health into the conversation, noting, "Penny also used to say that stress causes cancer," or, "Penny would always worry that stress can trigger relapses. Remember how Penny would say that?"

Within me, lesbian Terry knew the conversation she came to have with Patty about being Penny's partner was not going to happen. She could see then, as I only understood years later, that Patty was rushing through the meal, filling the time with questions to avoid the conversation. When I continued to talk about Penny, Patty would block me, knowing that I would not be able to speak to her directly if I thought it would stress her out. It seemed she had lunch with me to appease me and to deliver her own message: don't talk to me about Penny or the estate because it would be stressful, and we know stress could cause a relapse of my breast cancer. I always felt this technique, if that's what it was, was dirty, but I fell for it every time, never having the heart or courage to tell Patty about how she was betraying me as well as her sister. And the conversations ended with a hug, a kiss, and Patty saying: "Love you. You're welcome any time."

I finally had enough. I wrote her a letter on September 24, and I told her if she refused to sit down and work this out "I would move forward legally" to retrieve my things. The deadline was October 20, 2000. I copied Rod and Don Jr. I was sitting in the very quiet Supreme Court five days later, when the phone rang. Patty was very angry. This letter she had read. "Do you know what this is? This is libel! You are a lawyer, Terry, you know better than this. Is this serious? Are you *serious*?"

Perhaps out of habit from my reporting days, or because I was trying to distance myself from the brunt of the personal sting of the conversation, or because I wanted proof, I started to take notes on a legal pad.

Patty went on, "You copied Rod and Donnie, Terry? Rod and Donnie? Rod, Mr. Moneybags, who is only interested in money, and Donnie, who is off to who knows where? They weren't part of this. How dare you disclose this to them."

I thought the word "disclose" was interesting.

I said, "Patty, I thought including them might force you to sit down with me and give us a starting point, since you and I can't ever seem to get to talking about this."

"Talk about what?" she said, her disgust clear.

"How about with the fact that you locked me out of my own home?" I said.

"You wait right there. You were not locked out," she said.

"Patty, are you serious? You changed the locks. I didn't have a key to my own home. The doors were dead-bolted."

"You could get in and out through the garage," she said, adding "and it was not your house."

I felt like my body was deflating, as though I were soaring through the air like a popped balloon. I felt like I was watching myself in a movie, and I was cringing at the terrible pain I was witnessing.

"What about what you said the night before Penny died? That you considered it my home as much as Penny's," I said.

"That was *before*," she said.

"Yeah, before she died," I said.

"No, before I knew the *real* Terry," she said. "You libeled me to my brothers," she continued.

We both paused.

Then Patty let out a very weird sort of guffaw. "Oh, I get it. I see it very clearly now. And I see what you are really made of. I am just so glad that Penny can't see this," she said, almost in a monologue.

"Me too, Patty, because you know that she would have never, ever, ever have been happy about this. She wanted us to 'get through this together,' remember?"

"Penny would be so disappointed in you, Terry Mutchler," she said. Our voices had become both parched and high-pitched.

"No, Patty, Penny would have never wanted me to suffer like this or for you to suffer either. But you know what we all talked about. Let's talk about the will."

"Right, you're a lawyer, you want to talk about the will?" she said, and it seemed she was daring me to speak the fact that I had finished writing the will after Penny died and it was auto-penned.

"Patty, you were nice to me until the moment I wrote the will and gave it to you," I said. "And then you treated me like a common criminal."

"You lied about the suitcase," Patty said, raising this issue again.

I pushed back. "It was my own fucking house, and those were my own fucking things, Patty."

That crude language seemed to snap her back into a different place, that place of calm distance.

"Please don't use that language," she said. "This is just about money for you. Penny didn't mean anything to you. It was money. I am so glad Penny is not here to see who you really are, Terry."

I was too stunned to reply to that painful accusation. Patty kept talking and repeating what now was a mantra: "Terry, you can take me to the United States Supreme Court. I will never give you anything."

For more than a year and a half, I believed that Patty would eventually do the right thing. I believed that she was grief-stricken and had her hands full with her family. I never believed that Patty would betray me. I trusted her with my life. Penny and I trusted her with my life. Confusion and blackness filled me.

"Terry this *is* what Penny wanted," Patty said to me, bringing my every fiber to stillness, realizing that in fact her behavior was no mistake or misunderstanding. Patty was never going to recognize me as Penny's partner. In that moment, I had to leave no room for interpretation or error. Although I had written to her that Penny and I were partners, I knew I had to say those words aloud. I had to speak the words that I had been afraid to speak.

"Patty," I said deliberately. "Penny and I were partners. That is why we did the will the way we did it. That's why we talked about a public will and a private will. We were trying to hide that fact from the public." Then Patty said something very odd, which made me realize that I would never be able to reach her—for something deeper and darker was lurking in her refusal to acknowledge the true nature of my relationship with her sister.

"I know you had Penny for five years, but I had her for forty, and in vitro," she said.

I knew that Patty was hurting deeply, and I genuinely felt bad. I softened and said: "Patty, look, I know that you and Penny were close, and I can't imagine losing a twin. I can't. It's like a part of you has died."

"It is, Terry," she said, her voice cracking, softening herself.

This tender acknowledgement is where the conversation should have started. Instead, we were engaged in the grief Olympics, competing against each other to be recognized as the one who was hurting the most and who had meant the most to Penny. Instead of building on that fertile ground, I was trying to gain more ground.

Despite that moment of tenderness, I went on, "But, Patty, are you telling me that Penny wanted me to be locked out of our house, that she wanted me to be forced out of our home and not given one thing? And that she wanted me to be in a situation where I can barely live? Is that what you are saying?"

"This is what Penny wanted. She told me many times that if she died, she didn't care if I backed up a U-haul to the house and took everything."

I thought back to that joke Penny had made before we left on one of our trips. She'd told Patty to take everything if *we* died while *we* were away. I continued to try to reach Patty by stating an obvious question "Patty, do you honestly believe that Penny would want me to be suffering like this? I have the notes from our discussions between the three of us about what Penny wanted."

"I have notes too," Patty said, blocking the real discussion.

My final words to her in that conversation were, "Patty, you know in your heart how much we loved each other and what Penny wanted."

I canceled my meeting at the fundraiser and drove to Rod and Jane's. "Maybe," I cried aloud, "maybe Penny really didn't love me. Maybe she did tell Patty something different than she told me."

Rod and Jane worked very hard that night to soothe me and remind of all the ways that Penny loved me and to not let Patty or anyone poison that truth. But I couldn't break free of the pain and confusion. Once I made it home, I replayed the conversation with Patty over and over again. I paced. I couldn't sleep. I couldn't think.

I wanted to call in sick the next day, but the judge had specifically asked me to attend a women's bar association event the next night. There, I was preoccupied but noticed a very cute attorney named Lyn Schollett. She asked for my telephone number, and although I was too mired in my own hell to give serious thought to dating, I gave it to her.

That weekend, I went to find Penny in a place we shared alone: Allerton Park in Monticello, Illinois. She wasn't there. When I got home that night, a large yellow package from the Illinois Bar Admissions Committee stuck out of my mailbox. Finally, a reason to celebrate. I tore it open.

I had flunked by one point. The river of weeping raged immediate and long. I cried all night.

The next morning, my eyes were red, swollen, and puffy. At the event for Penny, I couldn't stop crying. Near the end of the event, Patty approached me. "Can I speak to you a minute?" she said. I said yes. "I'd rather not do it here," she said. "Would you come to the car?"

When everybody was filing out, we walked outside. It was raining. She asked Kristin to wait under a nearby pavilion so that we could talk privately in Penny's Volvo. It was a surreal experience to open the door to the Volvo.

The interior of the car looked so different from the pristine way that Penny and I kept it. We had washed it every week. Now the car was not vacuumed, and the inside was dirty.

I told her that I had flunked the bar, and she seemed genuinely hurt for me. At my feet on the floor of the passenger's side was a brown bag with handles. Patty reached over and picked up the bag, the contents clanked.

"I want you to have this," she said.

It was the silverware that I had written about in my March letter.

"Patty, I don't want that," I said truthfully. There was so much hurt and heartbreak associated with the fact that Patty had asked me to return this silverware. It made me sick.

"I really want you to have it," she said.

"Patty, I don't want it."

"Terry, is your letter serious?" she asked.

"Yes, it is. We need to talk about this."

"I decided to give you a check, Terry," she said. "All you have to do is sign this." She handed me a two-page document.

I scanned the words, which clearly had been written by a lawyer.

Agree that Penny did not want me to have anything.

Relinquish any rights I thought I had.

Identified as a friend and employee.

"It's a thousand dollars, Terry. It's right here." She showed me the check.

I shook my head in disgust. No one would ever believe that Patty, *Patty* had offered me a thousand dollars to walk away from my life with Penny. I needed to take this document with me.

"Patty, I'm not signing anything today. I'll take this with me and look it over."

"No, this is only good if you sign it today."

I looked at it again, trying to employ my reporting skills and memorize the language as much as possible, but my emotions were too high and the document was too long for that.

"Terry, look, I know you need money," she said, tapping right into my financial reality, and also my embarrassment and shame about money that lingered from my youth. While I had been working steadily as a law clerk, I had accumulated a great deal of debt while in law school, and I was terrible at money management. Despite that, I would never sell out my relationship with Penny for any amount of money, ever!

"Sign this, Terry. *Please*. You can have $1,000," she said, and she handed me Penny's black Mont Blanc pen, which immediately reminded me of the day that Penny and I got the news of her cancer's return.

"Patty, I'm not signing this. I'll just move forward with my lawyer."

"Terry," she said, her voice hardening. "I told you this before. You can take me to the Supreme Court. I will never give you anything."

"That's your decision. I'm just asking you to focus on Penny, not how much you like or dislike me, but to honor Penny's wishes."

"I am honoring Penny's wishes, 100 percent."

"Patty, how can you say that?" I said. "You were right there with us when we talked about the will."

She closed her eyes and shook her head and repeated: "This is exactly what Penny wanted."

I knew that wasn't true. I knew that I would never sign anything. I knew that I didn't have anything else to say. I wanted to sit for one more minute in our car—the car that we had still been trying to name when Penny died, the car that we toasted champagne over with the salesman we bought it from. I looked out the rain-splattered window at Kristin and sighed. I missed this family. I missed the fun I used to have with them and the way the kids loved to play with me.

"Good-bye, Patty," I said.

I opened the door as Patty said, "Please, Terry, sign this."

I reached past the document, momentarily thinking I should grab it. Instead, I picked up the silverware, and shut the door. I waved to Kristin, and said in a cracked voice, "I love you, Kristin." She smiled and waved.

Shaking and crying, I drove to Rod and Jane's and told them what happened. Rod offered to talk with Patty to try and resolve this, but I begged him not to; inexplicably, I felt like a child whose parents confront a teacher. I felt that my life would get worse if he intervened, and I didn't want to start another dispute amongst the siblings.

On Monday, I called Professor Closen. He wanted me to do some legal research about the issues I was experiencing. I thanked him but said I couldn't do it. I needed someone to do this for me.

On October 11, Patty called me and said she wanted to set up a time to talk about things. We arranged to meet two days later at my home.

Before we hung up, I tried again to explain myself. "Patty, I just want my things back, and I want you to honor Penny's wishes," I said.

"You got your things when you left. You want Penny's things. You want things that aren't yours."

I hung up. I felt cold and clammy. A very black darkness filled my mind and soul. I had no energy left. I had nothing left. And I knew I had no legal standing to fight this. Even if I did file a lawsuit, I wasn't sure I could publically admit that Penny and I were partners. A desperate despondency shadowed my mind. There was absolutely nothing left to live for. Penny was dead. I had flunked the bar, and although I was doing fine at work, I was struggling emotionally and felt as though I was making a complete mess of my life.

Maybe, I thought slowly, *I should just kill myself.* I lay on my couch, exhausted, too tired to weep with these thoughts swirling within me. The relief would be worth it; I would no longer have to struggle to do basic things. And, perhaps, I would find Penny. As all these thoughts started to gain ground, the phone rang.

Lyn Schollett, the lawyer from the bar association, called and asked me out on a date. The irony, the timing, was too much. A light seemed to pierce the darkness, and I even managed to laugh as I recalled Klint's phrase, "I could dig a ditch." *Hell,* I thought, starting to come back to myself, *I'm too tired to kill myself.*

"Sure, Lyn," I said. "I would like that." And we set up a date for the next week.

On October 13, Patty called me and said that one of the kids was sick and she couldn't be at my house in person, and she asked if it would be all right if we talked on the phone instead. I agreed, but we got nowhere. I never took legal action, but I never told Patty I wouldn't. In fact, I didn't speak to Patty for several years.

CHAPTER THIRTY

DATING AND THE ABYSS

Lyn and I started dating, but I was weighed down with grief and should not have ventured into a relationship. I hid my grief. Publically, I was gregarious and outgoing for short periods of time. Privately, I would often slip into something I called "the abyss" a state where I would be nearly catatonic and unable to function for days at a time. I would become clammy and extremely cold. My breath was shallow. I would be near comatose. These spells were usually triggered by a particularly distressing thought or a memory of Penny, often near an anniversary. The abyss frightened me deeply, I feared it would last. I tried to hide these episodes from everyone.

A few months later, Lyn and I decided it was time to disclose our relationship to our families: me at Thanksgiving, her at Christmas. My mother knew of my relationships with women, but I had not yet come out specifically about Penny. Standing on our front porch, she told me that she loved Penny. But, she said, I was in for a hard life, and she didn't wish that for me. "I will always love you—you're my daughter—but how are you going to get past the Man upstairs?" she asked, referring to God.

She begged me not to tell my father—forbade me, in fact. Unbelievably, I abided her wish until just prior to his death in 2002. Dad told me he knew I was gay and advised me not to fall into the trap of "thinking for God." He told me, "Nobody really knows what He is thinking, and we could be a million miles off." I was grateful, but I also remember thinking, *I wish you would have given me this sage piece of advice when I was young.*

Although Lyn had been in a previous relationship with a woman and was out in our local community, she had not yet made this disclosure to her family. She was both nervous and excited about her Christmas plans. She was shocked when she saw the abyss for the first time as we were preparing to leave for our parents' homes. I became extremely weak and was so tired I couldn't keep my eyes open. I was sitting on the floor in front of Lyn's wooden coffee table, staring at a legal opinion I was editing. I was so out of it that when a candle caught the papers—and then the table—on fire I didn't even notice.

"Oh my God, Terry," she said. "The table's on fire."

She extinguished the flames, but her table still bears the burn mark. I didn't know what was happening to me. I called my mother, crying. I was worried that I was going crazy and explained my symptoms to her.

"It sounds like you are in shock," she said, and advised me to tell my doctor that my partner had died. Dr. Burns examined me and said he believed that my body was starting to process this grief and I was experiencing symptoms of depression. He prescribed medicine, and he recommended that I try to reach accord with Patty. I was certain that if I just tried harder and forced myself to work and be happy, I could solve the symptoms of the abyss.

I finally made it home for Christmas, but I slept most of the time I was there. Lyn traveled to Michigan and came out to her parents. They initially had some concerns, but quickly became supportive of their daughter, and later of me.

We kept dating and Lyn took me to a party to meet her friends. There I met Carol Corgan, a woman who had dealt with a great deal of grief in her life. When Carol learned the truth of my relationship and its painful aftermath, she warned: "Don't become the gregarious version of me in ten years." I felt a kinship with Carol. We decided to keep a "grief journal," where I would reveal a story about Penny and she would write about her best friend who had died. The more I wrote, the more frequently the episodes of the abyss would occur—and the more Lyn was left to help pick up the pieces.

Since Penny's death, I had been in and out of therapy. Now, I decided that I needed to process the grief with a professional, not a pal. I wanted to "be done" before the next sitting of the bar exam. I had no idea that therapy would take years to unravel the many layers of grief and traumas of my youth.

That January, I devoted my attention to studying. The bar examination fell on the anniversary of Penny's death, and I feared the abyss would hit. In preparation, I employed a trick of the mind. I decided to give Penny my law license as a gift, and thus I was going to have to pass the bar exam. This mental game gave me the motivation to study even when I absolutely did not want to do anything but sleep.

When I walked out of the bar exam, I felt confident, happy, and exhausted. I was aching for Penny. I wanted to share this milestone with her. I realized I was still living for Penny, and Lyn was being shortchanged. Over the next few months, my depression seemed to deepen. Although I had successfully passed the bar, been sworn in as a lawyer, and was still dating Lyn, in some ways I felt as dead as Penny.

When the fourth anniversary of Penny's death approached, I actually shook and felt tremendous pain. A dark cloud seemed to physically envelope me.

Wanting to preempt the abyss on this anniversary, I chose to face the grief alone at a bed and breakfast on an island off the coast of Georgia. I had nightmares, dreaming I couldn't prove Penny and I were lovers. I wrote about the sensation that there was a werewolf of grief prowling my soul, tearing me apart. I spent the anniversary of Penny's death drunk. The next day, I decided that the only way to get closure was to conduct a funeral for Penny. Instead of friends and family mourning with me on the shoreline, it was nature in attendance of what I later called "Penny's Funeral by the Sea," during which I begged God to help me and show me how to heal and live a full life. The ritual made me feel better.

I returned to Illinois, relieved but not whole. I still felt like a painting by Picasso, a shell of misplaced body parts. I stopped looking for peace, and tried to focus on my relationship with Lyn and finding a job as the clerkship ended.

I landed a premier job with a major Chicago law firm slated to start in March 2001. The life of a young associate doesn't leave room for anything but work and focused precision. Despite the time restriction and my move to Chicago, Lyn and I decided to keep seeing each other. I should have taken time off, worked through the grief, and been alone instead of trying to work a ninety-hour-a-week job, commute on the weekends, and attempt to deal with everything. I chose to stay in motion, as fast as possible.

Though the first few months were excruciating, I got the swing of it. But by midsummer of 2001, the pain overtook me once again, and I felt as though I could not put one foot in front of the other. I contemplated quitting my job, but I enjoyed the incredible financial luxury that this type of position provided and the ways in which it enabled me to help my family. Golden handcuffs, to be sure.

Then 9/11 happened. Listening to people's "last words" to loved ones gave me courage. I had experienced the greatest love of my life to that point, and I was proud of it. I didn't need to hide the reality that I was a lesbian. I decided I didn't want to die without finding the courage to face Don and Patty directly and tell them that they were cruel to me.

I drove to Don's home, feeling brave. When I pulled in the driveway, the first thing I saw was our deck furniture. I felt the abyss coming on. My thoughts started to drift to Penny. This time, though, I started to think of Penny in a different way—I thought of all the pain and sadness that Don had caused Penny, and I began to let that advocacy flow into my veins. If I could stand up to him for me, then maybe I could also do it for her.

"Fuck it, it's only a table," I said and strode past our table, chairs and umbrella.

It was now or never. I asked Don if I could speak to him. I set a tape recorder on the deck rail in front of him. I knew I would not be able to remember everything I said to him, or that he said to me, so I decided to record our conversation as long as he had no objections.

I needed to know that I could find my voice and confront him. I was nervous and started out gently. "There's something I want to ask you." I prefaced with my love for Penny, and then said I needed to know why he and Patty had treated me poorly. I told him I didn't care what the answer was, I just needed to know.

He said he didn't think he'd treated me poorly, yet he honed in on all the things he did that had harmed me: taking Penny's purse; calling me about leaving the lights on; asking me whose shoes I had on. He remembered it all, but said he was simply protecting Penny and Patty. He rejected the idea that Penny and I were married. Then he recited his two major complaints: "You moved your family in," he said of the time my family attended the funeral. And, he was upset that I had tried to cash a campaign check after Penny had died. Interestingly, when I spoke of being locked out, he blamed Patty. "I had nothing to do with it." He thanked me for helping Penny, but then said, "I'm glad everything went to Patty as it should have."

I felt dizzy. As a reporter, I knew that I wasn't going to get any smoking gun or real answer from Don. What was important was my ability to express how I felt about how he behaved. I had done that. The last thing I wanted to do was faint and need his help. I shook his hand and left. When I got in the car I was shaking and crying in relief for having the courage to speak my mind and heart to a person who caused me great pain.

I knew I also needed to confront Patty. Two months later, I pulled into her driveway. I was flooded with emotion. I was afraid this would morph into a faux social call. I knocked, half hoping she wouldn't answer. She did and seemed a little stunned to see me.

"Hi, Patty," I said. "I was hoping that we could talk."

She seemed to hesitate but then said, "Come in."

I tried hard not to look into her living room, which was decorated with the furniture Penny and I had acquired and was set up in a nearly identical way. As I walked past the table that Penny and I had designed together, a bit of a yelp came from my throat. I couldn't help but run my hand over it.

"Penny would have loved that the kids do their homework at that table," Patty said, and I was disgusted that she tried to justify taking this table.

We sat in her dining room. Weston came in and with great enthusiasm said, "Hi, Terry!" as he rushed to hug and kiss me.

"Hey there, big man" I said with equal happiness. I hugged him and didn't want to let go. When Weston left the room, I regrouped, determined to keep this conversation on track. Once and for all, I needed to get to the heart of how Patty had behaved after Penny died.

Instead of declaring that what I thought she had done was wrong, as I had with Don, I simply asked her some questions. I told her I was hurt and confused by the way she treated me after Penny died. I repeated most of what I had written to her in the first letter I sent her. As I had with her father, I asked if I had done something to offend her.

To my surprise, she said, "yes" there were some things that had bothered her. Whatever I had done wrong, I was certain I could fix. She, too, cited the cashing of my campaign work checks after Penny had died and me purchasing newspapers announcing Penny's death out of campaign funds, and she claimed that I was giving things away from the home and causing things to move too fast.

"Patty, Penny did not want me cut out of everything," I said, going right to the heart of the matter.

"I am honoring Penny's wishes 100 percent," she said, and I could almost foretell the next line, which I had become so sick of hearing. "You can take me to the Supreme Court. I will never give you anything."

I tried to tap into Penny's love for me, that we were married, and I asked her look at our love letters, which she refused.

"Don't say you were married," she said shaking her head back and forth. "You were friends. Penny took you under her wing. That is all."

I felt defeated, and hoped at minimum I could get a few things back. "It would really help if you could find your way to let me have them," I said.

"Why, when we went to that restaurant in Indiana, did you make a point of telling me about the boy who asked you to marry him?" she asked. That was a fair question. When Penny's cancer had returned in 1996, Penny had asked me if I would arrange for her to meet my minister to be prayed for, and she wanted Patty to go with her for that blessing. The three of us had flown to Indiana, and beforehand, at a restaurant, I purposely pointed out the booth where my onetime boyfriend had asked me to marry him when we were teenagers.

I told her that I was nervous about the collision my faith and my reality were about to have by introducing my partner to my minister to seek his help. And I wanted to reinforce the story that Penny and I told everyone: that we were just friends.

"Patty, you're seriously not trying to tell me you didn't know we were partners. You treated us as a couple—you even put us in a twin bed together at your house."

I continued, "Let's say we were just friends. Let's just say that is what you truly believed. Do you believe you treated me like a friend? You let other people go through Penny's clothes. You gave away things and didn't even ask me or consult me. You cut me out, period, because you were afraid of what I represented to Penny, and you didn't want the public to know that she was a lesbian."

The room was filled with tension, and I felt dizzy and unable to stay focused. I was becoming angry. I felt that I was lost and would forever be tormented.

"Patty, please look at these love letters."

She refused.

I decided to recite my list. I asked for our bed, our desk, and the cherry kitchen table. Knowing she would never agree to give me our Chagalls or the Rafielli paintings, I asked for "some of our art." I asked for some of Penny's clothes. I asked for the leather driving gloves that I had bought Penny. And I said firmly, "I want that Tag Heuer watch. We considered those our anniversary watches."

For the first time, I knew I had not done anything to deserve this. I always believed that if Patty and I could talk honestly, she would say to me, "Terry, as painful as it is for me to say, here's why I behaved as I did." I thought she might tell me that she couldn't bring herself to go against her father. Anything.

"Patty," I said, "do you believe me that Penny and I were lovers?"

I could see pain in her face as she was thinking of whether or not to answer me truthfully. "Yes," she said.

I started to cry. Then, she spoke more openly.

"I used to stay up nights thinking about it. I wasn't able to sleep, wondering why Penny didn't tell me. Why didn't she tell me, Terry?"

"She said she was certain that you knew, and that you would be fine with it," I said. "Penny was worried that Doug wouldn't let us see the kids if he knew." We thought this because one of Doug's sisters had lived with a woman for many years but the fact was never discussed openly or honestly among us.

"Let's say you didn't know that Penny and I were lovers," I said quietly, believing I could make real progress. "But you know now. You have to know that Penny would not want this to have happened this way and that she wouldn't want me to be treated this way."

Our moment of true intersection passed. She repeated her mantra.

I began 2002 with the pledge that I would force myself to accept that Penny was dead and stop torturing myself about the things that I'd lost, or that I didn't have the strength to stick up for myself. I threw myself into my work as hard as I could. My doctor said that I had to rest and recover. He strongly recommended a leave of absence. I resisted. I saw it as "giving up."

Shortly after winning an eight-million-dollar estate appeal, I hit the wall and took a leave of absence. Within the first few weeks, I felt lost. By December, as rest started to seep into my being, instead of feeling better, I went into an even deeper depression. I stopped seeing friends and returning telephone calls. I was barely seeing Lyn. As Christmas approached, I could barely get out of bed. I bought a tree but left it on my porch. A friend at the firm, Therese King Nohos, had come by the house because I had not returned any of her phone calls. She knew my story, and that I had lost everything, including my Christmas ornaments. She brought the tree inside. While we sat and talked, she cut paper ornaments from my pastel paper, decorating my tree.

After the holidays, I decided to travel out west to escape my everyday world. I spent nearly two months camping alone in the desert, trying to force myself out of my depression by writing, praying, and painting pastels. As my time there came to a close, I felt as though I had finally made some headway with the grief. I was able to deal with it better; the abyss didn't last as long as it had before. I viewed that as success, no matter how small. As I returned east, I had two thoughts on my mind: Lyn and I needed to separate, and would there be a letter from Patty telling me that she wanted to return my belongings?

Nearly two decades later, I still do not have any of my things, not even the limited list that I asked for. I ran into Patty at the funeral of Senator Vince Demuzio in 2004. I ignored her. She spoke to me casually, but I was not interested. I never again spoke to Don, who died in 2013 at ninety years old.

I still ache for certain pieces of our life together, whether it's a jacket she wore, a book she read, or a piece of art we bought. I now know I possess the most cherished aspect of my life with Penny: our memories and our love. The things I lost are just things in a material sense, but somehow, things mean a great deal in death. Even the smallest item that belonged to a loved one becomes a token of the life shared, and the essence and elements of healing. You touch these items, you cry a little, you laugh a little, and you put them back down—they're conduits between this dimension and the memory of those we loved and lost.

CHAPTER THIRTY-ONE

THE SEASONS OF GRIEF

Anger and grief about the things we shared, and the things that were taken from me, are corded in me like a brown rope that splinters and burns your hands. Our shared life yanked through my fingertips. Our home, our dining room table, our couch, our bath towels, our sheets, our tablecloths, our dinner plates, our glasses, her favorite mugs, our coffee maker, our knives, our forks, our serving spoons, our books, our bed, our fireplace tools, our pottery, my favorite cookbooks, our pie dishes, our magazines, our music, our aluminum ladder, our grease-stained lawn mower, our rakes, our gas cans, our tools, our shovels, our cleaning rags, Penny's clothes, her around-the-house shirts, her toothbrush, her Borghese lotions and Bobbi Brown makeup, her brooches and rings and bracelets, her socks with holes in them, our blankets, our beach towels, our fingernail clippers, our art. The red-striped shirt she wore on our first date. The blue silk dress she bought for our first anniversary dinner that never got its public debut because, as we got ready to walk out the door, we stumbled into a kiss and never reached the car. Her favorite teal gardening shirt. Our gardening gloves. The yards of scarves that she playfully draped around my neck to pull me to her.

The rope burn of loss leaves me paralyzed, still, staring at my pained, red palms. I am unable to comprehend the speed of the loss. Clenching my fists, I try to grip the invisible rope. *If I am quicker, if I am better, if I am good. If I am visible, if I were loveable, surely I will be able to put the key in my front door, and this time, this time the key will turn. The house is still*

there on Sims Drive. I still have the key on the leather Coach key ring she gave
me, so surely I can walk back into my dismantled life.

Every fall, my body tightens at the scent of cool air, and I try to soothe the pain of losing our good books and warm sweaters and wool socks. Every winter, I try to forget the pain of losing every Christmas ornament we ever hung on an evergreen. Every spring, I wade through the muddy memory of our yard tools and lightweight jackets from Columbia and North Face, and every summer, like clockwork, my stomach and chest cord around each other, twisted and gnarled, as I face the anger of our lost outdoor furniture.

The inescapable seasons of grief.

Every year, pockets of happiness pop up, like delft-blue hyacinths or crocuses, in mailbox catalogues selling patio furniture. The silent pages boast a summer dinner party. Friends laughing. Women in white sundresses and hats. Broad-shouldered men in blue-striped shirts and boat shoes. Cherry tomatoes and quartered artichokes on the grill, with charcoal marks as evenly spaced as black lines in a composition notebook. For a moment, I forget my loss and I am stringing outdoor lights and lighting citronella candles.

I have come to terms with Penny's death, and I feel her love with me as an advocate and guide. But what I still struggle to accept or even make sense of is that I could not speak, or whisper a protest, even when the locks were changed on my own home with my things inside.

Somewhere inside my own being, I believed that because Penny and I were lesbians, we were second-class citizens. That is the most difficult grieving I do. I believed that because we broke a moral code, I didn't have a right to claim my own life; certainly, I was not entitled to the things that made our house a home. Things that I will never see or touch again. I am tormented by an inconsolable ache: if I hadn't been denied the mourning ritual afforded to any widow—to go through her spouse's things, touch them, smell them, hold them, as I could not hold Penny—the skin of my heart may have healed more quickly or differently. Healed at all.

I try to buy more yard furniture. Sometimes, I even get to the store and pick it out or find myself on the last confirm-purchase page. But like a ritual, each year, I walk away or close the screen. To purchase another set of outdoor furniture requires me to face the vivid memories of sitting in our deck chairs late at night, smelling the char of a New York strip and grilled vegetables. It requires me to come to terms with the fact that all the parties that Penny and I envisioned, the ones we planned aloud as a game to kill time and pain when she was hospitalized, will only ever be just that: imaginings. To let go of our deck furniture and let it rest where it now lives, with Penny's father and Penny's sister, requires me to accept the reality of what happened: I willingly walked into the windowless, bricked prison of our secret life, decorated with sweetness and shame, and I mistakenly handed that key to someone I loved and thought, at least, would be a benevolent warden.

The cycle of the seasons has changed for me now. Time is no longer marked by blushing leaves that give way to swirling snows, or a sopping wet yard that dries into the green grass of endless summer days. Instead, the quadrants of the equinox are hope, dashed hope, paralysis, and anger. Anger is sometimes my longest season. Even amid falling deeply in love again with Maria, a woman from Greece I have loved since the instant I laid eyes on her, I am sometimes still caught in the anger of my past life being lost and being locked from home.

Eventually, though, my white-hot anger cools, and I am calm. The werewolf of grief, exhausted and unsatisfied, tires of prowling and falls asleep inside me, and hope and belief bubble again within me. My heart gains momentum. I am able to love deeply and dream long into this future with Maria. I know that next year, yes, next year, certainly by my thirty-fifth, my fortieth, my forty-fifth, and now my fiftieth birthday, at the latest, I will possess the courage to demolish every brick and buy new Adirondack chairs, another grill, a colorful umbrella, and an array of outdoor candles, striking a match to the past and the future at once.

CHICAGO

In November 2013, the Illinois Legislature was considering a marriage equality bill to become the fifteenth state to legalize gay marriage. A very dear friend, Ann Williams, a representative in the Illinois House of Representatives, asked me if she could reveal my relationship with Penny on the House floor in support of this bill. Ann and I met while we worked for Illinois Attorney General Lisa Madigan. Early on in our friendship, I shared with Ann the story of my life with Penny, and I trusted that if she spoke, she would do it well.

I gave her permission. It was fitting that this public revelation of my life with Penny would be in the Illinois Capitol, which held so many memories for me, and on a bill of marriage equality. I wanted her to speak about it, but I began to worry that something would block her ability to tell our story. I felt that if Ann spoke about this on the House floor it would correct and ease the pain of my not being able to speak at Penny's funeral. I knew I wanted her to do this, and she wanted me to come witness it.

Originally, I was not going to go. I was too busy at work and I feared that it would negatively affect my relationship with Maria, although I had not spoken to her about it. A conversation with my chief counsel, Dena Lefkowitz, convinced me that I was off-base and needed to talk to Maria, which I did. "I think it's really critical and important for you to be there," Maria said when I spoke to her. So I asked her if she would come with me, because for me, it was equally important to honor and recognize my life with Maria, as well as close the circle on my past.

Unfortunately, the bill was delayed several times. When it was called last-minute months later, I was in Philadelphia. I watched on my iPhone. I called Maria, Rod, and Jane to let them know this was happening. I was scared. What would happen? Would she talk about Penny and me as planned? Would someone try and stop her? Would I feel relief? Would I feel as though I betrayed Penny? Would there be backlash? My stomach was jumping as I heard the House Speaker recognize Penny, the gentlewoman of Chicago:

> "One of the greatest love stories I have ever heard played out right here, under this beautiful dome. But it was a secret. Why? Because it happened nearly twenty years ago and it involved a state senator, the late Penny Severns, and one of my dearest friends, a woman named Terry Mutchler, at the time an AP reporter here at the Capitol. Penny served in the Senate from 1986 until her tragic and untimely death from breast cancer in 1998. For much of that time, there were no openly gay members in either chamber. So the relationship between Penny and Terry was pretty much a secret until after her death. Though I never met Penny, Terry said they considered themselves married—after all, they shared their lives through good times and terrible tragedy, and they were committed to each other as if they were married. But not in the eyes of society. In fact, Penny's death resolution in the Senate omitted any mention of their relationship. Can you imagine that? How heartbreaking. But Penny and Terry just wanted what so many people want—to express their love through marriage. I believe that today, their relationship would have played out much differently than it did twenty years ago. Because times have changed, and we all view things differently. But the law has not caught up with society."

As I listened to Ann speak about my life with Penny, my mind replayed the night that Penny talked with me about how beautiful the moonlight was through the dome. I smiled as I thought of her standing at the brass rail. I chuckled at her indignation when I thought she was a lobbyist. I felt a warm sensation, a wash of relief, and I felt as though the mangled, misplaced Picasso woman inside me began to shift. Ann's words brought comfort and deep relief. But still, for all my hopes, I realized that the wound inside me, while smaller, was still gaping—an unmistakable ache still existed within. Again, as I had when I held Penny's funeral by the sea in Tybee Island, I resigned myself to the fact that I would never completely heal. I told myself to be grateful with any measure of relief that Ann's remarks brought.

A week before Thanksgiving, Ann invited me to the bill signing. Again, I hesitated. Maria convinced me that it was important for me to be at that event, even though she could not go this time because of her schedule. I flew to Chicago the night before. Seeing the familiar landmarks and skyline, I felt homesick and confused, as though I was in a time warp. All the markings of my old life, with the exception of Penny, were present. Did I make a mistake in coming? *It is 2013,* I kept reminding myself, trying to ground myself and calm the internal little girl who felt abandoned. No matter how hard I tried to reassure myself, my mind and body were clearly in 1998 in a city that Penny and I explored regularly. I felt misaligned. Out of place. I hurt. I called Maria. She was heading to bed. I felt terribly sad, again standing in the two separate worlds of death and life. I called Rod and Jane. Standing in the Chicago cold, I felt better hearing their voices of reassurance that this was a good thing and that all would be well. "You're doing this for all of us," Rod counseled. "We are all going to heal from this."

The next day, as we prepared to join thousands of people at the signing of the Marriage Equality legislation, I felt happy. I felt proud of the work that Ann had done on the bill, and I felt a deep thanks for her personal remarks about my life. Yet as we stood in the VIP line to enter the event, I couldn't shake the feeling of being out of place. As we were escorted to our seats by a state police officer, I thought back to the day of Penny's funeral and the cop in the bedroom. *How different everything was then.* I saw many old friends and Penny's former colleagues, who spoke so kindly and gently to me with fond memories of Penny. I was surprised at how many of them expressed sorrow for my loss, a simple and yet profound recognition even all these years later. Shaking hands, I felt as though I were campaigning, but this time, unlike the countless times since Penny's death, it felt good, energizing. I choked up when Senator Terry Link shook my hand and said, "I'm really sorry for your loss. I never knew you and Penny were together. I just knew she was happy."

As the ceremony began, the state's constitutional officers were introduced and walked on stage past President Lincoln's desk, where, as the sixteenth president, he had written the Gettysburg Address. I realized that many of these people had also attended Penny's funeral. I trembled inside as I saw them, having painful flashes of that day. Judy Baar Topinka, the state's treasurer, walked out on the stage. She pointed to me and said hello. Then she bowed her head and put her hand on her heart, patting it, the same gesture she had made to me at Penny's funeral, fifteen years before. Secretary of State Jesse White also pointed and waved. After the speeches, Governor Pat Quinn sat at Lincoln's desk, and the constitutional officers surrounded him. With a plethora of pens, Governor Quinn signed the bill into law.

I was in the front row, watching him on the stage. Attorney General Lisa Madigan, my old boss, caught my eye and waved. She leaned into the governor and said, "Let's give one of these pens to Terry Mutchler." He nodded, made a stroke with another pen, and handed it to her. She walked over, knelt down, and handed me the pen. With a hug, she said, "I hope this helps." Secretary White also motioned for me, and as I hugged him, he also gave me a pen that the governor had signed the bill with. "I think of her every day, Terry," Jesse said. Later, Governor Quinn shook my hand and said, "Terry, it's nice to see you. We still miss Penny very much. We could use her around here."

I leaned over to Ann, who was sitting to my left, and, tearing up, I said, "At Penny's funeral, I was fifteen rows back. Here, I am sitting in the front row, the dead-center seat. Thank you for this." She gripped my hand tightly, and we cried. In that moment, an old pain was eased. I realized my effort to force healing for so many years was as ineffective as standing over a flower and commanding it to bloom. Nature has its own schedule. And, while I couldn't explain it well, I felt as though the gaping hole of grief within had finally, fifteen years later, healed.

"You know, Ann," I said. "I'll see Penny again someday. I do believe that. But I am ready to leave her in the dimension she is in, and I am ready to live in this dimension, fully. I have a great life. I'm in love with Maria, and today, I finally feel like I've found the missing piece of myself. Everything is in the right place."

ACKNOWLEDGMENTS

I never intended to write a book about Penny and me. Writing *Under This Beautiful Dome* began as grief therapy. Six years after Penny's death, I was still greatly mired in grief and suffering. In 2004, a college friend, Kirsten Lee Soares, encouraged me to apply to an intensive writing retreat in Pine Mountain, California, as an effort to shift the grief. I balked. Without my knowing it, she applied for me. After much tumult, I showed up, thinking I would leave the first day.

I ended up sticking it out, and incredibly, two life-altering events happened at that ten-day retreat. First, I shared my story publically for the first time, and those powerful writing women convinced me that I needed to make this story visible. Second, I fell completely in love with an elegant Greek poet who was also attending the retreat.

For holding my personality and my prose, my deep thanks to the women of Pine Mountain: Deena Metzger, the facilitator; Kirsten Soares; Laurie Wagner; Maya Stein; and Meg Tilly, who taught me that writing a book consists of just writing little stories, one at a time. To Dena Lefkowitz, without whom this book would still be a dusty, unfinished manuscript and without whom I would have never considered going to Chicago for the signing of the law. To my agent, Jill Marsal of Marsal Lyon Literary Agency, who took special care with this story, and to Catherine Knepper, a deft editor who gave the book early structure. To the entire team at Seal Press, particularly Barrett Briske, who tirelessly edited with a keen eye and a gentle hand, and Executive Editor Laura Mazer, a true sculptor. To Eva

Zimmerman, an incredibly talented, tireless, and enthusiastic publicist. And, finally, thanks to Publisher Krista Lyons. Her immediate faith in this love story was unmatched, and she tirelessly worked to create an elegant and regal package for the reader. To my friend and fellow writer Anita Huslin, an early believer in both me and the book. To my Illinois friends, especially Klint Bruno, Ann Williams, and Lyn Schollett, whose friendship survived Chapter 30. To Carol Corgan, the first person to help me look at grief straight in the eye. To a talented group of doctors who helped me at various points in the healing process: George Burns, Marcia Pavlou, Eva Muller, Lori McKenzie, and Carol Brockman. And a crowning thanks to Dr. Marilyn Luber, who helped get me quiet enough to write.

To my father Donald Mutchler, and to my mother, Star Brundle Mutchler, who at eighty-three was thrilled that I was finally going to tell this story. Profound thanks to my sister and friend Star Donna Parker, a Christian in the truest sense of the word. Her unfailing love and kindnesses to me are too immeasurable to count. To Rod and Jane Severns, who opened their hearts to me and honored the love that Penny and I shared. They support my every effort, including this book, even though it is sometimes difficult to read about those that we love. More than once their wisdom kept the book moving and I thank them for every "mercy run." To Maria's children, my friends: Artemis Brod, a constant encouragement and fellow writer, and Alexi Brod, whose technology expertise helped many times.

Lastly, you would not be holding this book in your hands if it were not for my partner, Maria Papacostaki, whom I love. She pushed me when I was unpushable and held gently the struggles and personal and painful insights that I discovered on this writing journey. Unselfishly, Maria gave up countless weekends and nights and altered our own life together for several years for the sake of getting this book into the world. I could not have had the same unending grace and unfailing support for such a book. Not only did she support me in every way, but her editing and insight were also superior. She has spared the reader much.

© DIANA ROBINSON

ABOUT THE AUTHOR

Terry Mutchler is an attorney and former award-winning journalist who was appointed as Pennsylvania's first Executive Director of the Office of Open Records, ensuring government transparency. A writer for The Associated Press, she covered politics in Pennsylvania, New Jersey, Alaska, and Illinois, where she was the first woman appointed AP Statehouse Correspondent. She won several Keystone Awards, Pennsylvania's top honor for reporting, and was the AP's state nominee for Young Writer of the Year.

Mutchler clerked for the Supreme Court of Illinois and for the Executive Office of the President during the Clinton Administration. She was a Chicago trial lawyer at a major national law firm before returning to public service as a speechwriter and senior advisor for the Illinois Attorney General. Governor Ed Rendell appointed Mutchler to her current six-year post.

Mutchler received her BA from Pennsylvania State University and her JD from John Marshall School of Law in Chicago. She was a Bohnett Fellow for Senior Executives in State and Local Government at Harvard's Kennedy School of Government. She lives in the suburbs of Philadelphia, PA.

SELECTED TITLES FROM SEAL PRESS

Hillary Clinton in Her Own Words, edited by Lisa Rogak. $14.00, 978-1-58005-533-8. This timely collection of Clinton quotes captures her evolving role in American politics and culture.

We Hope You Like This Song: An Overly Honest Story about Friendship, Death, and Mix Tapes, by Bree Housley. $16.00, 978-1-58005-431-7. Bree Housley's sweet, quirky, and hilarious tribute to her lifelong friend, and her chronicle of how she honored her after her premature death.

What Will It Take to Make a Woman President?: Conversations about Women, Leadership, and Power, by Marianne Schnall. $16.00, 978-1-58005-496-6. This timely discussion features interviews with more than twenty leading politicians, writers, artists, and activists about why America has not yet elected a female president.

Lesbian Couples: A Guide to Creating Healthy Relationships, by D. Merilee Clunis and G. Dorsey Green. $16.95, 978-1-58005-131-6. Drawing from a decade of research, this helpful and readable resource covers topics from conflict-resolution to commitment ceremonies, using a variety of examples and problem-solving techniques.

Intimate Politics: How I Grew Up Red, Fought for Free Speech, and Became a Feminist Rebel, by Bettina F. Aptheker. $16.95, 978-1-58005-160-6. A courageous and uncompromising account of one woman's personal and political transformation, and a fascinating portrayal of a key chapter in our nation's history.

Riding Fury Home: A Memoir, by Chana Wilson. $17.00, 978-1-58005-432-4. A shattering, exquisitely written account of one family's struggle against homophobia and mental illness in a changing world—and a powerful story of healing, forgiveness, and redemption.

FIND SEAL PRESS ONLINE
www.SealPress.com
www.Facebook.com/SealPress
Twitter: @SealPress